Representations of Nature in Middle-earth

Representations of Nature in Middle-earth

edited by
Martin Simonson

2015

Cormarë Series No. 34

Series Editors: Peter Buchs • Thomas Honegger • Andrew Moglestue • Johanna Schön

Series Editor responsible for this volume: Thomas Honegger

Library of Congress Cataloging-in-Publication Data

Martin Simonson (ed.):
Representations of Nature in Middle-earth
ISBN 978-3-905703-34-4

Subject headings:
Tolkien, J.R.R. (John Ronald Reuel), 1892-1973
Nature
Middle-earth
Ecocriticism
Ecology
The Lord of the Rings
The Hobbit
The Silmarillion

Cormarë Series No. 34

First published 2015

© Walking Tree Publishers, Zurich and Jena, 2015

All rights reserved. No portion of this book may be reproduced, by any process or technique, without the express written consent of the publisher

Cover illustration-picture 'Zaldiaran' by Martin Simonson.
Reproduced by permission of the artist. Copyright 2015

Set in Adobe Garamond Pro and Shannon by Walking Tree Publishers
Printed by Lightning Source in the United Kingdom and United States

Board of Advisors

Academic Advisors

Douglas A. Anderson (independent scholar)

Dieter Bachmann (Universität Zürich)

Patrick Curry (independent scholar)

Michael D.C. Drout (Wheaton College)

Vincent Ferré (Université de Paris-Est Créteil UPEC)

Verlyn Flieger (University of Maryland)

Thomas Fornet-Ponse (Rheinische Friedrich-Wilhelms-Universität Bonn)

Christopher Garbowski (University of Lublin, Poland)

Mark T. Hooker (Indiana University)

Andrew James Johnston (Freie Universität Berlin)

Rainer Nagel (Johannes Gutenberg-Universität Mainz)

Helmut W. Pesch (independent scholar)

Tom A. Shippey (University of Winchester)

Allan G. Turner (Friedrich-Schiller-Universität Jena)

Frank Weinreich (independent scholar)

General Readers

Johan Boots

Jean Chausse

Friedhelm Schneidewind

Isaac Juan Tomas

Patrick Van den hole

Johan Vanhecke (Letterenhuis, Antwerp)

Acknowledgments

Many thanks to all those who worked with us to make this volume possible – most prominently, of course, the contributors!

A great 'thank you' also to Christoph Rzymski for assembling the index, and to Tamara Schmidt who helped layouting and proofreading the text and who proved an expert typo-hunter.

    Martin Simonson & Thomas Honegger

Contents

Martin Simonson
Introduction ... i

Andrea Denekamp
"Transform stalwart trees":
Sylvan Biocentrism in *The Lord of the Rings* ... 1

Jessica Seymour
"As we draw near mountains":
Nature and Beauty in the Hearts of Dwarves ... 29

Gabriela Silva Rivero
"Behind a grey rain-curtain":
Water, Melancholy and Healing in *The Lord of the Rings* ... 49

Yannick Imbert
Eru will enter Ëa:
The Creational-Eschatological Hope of J.R.R. Tolkien ... 73

Christopher Roman
Thinking with the Elements:
J.R.R. Tolkien's Ecology and Object-Oriented Ontology ... 95

Magdalena Mączyńska
On Trees of Middle-earth:
J.R.R. Tolkien's Mythical Creation ... 119

Doris McGonagill
In Living Memory: Tolkien's Trees and
Sylvan Landscapes as Metaphors of Cultural Memory ... 139

Peter Hodder
A New Zealand Perspective on the Tectonics of Middle-earth ... 171

Gabriel Ertsgaard
"Leaves of Gold There Grew":
Lothlórien, Postcolonialism, and Ecology ... 207

Index ... 231

Martin Simonson

Introduction

> *We should look at green again, and be startled anew (but not blinded) by blue and yellow and red...*
> J.R.R. Tolkien, "On Fairy-stories"

Middle-earth is for many people synonymous with nature – whether it be vast stretches of wild nature, enclaves of garden-like cultivated nature, or forests and hills that have been destroyed and contaminated. Apart from green, blue, yellow and red, we thus also get plenty of strokes in less gay colours, such as brown, gray and black. In spite of this variety, which reflect both the promises and pitfalls of our engagement with the natural world, Tolkien's secondary world has in popular culture become an epitome of outstanding natural beauty – partly, of course, due to the spectacular locations chosen for Peter Jackson's film adaptations. However, to centre on the 'merely' beautiful betrays a far too simplistic view of Middle-earth. While many of the sceneries described by Tolkien could certainly be construed as sublime and awe-inspiring in the best Romantic tradition – Rivendell, the Misty Mountains and the Falls of Rauros are among the first to come to mind – others, such as the Brown Lands or the Midgewater Marshes, are simply dreary, tedious and uncomfortable. The bottom line is that the descriptions of nature in Middle-earth are nuanced and multi-layered, realistically heterogeneous, awake to a restless spirit of creation or subjugated by wilful acts of destruction. All of this makes the physical setting of Tolkien's works compelling and open to many different interpretations.

Books such as Patrick Curry's *Defending Middle-earth* (1997) and his most recent collection of essays, *Deep Roots in a Time of Frost* (2014), Matthew Dickerson and Jonathan Evans' *Ents, Elves and Eriador* (2006), and Liam Campbell's *The Ecological Augury in the Works of J.R.R. Tolkien* (2011), have seen Middle-earth as an artistically expressed predecessor of the Green movement's agenda in the face of industrial abuse. Others, such as Siewers, Flieger and Dufau, have read nature in Tolkien's work in terms of old myths, folklore and religion; and yet others take the elaborate descriptions of the physical environment, textual and cartographic, as a sign that Middle-earth itself is the central protagonist of *The Lord of the Rings*.

Tolkien himself leaves the field open for interpretation, as long as we do not single out one particular perspective as more valid than any other – as the Professor states in his famous 1966 foreword to *The Lord of the Rings*, applicability not allegory is key to the understanding of his tale.

For all these different approaches, it seems safe to say that nature in Middle-earth plays a crucial role not only in the creation of atmospheres and settings that enhance both the realism and the emotional appeal of the secondary world – it also acts as an agent of change within the stories. It is equally important to stress that in general terms, nature as a concept (that is, nature interpreted in human terms) really belongs to the realm of culture. This is consistently reflected in Tolkien's writings: the presence of past civilizations and different races' intervention in nature is rarely absent from the sceneries – something which is seen in place-names, the ruined remains of past civilizations and other cultural impressions on the natural world. In fact, the tales show an ongoing and intensive dialogue between nature and culture, motivated by different needs – gardens, tilled fields, grazed heathlands, mines, cities hewn out of rock, roads, dams, waterways, architecture and artwork all testify to this intense interaction.

From this point of view, Tolkien's Middle-earth engages with historical, economic and social conditions in much the same way as many realist narratives. However, what makes the dimension of nature in this imagined setting particularly compelling is that it is interpreted not only by humans, but also by beings affected by conditions alien to the human race. This implies an even larger amount of visions and positions within a web of interrelated concerns – whether they be cultural, psychological, economic, aesthetic, philosophical or theological. The present collection of essays sets out to explore Middle-earth as an enhanced ecological entity: enhanced because of the multitude of non-human perspectives, and ecological in the sense that it shows "the relationships between a group of living things and their environment," to use Merriam Webster's definition.

The first part of the collection deals precisely with the different ways in which non-human beings in Middle-earth respond to their physical environment. First, Andrea Denekamp offers a vision of how Ents articulate a sylvan biocentrism that questions the cornerstones of a conventional human understanding of stewardship. Jessica Seymour then explores the relationship of Dwarves with the mineral world, and outlines an aesthetic vision that subverts common assumptions of beauty shared by other races in Middle-earth. Finally, Gabriela Silva takes a look at how water can be both the source of healing and melancholy, particularly for Elves and Hobbits, and how it anticipates transcendence in Middle-earth.

The next part is made up of two essays devoted to metaphysical readings of nature in Middle-earth. Yannick Imbert proposes a Thomist approach, highlighting the expression of hope for the restoration of the natural world as key to his interpretation, while Christopher Roman takes the part of "inanimate" matter to argue for the presence of what he labels an "object-oriented ontology", referring to the active interaction of objects with other elements in Middle-earth.

Part three, then, looks back to the past in order to come to terms with the prominent role of trees and forests in Tolkien's oeuvre. Magdalena Mączyńska highlights the mythical resonances in Tolkien's depiction of the arboreal world, establishing a set of parallelisms between Tolkien's own mythology and real-world mythologies. Doris McGonagill, for her part, uses the lens of modern thinkers and cultural historians such as Hans Blumendal, Robert Pogue Harrison and Simon Schama to stress the intimate connection between Tolkien's forests and cultural memory.

The final part of the book centres on various kinds of transfers of Middle-earth as a physical space. Peter Hodder outlines the parallels between the tectonic evolution of Middle-earth and that of New Zealand, arguing that the real-world locations where Jackson's films were shot actually reflect the geological history of the secondary world rather well. Finally, Gabriel Ertsgaard situates the Elves' withdrawal from Middle-earth within an ecocritical and postcolonial framework, arguing that the Elvish stance shows an ideal sense of stewardship that embraces limits and finitude, which in turn is linked to Tolkien's general idea of death as a gift – in contrast to the questionable response of the real-world Western civilization to the current ecological crisis.

I am convinced that these new explorations of Middle-earth as an enhanced ecological entity, a scene for metaphysical speculation, an arboreal depository of cultural memory and a reflection of real-world natural and imperialistic processes, will open up new vistas and prepare the way for future scholarly expeditions in the rich and still unfolding setting that Tolkien devised for his literary creations.

Martin Simonson
Vitoria, November 2014

Works Cited

CAMPBELL, Liam. *The Ecological Augury in the Works of J.R.R. Tolkien*. Cormarë Series 21. Zurich and Jena: Walking Tree Publishers, 2011.

CURRY, Patrick. *Defending Middle-earth. Tolkien, Myth and Modernity*. Edinburgh: Floris Books, 1997.

Deep Roots in a Time of Frost. Essays on Tolkien. Cormarë Series 33. Zurich and Jena: Walking Tree Publishers, 2014

DICKERSON, Matthew and Jonathan Evans. *Ents, Elves, and Eriador. The Environmental Vision of J.R.R. Tolkien*. Lexington KY: The University Press of Kentucky, 2006.

Andrea Denekamp

"Transform stalwart trees": Sylvan Biocentrism in *The Lord of the Rings*

Abstract

Tolkien's writing reflects twentieth-century debates about the definition of wilderness and responds to the increasing deforestation and science of forestry that arose in Great Britain as a result of the war. Using Robert Pogue Harrison's *Forests: The Shadow of Civilization* (1993), geographer Douglass Davies's "The Evocative Symbolism of Trees" (1988), and E. P. Stebbings's *Commercial Forestry in Britain* (1919), this essay proposes to examine how Ents, being neither trees nor Men, demonstrate the biocentrism of the biotic Other as central components of ethical stewardship. As separation of place and culture is a cornerstone of his mythos, Tolkien portrays Ents as a sustainable cultural community – one that cares less for humanity than the biotic and ecological environments. They have their own history, language, artifacts, and architecture – all heavily steeped in silvaculture. Further, Ents represent a geography of non-planning (the anarchical development favored half-jokingly by Tolkien). Their stance is that of a culture on the brink of extinction. Further, the Ents act as a barrier between other cultural groups of Middle-earth, separating cultures and regions physically in a way that fosters diversity of local communities.

> I sang in the army of the trees' branches before the ruler of Britain...
> The Lord replied in language and in the land:
> Transform stalwart trees into armies...
> Cad Goddeu

The way trees, forests, and Ents (the shepherds of the trees) are described in *The Lord of the Rings* – as independent, active voices doomed to waning in the face of cultural collision – is indicative of Tolkien's ethic of forest stewardship. Because stewardship is a matter of perception, understanding how wilderness (the physical environment not directly controlled by human interference) informs cultural imagination and influences human interaction with nature is important in developing a complete stewardship ethic. As Robert Pogue Harrison points out in his study of forests in Western culture, *Forests: The Shadow of Civilizations*, "nature derives its mode of presence from the man-made world [...] The modes of nature's presence derive from modes of human consciousness, and these latter are historically determined" (163). It has been argued in many books that wilderness – nature separate from the influences of human culture – does not exist as anything other than a social construct. Among the most notable of these are William Cronon's "The Trouble with Wilderness; or Getting Back to the Wrong Nature" and Loren Eiseley's "How Natural is Natural?" which argue that all places, even un-peopled ones, are shaped by the interference of man. Cronon sees wilderness as Harrison does – as a shadow of civilization, the antithesis of ordered city values. In a similar fashion, Eiseley sees nature as an idol set up by man – a desire for a copy of Platonic nature – which cannot exist. Tolkien's portrayal of forests and Ent culture, influenced by his environmental perceptions and historical context, is in part an imagining of what the platonic ideal of a wilderness of trees would look like and also an acknowledgement that the ideal is unattainable. Though Ents give trees their own historically-determined voice, in the end, the Entish perspective is a human-derived vision of what the voice of the biotic Other might encompass and is influenced by the context of authorial experience. The stewardship ethic of the Ents, which is to allow wilderness to develop chaotically according to its own laws, is not sustainable in a world also inhabited by human(-like) cultures which seek to shape nature.

Critics have glossed over the implications to the text of considering the Ents an independent culture akin to that of Hobbits, Dwarves, Orcs, Elves, and Men. Yet, the richness in Tolkien's portrayal of Ents, trees, and forests is in the interplay between anthropocentric cultures with that of the Ent-culture. His inclusion of the Ents into the cultural and regional make-up of Middle-earth suggests that, for Tolkien, ecological diversity must be included in stewardship ethics. Tolkien's Ents, being neither trees nor men, demonstrate the biocentrism of the biotic Other. Biocentrism is the view that the rights and needs of humans are not more important than those of other living things; plants, animals, and humans all have rights and needs which need to be considered equally. The Ents comprise a distinct community within the world of diverse locales in *The Lord of the Rings*. In their increasing finitude, the Ents and the wilderness forests they inhabit represent both a dying culture and a distinct ecological region. Tolkien is inconclusive about whether the Ents partially bring about their own demise through the loss of the Entwives – which stems in part from stubborn, unresolved debates over whose view of nature is correct (that of the conservationist Ents or the horticulturist Entwives). However, Tolkien clearly concludes that Orcs and Men bear the largest responsibility for the decimation of the forests and Ents and, in the end, the biocentric discourse of the Ents goes extinct, indicating that it is unlikely men and trees can sustainably coexist. Tolkien's forests, in addition to acting as a dividing force, by means of a physical barrier, between the other cultural regions of Middle-earth, also highlight the cultural differences between those who interact (or fail to interact) with them as a community in their own right.

An Entish Stance

Tolkien portrays Ents as a distinctive cultural community – one that cares less for humanity than for the biotic and ecological environments. Rather than being trees, Ents *represent* trees. However, they have their own culture, history, language, artifacts, and architecture which is heavily steeped in silva-culture. The Ents are a self-sustaining culture in Middle-earth and represent a geography of non-planning (the anarchical development favored half-jokingly by Tolkien) (*L* 63). The external appearance of the Ents, the environment in which they choose to live, and the architecture of their homes are indicative of their desire to blend in with, rather than dominate, their environment. The textual argument, based on their stance as a culture on the brink of extinction, is that the biocentric voice will always be subservient in an anthropocentric world. Tolkien was concerned with how man lives in and with the world; the Ents are a new vision of what that relationship could look like to a species less self-centered than humans.

Though the forests seem vast – at one point in their journey the hobbits "were on an island in a sea of trees" (*LotR* 111) – the hobbits are experiencing the last remnants of an ancient and endangered wilderness: "It was […] a survivor of vast forgotten woods; and in it there lived yet, ageing no quicker than the hills, the fathers of the fathers of trees, remembering times when they were lords" (*LotR* 127-128). But many acts of violence have reduced the forest. Quickbeam recounts: "Orcs came with axes and cut down my trees. I came and called them by their long names, but they did not quiver, they did not hear or answer: they lay dead" (*LotR* 472). The felling of the Rowan trees is a genocide carried out by Saruman and his army of Orcs. Yet, it is only one episode in a long history of forest destruction.

In *The Silmarillion*, Yavanna, a queen of the Valar associated with nature, asks of Eru "Shall nothing that I have devised be free from the dominion of others?" (*S* 45). She fears the axes of her husband Aulë's dwarves:

> the *kelvar* can flee or defend themselves, whereas the *olvar* that grow cannot. And among these I hold trees dear. Long in the growing, swift shall they be in the felling, and unless they pay toll with fruit upon bough little mourned in their passing. [...] Would that the trees might speak on behalf of all things that have roots, and punish those that wrong them! (*S* 45)

In response to Yavanna's pleas, Manwë responds that "spirits from afar [...] will go among the *kelvar* and the *olvar*, and some will dwell therein, and be held in reverence, and their just anger shall be feared. [...] But in the forests shall walk the Shepherds of the Trees" (*S* 46). This implies that the Ents are not trees; rather, they are "a power in the forests whose wrath [the Dwarves] will arouse at their peril" (*S* 46). The age-old struggle between the forest as its own entity with rights and the forest as commodity for consumption is born in Middle-earth when Aulë responds in *The Silmarillion* to his wife by saying, "Nonetheless [the Dwarves] will have need of wood" (*S* 46). So, the Ents of Tolkien's mythology were brought into existence to provide balance. As Cynthia Cohen explains, Tolkien's creation of Ents is unique:

> Ents, by the time they emerged as tree-herds, [had been] afforded [...] the odd distinction of looking like trees, being associated with trees, living among trees, and being charged with the responsibility to protect trees, but not actually being trees – a situation not imagined in literature before Tolkien's time. (Cohen 114-115)

Rather than being trees, Ents live among and protect trees of the forest. At some point in Tolkien's development of Middle-earth, Ents transformed into a cultural community replete with history, language, artifacts, and architecture steeped in silvaculture.

It is significant that Ents can be figured as a Middle-earth culture and their environment as a home. It gives them legitimacy and authority equal to that of the other cultures. Ents have agency, the ability to act. They are not subject to human control, so they remain the voice of non-human nature. Ents can therefore be examined under the framework of cultural and behavioral literary geography. As Cohen asserts:

> Ents demonstrate cultural development, evident in their linguistic prowess, and in the system of government followed at Entmoot. [...] The memory of the presence of Entwives and Entings demonstrates not only that Ents have family structure, but also that they experience love, disagreement, and longing. Expressed in songs, chants and poems, these emotions are captured in a body of literature that further asserts the human side of Ents. (Cohen 115-116)

While Cohen is correct in most of her claims, it is not true that Ents have a "human side." The intent behind the Ents seems to be their distance from humanity. Though Cohen expresses that Ents have culture, it is necessary to assessing Tolkien's stewardship ethic to more fully develop the parameters of Entish culture. For instance, Ents break down into tribes or smaller groups: "[The hobbits] learned that [Bregalad/Quickbeam] belonged to Skinbark's people" (*LotR* 472). The existence of place-based communities means that Ents can be considered one of the diverse place-based cultures of Middle-earth. Further, their habitat, Fangorn Forest, is a locale which can be examined culturally and regionally.

Ents have an unusually strong attachment to bioregion – a geographical area defined by biological or environmental characteristics, such as geology or topography, rather than by political or administrative boundaries. They are a true silvaculture, even resembling in body their physical environment. When Merry and Pippin inadvertently insult one of the forest inhabitants, they are accosted with sarcasm: "'Almost felt you liked the Forest! That's good! That's uncommonly kind of you,' said a strange voice" (*LotR* 452). After all, the Forest is the home of *the Ent*, aka Treebeard and Fangorn. Treebeard is the oldest living inhabitant of Middle-earth: "Treebeard is Fangorn, the guardian of the forest; he is the oldest of the ents, the oldest living thing that still walks beneath the Sun upon this Middle-earth" (*LotR* 488). It logically follows that Fangorn Forest is the oldest inhabited region in Middle-earth (though the rest of Middle-earth seems to have forgotten the fact). The Ent is so suited to his environment that he blends in with it:

> They found that they were looking at a most extraordinary face. It belonged to a large man-like, almost Troll-like, figure at least fourteen foot high, very sturdy, with a tall head, and hardly any neck. Whether it was clad in stuff like green and grey bark, or whether that was its hide, was difficult to say. At any rate the arms, at a short distance from the trunk, were not wrinkled, but covered with a brown smooth skin. […] The lower part of the long face was covered with a sweeping grey beard, bushy, almost twiggy at the roots, thin and mossy at the ends. (*LotR* 452)

Though all Ents resemble trees, they are a physically diverse ethnic group: "Ents were as different from one another as trees from trees: some as different as one tree is from another of the same name but quite different growth and history; and some as different as one tree-kind from another, as birch from beech, oak from fir" (*LotR* 468-469). And yet, they are "kindred" (*LotR* 469). Over thousands of years of living in a bioregion for which they were created, the Ents have merged seamlessly into their environment.

Their culture is an extension of the place they inhabit; Fangorn Forest is architecturally and aesthetically *treeish*: "Look at all those weeping, trailing, beards and whiskers of lichen! And most of the trees seem to be half covered with ragged dry leaves that have never fallen. Untidy" (*LotR* 450). Treebeard leads Merry and Pippin to his home, designated as Wellinghall: "Two great trees stood there, one on either side, like living gate-posts; but there was no gate save their crossing and interwoven boughs" (*LotR* 458-459). The hobbits find that "the floor of a great hall had been cut in the side of the hill. On either hand the walls sloped upwards, until they were fifty feet high or more, and along each wall stood an aisle of trees that also increased in height as they marched upwards" (*LotR* 459). The house was well-supplied with water (indoor plumbing): "A little stream escaped from the springs above, and leaving the main water, fell tinkling down the sheer face of the wall, pouring in silver drops, like a fine curtain in front of the arched bay" (*LotR* 459). The waterfall serves as a welcoming entrance from the outer hall into the Ent-house proper where "a great stone table stood there, but no chairs" (*LotR* 459). Ents possess artifacts in the form of "great vessels" which produce light, "tall stone jars […] with heavy lids," "bowls," and "a great bed on low legs […] covered deep in dried grass and bracken" with "pillows of grass" (*LotR* 459, 460). Without modern plumbing, electricity, furniture made from wood, or fossil fuels, the Ent-home possesses water, light, and furniture, as well as its own aesthetic charm. Because their method of living has been successful (they are the oldest beings in Middle-earth), their culture is sustainable.

Ents represent a geography of non-planning (the anarchical development favored by Tolkien); the Entwives, who are planners and planters, have gone missing. The Entwives "ordered [plants] to grow according to their wishes [...] The Entwives desired order, and plenty, and peace (by which they meant that things should remain where they had set them). So the Entwives made gardens to live in" (*LotR* 465). The Ents, in contrast, "ate only such fruit as the trees let fall in their path," and, as we have already seen, desire to live in the naturally unkempt forest (*LotR* 464). By living wild, Ents hope to preserve their environment and the heart of their culture. As Dickerson and Evans explain in *Ents, Elves, and Eriador: The Environmental Vision of J.R.R. Tolkien* (251): "The Ents are not interested in *sustainable* forestry, agriculture, or horticulture because they are not interested in forestry, agriculture, or horticulture of *any* kind. They want to preserve Fangorn as it is: wild." Any force that wishes to control nature, even the Entwives, violates the sustainability of wild, un-ordered nature. The struggle of humanity to bend the natural world to do its bidding results in a harnessing of wilderness which leads to the destruction of all that is wild. Tamed, human-influenced nature is what remains, in the form of horticulture, agriculture, and the science of forestry. In Tolkien's mythopoeic world, human dominion over the earth has led to the near (and eventual) extinction of Ents, the embodiment of wilderness: "Only three remain of the first Ents that walked in the woods before the Darkness," Treebeard laments (*LotR* 463).

The inability of the Ents (wilderness) and Entwives (horticulture) to find a common ground is ironic, because both are stewards of nature, trees in particular. Treebeard elucidates the objectives of the Ents: "We keep off strangers and the foolhardy; and we train and we teach, we walk and we weed" (*LotR* 457). In his essay, "Tolkien's Imaginary Nature", Michael Brisbois (203) points out: "The treeherd Ents, the Elves, and the Hobbits all live in a relationship of stewardship with nature; however, this relationship is not one of blissful harmony. Elves and Ents seem to co-exist with nature and are not viewed as the ideal in Tolkien's work." Brisbois is off-target here. The Ents (and Elves) are representative of the ideal, in so far as they exist in accord with the natural world. Rather, the eventual waning of the Ents and their departure can be read as a sign that the ideal is unattainable in a human world, under failed human stewardship. Even mostly-successful human stewardship will fail in the end, because any system which puts humans first is bound to serve human ends first. Brisbois's break-down of nature, however, is useful. The Ents dwell in passive nature but are themselves an example of active, wrathful nature. Brisbois argues that, in Tolkien's novel, nature strikes back to punish "those who would abuse it" (213) – like the Balrog which rises from the depths to assault the dwarves of Moria and like the ents and huorns (wild and ambulatory trees under the control of the Ents) which dispossess Saruman of Isengard. The Entish goal is to preserve the forests; they do not care whether or not the destruction of forests is carried out for practical reasons or caused by greed. They do not even care about the War of the Ring, except as it relates to the felling of trees. As Dickerson and Evans (123) contend: "Ents care for these places, expressing their respect for them by letting plants, flowers, and trees grow according to the principles inherent in their nature, countenancing neither the conversion of these lands to civilized use nor the organized cultivation of growing things." Ents have no forestry plan, seek to be left mostly to themselves, and ask that trees be left to themselves.

The invasion of Orcs into Fangorn, encouraged by Saruman, is an act of war. As the oldest inhabitants of Middle-earth, the Ents feel that they have been betrayed by a close neighbor with whom they were friendly and shared cultural knowledge. Treebeard explains that Saruman "used to give no trouble to his neighbours. [...] There was a time when he was always walking about my woods. He was polite in those days, always asking my leave (at least when he met me); and always eager to listen. I told him many things that he would never have found out by himself; but he never repaid me in like kind" (*LotR* 462). Saruman, who sides with Sauron in the battle against the other cultures of Middle-earth, has gone from a well-disposed neighbor who respects the lands and homes of those bordering his own, to a greedy, encroaching neighbor who takes resources from another's property without permission or apology: "Down on the borders they are felling trees – good trees. Some of the trees they just cut down and leave to rot – orc-mischief that; but most are hewn up and carried off to feed the fires of Orthanc. There is always a smoke rising from Isengard these days" (*LotR* 462). Here we have an example of one culture invading another, of beings with anthropocentric consciousness invading the wilderness. Treebeard, the voice of biocentrism, is moved to indignation: "It is orc-work, the wanton hewing [...] without even the bad excuse of feeding the fires, that has so angered us; and the treachery of a neighbour, who should have helped us. Wizards ought to know better: they do know better. There is no curse in Elvish, Entish, or the tongues of Men bad enough for such treachery" (*LotR* 474). It is this lack of respect for the Ents, their boundaries, and their culture of stewardship that eventually spurs the Ents to action. There is a cultural collision, as a secondary war erupts over the rights of trees.

When Merry and Pippin seek to enlist the help of the Ents in the war, Treebeard initially responds: "I am not altogether on anybody's *side*, because nobody is altogether on my *side*, if you understand me: nobody cares for the woods as I care for them, not even Elves nowadays. [...] And there are some things, of course, whose side I am altogether not on; I am against them altogether: these [...] Orcs, and their masters" (*LotR* 461). Ents cannot be influenced to action by the reasoning of other cultural groups in Middle-earth, because their perspective is not a human one. Elves, Dwarves, Hobbits, and Men are all selfish, human-like, civilized cultures. Ents are completely outside of civilization. Because the Fellowship of the Ring is decidedly against the Orcs and their master, there is a temporary, tacit alliance formed between the ents and the men of Rohan: "For if Sauron of old destroyed the gardens [of the Entwives], the Enemy today seems likely to wither all the woods" (*LotR* 465). The Ents are apprised that "there are wastes of stump and bramble where once there were singing groves" (*LotR* 463). In a moment of decisiveness (to which Ents are not often prone), Treebeard booms, "I will stop it!" (*LotR* 463). The Ents enter the War of the Ring to save the trees of Fangorn, exemplifying the protection Yavanna had once begged for them.

The inhabitants of Middle-earth, for the most part, are unfamiliar with the strength of the Ents. The Ents have not interacted with the other cultures of Middle-earth for some time and have been mostly relegated to myth. The boundaries of the forest are best protected in the Third Age by the legacy of fear associated with them. The Ents themselves seem not to have flexed their muscles in a while. Treebeard describes their physical strength: "We are made of the bones of the earth. We can split stone like the roots of trees, only quicker, far quicker, if our minds are roused" (*LotR* 474). Merry and Pippin find that "an angry Ent is terrifying. Their fingers, and their toes, just freeze on to rock; and they tear it up like bread-crust. It was like watching the work of great tree-roots in a hundred years, all packed into a few moments" (*LotR* 553). Ents are far stronger than the trees they protect, as Manwë promised they would be: "An Ent can be stuck as full of orc-arrows as a pin-cushion, and take no serious harm. They cannot be poisoned [...]. It takes a very heavy axe-stroke to wound them seriously. [...] A man that hacks once at an Ent never gets a chance of a second blow. A punch from an Ent-fist crumples up iron like thin tin" (*LotR* 552-553). The Ents are a formidable enemy and fighting force. Out of Fangorn Ents and Huorns go to their own defense and to the aid of Rohan. They destroy (and bury) Orcs: "Wailing they passed under the waiting shadow of the trees; and from that shadow none ever came again" (*LotR* 529). The Ents become an unbeatable army that assists its neighbors. However, the Ents know they are fighting the long retreat: "Aye, aye, there was all one wood once upon a time from here to the Mountains of Lune, and this was just the East End" (*LotR* 457). Orcs of the Third Age are not responsible for all of the destruction; Men, Hobbits, and Dwarves also share culpability for deforestation.

The Ents act as a barrier between the other cultural groups of Middle-earth, separating cultures and regions physically, in a way that fosters diversity of local communities. The unresolved debate between the Ents (wilderness) and the Entwives (horticulture) is consistent with the text's inner debate over the rights Tolkien endows wilderness with and the expressed love of the beauty of cultivated nature. The ethic of the shepherds of the trees comes back to Tolkien's Christian environmental stewardship ethic, which acknowledges the validity of wilderness to exist according to its own laws, as endowed by the Creator, but despairs that all the Earth will eventually be subject to the control of fallen humans. In the end, it seems that the Ents' biocentric cultural version of stewardship – which allows the flora and fauna of the wilderness to develop along its own chaotic laws – is ideal and sufficient to the Ents but fails when it comes in contact with the anthropocentric cultural ethics of Men, Dwarves, Orcs, Hobbits, and Saruman and Sauron.

Forests as Shadows of Cultural Perception

To better understand Tolkien's ethics of forest stewardship, let us examine how the cultures of Middle-earth perceive forests. The Ents, the shepherds of the trees, are conservationists in the sense that they seek continuance of forests while allowing trees to develop organically. In this regard, the Ents are as focused on conserving their culture and home as the Elves or Hobbits are concerned with maintaining theirs. Each perspective is in some way self-serving. That the anthropocentric world-view dominates Middle-earth by the end of *The Lord of the Rings* is telling of Tolkien's opinion of the direction of development – it is to be human-controlled, as it is in the primary world. The cultural validity of the Elves and Ents, however, stresses the importance of considering the value of biocentrism and ecocentrism to the health, vitality, and variety of the natural world in an anthropocentric discourse so that man may be the best possible steward of the whole earth. By the end of *The Lord of the Rings*, however mysterious they still are, Ents are viewed by external cultures as an active, self-determining force. These shepherds of the forest represent a biocentric sylvan world-view that, however limited in number, influences external cultures.

How a culture interacts with and defines forests is more indicative of the culture than the nature of the forest. In popular imagination, forests are traditionally places of darkness and fear, concealment, enchantment, awe, wonder, and harbingers of the threatening or alien outsider. Wilderness is a place separate from human culture and, as such, not ruled by human laws. The laws that rule nature are not apparent. For Frodo and Sam traveling in secret to Mordor, the forest is a place of concealment – for them as well as their enemies. When Faramir and his soldiers capture the two hobbits in the no-man's land of Ithilien, each group is suspicious of the other's intentions. Faramir in the wild represents a Robin Hood trope, what Martin Simonson (207-208) refers to in *The Lord of the Rings and the Western Narrative Tradition* as an instance of "nineteenth-century 'pseudomedieval' romance" in which the cultivated "outlaw" in the woodland setting indicates a sense of adventure and mystery. Faramir and his men hide themselves in the forests of Ithilien, using its cover as a disguise to fight off Orcs. As Harrison points out,

> the first and most essential cover of all for the outlaw is none other than the forest itself. The forest represents his locus of concealment. […] In its shadows the outlaw finds safe haven from the established order and can harass his enemies like an invisible presence that every now and then reveals itself, suddenly and unexpectedly, only to withdraw again under the forest's cover. (79-80)

The same is true of Gollum who disappears within the cover of the forest so well he is initially concealed from Faramir and his party.

If we consider the forests of Middle-earth as Harrison considers them, allowing that the cultural perception of forests tells us a great deal about the values of the society doing the perceiving, then the Old Forest and Fangorn represent all those elements of reality Hobbits shy away from in fear – darkness, confusion, constriction, threat from the unknown Other, verticality, etc. Verlyn Flieger in "Taking the Part of the Trees: Eco-Conflict in Middle-earth" argues that the Old Forest is "Tolkien's version of the standard fairy-tale dark wood" (149). In some respects, this is correct. Like forests of fairy, the Old Forest is associated with warnings and lessons. In speaking of Buckland, a hobbit claims that it is no wonder that hobbits from Buckland are odd, "if they live on the wrong side of the Brandywine River and right agin the Old Forest. That's a dark bad place […]" (*LotR* 22). The hobbits of Buckland see the Old Forest as an enemy, building a hedge to separate their civilization from the wilderness of the forest: "But, of course, it was not a complete protection. The Forest drew close to the hedge in many places. The Bucklanders kept their doors locked after dark, and that also was not usual in the Shire" (*LotR* 97). The perceived threat might be the dangers which the forest can conceal from sight – like thieves and vagabonds. However, as we read on, we learn that the threat is actually the forest itself. The forest is clearly a wilderness, in many ways unknown, unexplored, and uninviting to the hobbits: "'But that can only mean going into the Old Forest!' said Fredegar horrified" (*LotR* 105) as Frodo explains his plan of secret escape from Buckland. "It is quite as dangerous as Black Riders. […] You won't have any luck in the Old Forest […]. No one ever has luck in there. You'll get lost. People don't go in there" (*LotR* 105). The comparison of the forest to the Black Riders, the most powerful of Sauron's forces, is indicative of just how deeply-seated the hobbits' fear of forests is. Merry disagrees, claiming that the Brandybucks venture in on occasion – "usually in daylight, of course, when the trees are sleepy and fairly quiet" (*LotR* 105). However Merry also finds the forest troubling:

> But the Forest *is* queer. Everything in it is very much more alive, more aware of what is going on, so to speak, than things are in the Shire. And the trees do not like strangers. They watch you. [...] They do say the trees do actually move, and can surround strangers and hem them in. In fact long ago they attacked the Hedge [...] But the hobbits came and cut down hundreds of trees, and made a great bonfire in the Forest [...]. After that the trees gave up the attack, but they became very unfriendly. (*LotR* 108)

By Merry's admission, hobbits have harmed the Old Forest in an attempt to keep the wilderness of trees from encroaching on settled lands. In a Tolkienian twist, the forest also seems to view the hobbits as unwelcome outsiders. Flieger attributes this tension to the conflict between civilization and wilderness which is necessary if human communities are to survive but which is regrettable nonetheless. The hobbits, attempting to travel north, are forced east and into the deepest part of the forest by unrelenting trees and eventually fall prey to Old Man Willow, who embodies the menacing traits hobbits ascribe to the forest. Old Man Willow is the biotic Other, the tree-being that despises the hackers and burners – a category which the hobbits fit into – and is able to cast a "spell" over the hobbits, causing them to fall asleep (*LotR* 114). Before long, the roots of the tree throw Frodo in the water and hold him down; Pippin has vanished as a crack in the tree closes over him; and Merry is trapped in a crevice "the edges of which gripped like a pair of pincers" (*LotR* 115). Sam and Frodo beat at the tree and "the leaves rustled and whispered, but with a sound now of faint and far-off laughter" (*LotR* 115). Though we sympathize with the hobbits, we can see Old Man Willow's justification, as well, in the story of the massacre. So far, experience justifies the hobbits' fear of forests and demonstrates how fear of the forest makes forests a physical barrier between communities.

Through Tom Bombadil (the master of the Old Forest), the hobbits begin

> to understand the lives of the Forest, apart from themselves, indeed to feel themselves as the strangers where all other things were at home [...] Tom's words laid bare the hearts of trees and their thoughts, which were often dark and strange, and filled with a hatred of things that go free upon the earth, gnawing, biting, breaking, hacking, burning: destroyers and usurpers. (*LotR* 127)

The adjectives describe the trees' dislike of Orcs, Dwarves, Hobbits, and Men – all those who use wood as fuel for fire. Which trees have "hearts" and "thoughts" remains unclear. Tom Bombadil seems to be referring to trees that appear non-sentient. Tolkien never clarifies. Yet, the interaction with Tom Bombadil expands the hobbits' perspective of the forests beyond their own cultural awareness.

In the Shire, individual "tame" trees denuded of their "wild" associations are harmless, picturesque, and highly valued. At Frodo and Bilbo's birthday party, the party tree is central to the action: "There was a specially large pavilion, so big that the tree that grew in the field was right inside it, and stood proudly near one end, at the head of the chief table" (*LotR* 26). The tree as symbol of community, continuity, and unity is both mythical and literal. Among the fireworks Gandalf brings to Bilbo's party for the appreciation of the hobbits are "green trees with trunks of dark smoke: their leaves opened like a whole spring unfolding in a moment, and their shining branches dropped glowing flowers down upon the astonished hobbits, disappearing with a sweet scent just before they touched their upturned faces" (*LotR* 27). The tree, it seems, is an important symbol for the familial hobbits, evoking a sense of community and attachment. In "The Evocative Symbolism of Trees," geographer Douglas Davies (41) directs our attention to the fact that "after all is said it remains true that grass, the most universal and successful of plants, has seldom fed the flames of creative thought to any marked extent. Trees have done so because they possess not only a variety of parts but because they stand over and against human generations in a way which demands acknowledgement." The variety of individual trees and trees in forests makes them prime candidates for taking on an array of symbolic meanings – from the grandeur and sheltering aspects of the Party Tree, to the fearsome Old Man Willow in the confusing and untidy Old Forest, to the regenerative Mallorn planted by Sam which marks the renewal of the Shire's fertility.

The interaction of Merry and Pippin with the Ents of Fangorn leads to new knowledge and potential symbolism of trees and forests in the Hobbit imagination. At the outset, Ents are nothing more than a fable to them. When one of the hobbits at the inn talks of a walking tree his cousin had seen, he has to defend himself, claiming, "But this one was as big as an elm tree, and walking – walking seven yards to a stride, if it was an inch" (*LotR* 43). The others believe the story is a tall tale. Merry and Pippin learn that the stories are true when they stumble into Fangorn. The Entin forest evokes fear; the cultural memory of Hobbits and Men remembers Fangorn Forest as dark, angry, and dangerous. Yet, it is also majestic, awe-inspiring, sad, mysterious, and powerful.

The perception Men of Middle-earth have of forests is similar to that of the Hobbits'. As the Men of Middle-earth become increasingly rational, they fear more and more that which cannot be explained rationally – like the Ents. It is the subconscious fear that keeps the Riders of Rohan from breaching the forest boundaries and makes the hobbits, at first, fear the wood. Hobbits, with their love of stories, are less resistant to the possibility of Ents than men like Denethor, Théoden, or the Riders of Rohan. Forests are dark and foreboding – in opposition to the open fields of the Mark. Harrison (6; author's emphasis) explains that "we have been a civilization of sky-worshipers, children of a celestial father. *Where divinity has been identified with the sky, or with the eternal geometry of the stars, or with cosmic infinity, or with 'heaven,' the forests become monstrous, for they hide the prospect of god.*" And yet, in both Christian tradition and Tolkien's religious conception, the forests are also the creation of God and embody His design. As Aragorn, Legolas, and Gimli camp on the borders of the forest, it seems to them that the wood "felt as a great brooding presence, full of secret purpose" (*LotR* 431). Aragorn, the representative of Middle-earth's greatest civilized city, says, "it is perilous to touch the trees of that wood" (*LotR* 430). He explains: "it is old […] as old as the forest by the Barrow-downs, and it is far greater. […] [it is] the last strongholds of the mighty woods of the Elder Days […] Yet Fangorn holds some secret of its own" (431). It may seem odd that Aragorn, who has spent so much time with the Elves, should express fear of the forest. But, if we consider that Aragorn has more respect for and knowledge of the individual cultures of Middle-earth than any other character excepting Gandalf, his statement is more evocative of wisdom than fear. He understands that Fangorn is often wronged by outsiders. The White Tree of Gondor is Aragorn's birthright; yet, as in the Shire with the Party Tree, the forest is "Other". The single tree is evocative of positive symbolism, while the forest is unfathomable, sublime rather than beautiful, and often negative in its associations. While walking through the Old Forest, Frodo sings a song: "[…] For though dark they stand/all woods there be must end at last,/and see the open sun go past […]" (*LotR* 110). In *The Road to Middle-earth* Shippey interprets this song literally as referring to the hobbits' desire to be free from the confines of the forest and, figuratively, as a reference to the life and death, in which death will "end in some vision of cosmic order which can only be hinted at in stars or 'sun'" (190). Forests, though part of creation, seem to be a barrier to connectedness with an ordered cosmos which an unobstructed sky full of stars seems to represent.

The forces of Fangorn Forest, of which everyone but Gandalf and Legolas has some fear, help the men of Rohan in their battle against Isengard because their goals are the same. But the men of Rohan fear the movable forest of Huorns, refusing to enter it: "The ends of their long sweeping boughs hung down like searching fingers, their roots stood up from the ground like the limbs of strange monsters, and dark caverns opened beneath them" (*LotR* 533). Gandalf explains the appearance of the trees: "'It is not wizardry, but a power far older […] a power that walked the earth, ere elf sang or hammer rang'" (*LotR* 531). The trees were a part of Middle-earth long before men. When the Ents begin to walk among the fields and the trees on the outskirts of Helm's Deep after disposing of the orc army, Gandalf explains that "indeed they are not concerned with us" (*LotR* 536). A forest that can decimate an army is fearsome, indeed. It is not likely, nor is it implied, that the perception of the forests by the Men of Middle-earth has changed with their encounters, helpful to their cause though the outcome may be.

Other than as destroyers of trees, the Orcs' perceptions of trees in *The Lord of the Rings* have not been examined, to my knowledge. Orcs are unique in Middle-earth for being killed by trees (out of revenge for trees they have hewn). They kill and are killed by Ents and Huorns. Orcs are a shadow of the sinister side of forests. Unlike the other cultures of Middle-earth which destroy forests based largely on need for wood or farmland, the Orcs take pleasure in the destruction and are purposefully wasteful – leaving trees cut down to rot. The green life of the forest is seen wholly as a commodity. Orcs inhabit nearly barren landscapes – places where barriers to sight do not exist. Harrison associates the rise of technological advancements with the creation of clearings for habitation and agriculture which parallels orc-ish associations with trees in industrialized landscapes, like Isengard and Mordor: "Technology appropriated its uses for the purpose of deforestation. Hence technology too takes its origins from the sky" (Harrison 10). Orcs, created in and living among a warrior culture where their own lives are unquestionably expendable, show a loathing for all those creations which have sustainable life, whether it be in the form of an enduring culture like that of Rohan (whom they raid and pillage) or in the form of the timeless forest of Fangorn (which they cut trees from). It is as true of Orcs as it is of humankind that, "[t]here is too often a deliberate rage and vengefulness at work in the assault on nature and its species, as if one would project onto the natural world the intolerable anxieties of finitude which hold humanity hostage to death" (Harrison 18). The lives of Orcs are nasty, brutish, and short; in consequence, they cannot abide the longevity of the forest.

It is impossible to talk of forest perception in *The Lord of the Rings* without mentioning Elves. Orcs themselves are a foil to the Elves – representing a disregard for nature and complete disenchantment from the world, as well as living a short, finite existence. The Elves, the most horticulturally-minded of the inhabitants of Middle-earth, revere trees. The Elves of Mirkwood and the Galadhrim of Lothlórien live in great, treed cities. Their respect for the trees, their desire to know more about them and live in harmony with them, led the Eldar to awaken the trees to speech. The cultural memory of the sylvan Elves harkens back the openness of the seas and shores which allow an unobstructed view of the stars: "We still remember, we who dwell/In this far land beneath the trees,/Thy starlight on the Western Seas" (*LotR* 78). As Shippey points out, "As for the wood, its beauty is a net and a barrier; starlight and memory alone pierce through 'to us that wander here/Amid the world of woven trees'" (189). Elves, though, see both the beauties and the limitations of the forests. We can presume, since they are the oldest human-like race in Middle-earth, that living within the forests was a conscious choice they made. Yet, even to the Elves, Fangorn Forest is mysterious. Celeborn tells the fellowship that "they should not [...] risk becoming entangled in the Forest of Fangorn. That is a strange land, and is now little known" (*LotR* 364). Celeborn hints that the opinions of the Ents towards ousiders are no longer known, that no one has alliances with the Ents which guarantee safe passage through the forest. Yet, it is Legolas, a Mirkwood elf, who wishes to return to Fangorn after the War of the Rings, to learn more about it. He desires Gimli to return with him, so that Gimli may learn the truth of the forest – that it is not as treacherous as axe-wielding Dwarves believe.

In summation, Men, Hobbits, Dwarves, and Orcs – who utilize the forest as commodity and fuel – perceive the forests as dangerous and hostile because civilization exists in a state of war against wilderness. Cultural memory, distanced from experience, maintains that the forests are to be feared and that strange beings live in the shadows. Strictly speaking, cultural memory is correct: Huorns, Ents, and trees like Old Man Willow are indeed sentient, angry, mysterious, and powerful. Ents and the forests they inhabit enhance and expand the perceptive boundaries of the other cultures they come into contact with. The Elves, who appreciate ecological balance and have a longer view of history, perceive the forests as part of the necessary ecology of Middle-earth and the Ents as a part of the cultural heterogeneity. Elves can better comprehend the stance of the biotic Other which perceives the other cultures of Middle-earth as a threat. By including the reader in the hobbits' journey into the forest, Tolkien initiates him or her into the cultural consciousness of the biotic Other (which is an essential to a stewardship ethic). Merry and Pippin come away from their experience in Fangorn with a new understanding of Ents. They know the Ents, like most beings, possess the potential to be dangerous, but they have also visited in two Ent-houses and made friends among the Ents. They recognize the Ents as a cultural group belonging to an ecologically diverse and distinct locale.

The Tolkienian Perspective

What does all this exegesis indicate about Tolkien's conscious (or unconscious) sylvan stewardship ethic? First, it is crucial to have an understanding of the role trees play in the English literary tradition which informed Tolkien's imagination, the cultural context of World War I and post-war forestry, and in his interaction with the natural world. In both Tolkien's personal and authorial lives, trees are integral to aesthetic, cultural, mental, and moral well-being. Tolkien upholds his love of trees: "I am (obviously) much in love with plants and above all trees, and always have been; and I find human maltreatment of them as hard to bear as some find ill-treatment of animals" (*L* 220). Further, his writing is in line with many of the debates that arose in the twentieth-century about the definition of wilderness and the voice of the biotic Other and responds to the increasing deforestation and science of forestry that arose in Great Britain as a result of the war.

Because he enjoyed being among the flora, Tolkien was observant of changes to the landscape. He did not fail to notice the increasing deforestation of Great Britain during and after World Wars I and II. Timber was needed for the war effort, especially as imports decreased. As a result, deforestation was apparent in the countryside, in the papers, and in the rising cost of commodities like wood and paper. *The Lord of the Rings* could not be published as one book (as he wrote it and desired it to be produced) due to paper shortages caused by World War II.

To better understand the scope of the forestry problem in Great Britain after World War I, let us examine a representative work: the head of the Department of Forestry at the University of Edinburgh E. P. Stebbings's *Commercial Forestry in Britain: Its Decline and Revival* (1919). The frontispiece is a photograph of old-growth larch and spruce trees in Perthshire before the war with a contrasting image of the same area in July of 1918: all the trees have been felled and only a few remain on the ground, devoid of branches, as loggers load them (6). Not a single standing tree remains in the 1918 photograph; the landscape is unrecognizable from its pre-war condition. Stebbing most laments that "we did not think it necessary to grow woods for purely commercial reason – that is, for the sake of the timber and pit wood and paper pulp they would yield" (10). The Royal Institution of Chartered Surveyors published a report in which they outline a proposal to increase homeland timber (13). The Surveyors claim that most existing forests contain only a quarter of the timber they potentially could support. Further, the limiting of foreign timber supplies led to an over-harvesting of native timber (43). The government of Great Britain, as represented by this report, is interested in the scientific management and the financial rewards of forestry. They express no other value in forests: "properly managed woodlands may be said to furnish two sources of wealth: […] livelihood […] and […] capital" (43). Of all the characters in *The Lord of the Rings* this type of capitalist bottom-line economic thinking is most exemplified by Saruman. Progressive and necessary as commercial forestry is, it fails to adequately address the conservation of wilderness for its intrinsic value.

Tolkien was aware of the forestry debates raging around him. In a response to a leader in the *Daily Telegraph*, he writes:

> It would be unfair to compare the Forestry Commission with Sauron because as you observe it is capable of repentance; but nothing it has done that is stupid compares with the destruction, torture and murder of trees perpetrated by private individuals and minor official bodies. The savage sound of the electric saw is never silent wherever trees are still found growing. (*L* 420)

Certainly this letter expresses Tolkien's disfavor with the practices of the Forestry Commission as described by Stebbing. In literature and culture, trees were tended to and adored; in a post-war economy, they were more valued as commodities. Forest commoditization, progressive in its foresight of growing timber for necessary commodities and lessening of wasteful use, is one of the triumphs of modern forestry. Stebbing divides the "utility of forests to a nation" into direct (timber) and indirect utility (i.e. climate moderations, game preserves, etc.): "The direct utility of the forest is dependent upon the produce which it yields, the capital it represents, and the amount of labour it employs" (12). Such commodification of trees, however progressive or necessary, fails to address intrinsic, aesthetic, and other values of trees and fosters homogenous forests. As is evident to ecocritics, Ents and trees are not merely commodities in *The Lord of the Rings*; they cannot be "owned." When asked if Tom Bombadil is the owner of the Old Forest, Goldberry responds: "The trees and grasses and all things growing or living in the land belong each to themselves" (*LotR* 122). This statement, along with the journey into the thoughts of the fox (a hint of post-humanism), suggests that Tolkien views the forests as something outside of human control and ownership. Control and ownership of forests leads to deforestation.

Primal boreal forests no longer exist in England – nor did they long before Tolkien's era. Such forests are relegated to England's far history. And yet, they are part of the English collective consciousness. Peter Ackroyd, author of *Albion: The Origins of the English Imagination*, tellingly opens his work with a chapter entitled "Trees." He traces the culture of trees through poetry and history:

"The mark or symbol of the hawthorn tree is to be found in the runic alphabet of the ancient British tribes, as if the landscape propelled them into speech" (3). The tree is so integral to culture that it "encloses a communal memory [...] and from it derives that sense of place, of literal rootedness, which is one of the great themes of the English imagination" (Ackroyd 6). Lending credence to this theory is the Norse belief in Yggdrasil – with which Tolkien was well-familiar – which locates the axis of the world in the root of the enormous ash which connects to the realm of the gods. Such beliefs stemmed from cultural awe of gigantic trees which were once prolific in north-western Europe. Indeed, the tree is a powerful symbol of connection and regeneration in the European imagination and provides a link for the modern audience to the once-forested regions of their homeland.

Tolkien's passion was to create a mythology for England based on authentic language and motifs, lamenting that there was "nothing English" among the popular mythologies (*L* 144). Tolkien depicts an aspect of a mythological tree-trope which is distinctly English: the sentient tree that walks, talks, and sometimes marches to war. In "Treebeard's Roots in Medieval European Tradition", Edward Pettit outlines the early English (and European) belief in walking and talking flora, tracing references through medieval English literature's "The Wanderer," "The Ruin," *Andreas, Beowulf,* the homilies of Ælfric, *Sir Gawain and the Green Knight,* the "Nine Herbs Charm", the Welsh "Cad Goddeu", the Norse *Prose Edda, Völsunga Saga,* and the *Orkneyinga Saga.* In this manner, "the tree grows through the literature of the English" and represents a foundational element of the English imagination (Ackroyd 8).

One of the Ents' strongest connections to early mythology is "Cad Goddeu" ("The Army of the Trees" or the "Battle of the Trees"), which tells the tale of the shape-shifting poet Taliesin and the delineation of the powers of trees in battle (Ford 183). The poet describes a battle field "where grass and trees attacked" and "stalwart trees" were transformed "into armies" (Ford 183). It seems likely that Tolkien was familiar with such myths; despite his expressed distaste for Celtic myths, his library contained a substantial number of Celtic texts and many of his ideas represent a merging of Anglo-Saxon and Celtic myths, as Dimitra Fimi argues in "Tolkien's 'Celtic type of Legends': Merging Traditions." In fact, his friend G. B. Smith bequeathed him a copy of *The Mabinogi*, in which "Cad Goddeu" appears (Fimi 51-52). As a man fascinated by trees, it is likely that a famous army of marching trees would have captured his attention and generated a reaction. This trope of the tree that has mobility is prevalent. For example: "fifteenth-century English mystics saw trees as men walking" (Ackroyd 7). In the seventeenth-century, Shakespeare's Macbeth queries, "Who can impress the forest, bid the tree/ Unfix his earthbound root?" (6.1). The answer, of course, is Tolkien who, in a letter to W. H. Auden, once wrote that the use of the Ents "is due, I think, to my bitter disappointment and disgust from schooldays with the shabby use made in Shakespeare of the coming of 'Great Birnam wood to high Dunsinane hill:' I longed to devise a setting in which the trees might really march to war" (*L* 212). Tolkien's Ents and Huorns do, of course, engage in combat. In fact, they are efficient warriors, razing Isengard, driving a wedge of fear into the consciousness of Saruman's army, and inhuming the mounds of dead after the battle for Helm's Deep. Yet, Tolkien's trees represent far more than warring trees – Ents are complex metaphysical beings.

Tolkien's imagination, steeped in medieval and ancient literature and longing for a mythology which would make the past come alive, was capable of revitalizing the old imagery in a new context which speaks to current issues. In talking of Númenor, Dickerson and Evans (136) point out that "Long before the modern environmental concern over destruction of the tree cover in U.S. cities or South American rain forests, Tolkien had already associated the downfall of a great civilization with its lust for lumber. And he expressed this in chilling descriptions that could apply equally well to modern clear-cutting practices." In reading over the script for a planned movie adaptation of *The Lord of the Rings* in 1958, Tolkien laments a suspected non-interest in trees and Treebeard because "the story is so largely concerned with them" (*L* 275). Recall that, in Tolkien's mythology, the two trees of Valinor contained a light more pure and beautiful than that of the sun and the moon. The darkness chooses to devour these trees, above all else. Tolkien created trees so radiant that stars pale in comparison.

Tolkien disagrees with the Enlightenment view of forestry as determining merely the "usefulness" of trees (Harrison 120). Morality and aesthetics are taken out of forestry, and commercial economy becomes the dominant ideology. Messiness, variables, and biodiversity are limited. Conversely, Tolkien's Entish forests are an anarchy of non-planning; this is his comment on what a forest *is*. While outlining the tenets of landscape criticism in *The Aesthetics of Landscape*, Steven Bourassa claims that a landscape expert:

> should [...] be able to explain how a landscape was in the past, how it came to be the way it is, how it functions today and what it is likely to become in the future. [...] should also be able to read and interpret the layers of cultural meaning in the landscape and assess their significance vis-a-vis other cultural values, social, political, and economic issues [...]. The expert may be able to enlighten the public and thereby change landscape perceptions and attitudes. (Bourassa 121-122)

Tolkien is such a landscape expert. Tolkien's letters also demonstrate familiarity with local species; as a man with knowledge of the local flora, Tolkien is well-placed as a landscape expert – a local geographer. The portrayal of trees/forests in his mythology argues against the industrial view of forests as something solely to be managed, cultivated, and commodified for purely economic gain. Ents (and by extension forests) are, at least in the novel, entities in their own right. Reader response to trees, forests, and Ents, as evidenced by the volume of criticism and popular representations, has had a lasting impact on cultural perceptions of trees – mirroring, in some respects, the alteration in the perspectives of the hobbits, Merry and Pippin.

As our reading of Tolkien's depictions of nature has shown, Tolkien believes humans have been given a divine initiative to care for (and cultivate) the world. Part of Tolkien's stewardship ethic presses for a lack of excess – living without waste. This is one of the greatest strengths of the sustainable ethics of Ents and Elves. *The Lord of the Rings* was written by a man disturbed by the implications of industrialism and modernism on the natural world and to the human spirit, a man living in a fallen world and in search of a recovery or a re-enchantment. In "On Fairy-Stories" Tolkien claims:

> Recovery (which includes renewal of health) is a re-gaining – regaining of a clear view. I do not say 'seeing things as they are' and involve myself with the philosophers, though I might venture to say 'seeing things as we are (or were) meant to see them' – as things apart from ourselves. We need, in any case, to clean our windows; so that the things seen clearly may be freed from the drab blur of triteness or familiarity – from possessiveness (OFS 146).

Tolkien contends that such recovery can be found in fantastic literature. The key to how *The Lord of the Rings* has acted as a counterbalance to modernism can be found in the language Tolkien employs. Miracles can be perceived when we view the world as we were "meant" to see it, free of our "possessiveness." Seeing clearly is part of re-enchantment. It is this possessiveness that Tolkien frees his audience from, with regards to trees and forests. When he professes that, "We say we know them. They have become like the things which once attracted us by their glitter, or their colour, or their shape, and we laid hands on them, and then locked them in our hoard, acquired them, and acquiring ceased to look at them" (OFS 146), he could easily be referring to the trees which have ceased to carry portent for modern humans. Through the Ents, Tolkien encourages mankind to see wilderness as an entity "apart from ourselves."

Tolkien's trees are complex and his renderings sometimes seem contradictory, i.e. trees are to be respected and sustained, but some of them are angry and dangerous, like Old Man Willow and some of the ents. In "Taking the Part of the Trees: Eco-Conflict in Middle-earth" Verlyn Flieger succinctly states: "Here is the sticking point: wild nature and the human community do not coexist easily. Perhaps in an ideal world they should, but in the real world they simply don't" (150). Tolkien's world is ultimately more realistic than ideal. As a result, Tolkien's Ents and forests are complex; they have suffered much and their perspective is outside of the human perspective – which views trees as resources for human consumption. Yet, Tolkien has been accused of making his trees dangerous and threatening in his appeal for their value, rather than pleasant and friendly. In this, Tolkien aligns himself with the Romantic concept of sublime nature – the idea that there should be some awe, fear, and humility in human interaction with un-tamed nature. There is behind these notions the recognition that humans do not comprehend God's creations but should acknowledge value in them, whether understood or not.

Flieger argues that the portrayal of trees in Tolkien is at odds with his proclaimed love of trees. This type of thinking supposes that Tolkien loves only what is innocent and beautiful in trees, without loving also those elements which are dark, gnarled, or threatening. It is because he loves trees that his depiction of them is sometimes unflattering. In response to a reference to himself, trees, and gloom, in *The Daily Telegraph* on June 29, 1972, Tolkien responded:

> I feel that it is unfair to use my name as an adjective qualifying 'gloom,' especially in a context dealing with trees. In all my works, I take the part of the trees as against all their enemies. Lothlórien is beautiful because there the trees were loved; elsewhere forests are represented as awakening to consciousness of themselves. The Old Forest was hostile to two legged creatures because of the memory of many injuries. Fangorn Forest was old and beautiful, but at the time of the story tense with hostility because it was threatened by a machine-loving enemy. (*L* 419-420)

Most cultures, if threatened by some enemy (like Orcs), become hostile to outsiders. It is as much the case in Fangorn or the Old Forest as in Bree and Rohan. Tolkien's letters contain myriad references to trees which demonstrate his concern for their welfare: "Every tree has its enemy, few have an advocate. (Too often the hate is irrational, a fear of anything large and alive, and not easily tamed or destroyed, though it may clothe itself in pseudo-rational terms)" (*L* 321). The pseudo-rational for Tolkien would have been the destruction of trees to make roadways or clear a view. As Harrison (245) contends in his study of forests: "As the order of institutions follows its course, or as huts give way to villages and then to cities and finally to cosmopolitan academies, the forests move further and further away from the center of the clearings. At the center one eventually forgets that one is dwelling in a clearing." Few in England live in forests. The forests have been tamed or eliminated.

Tolkien was a practical man; he certainly realized that wood was necessary for fires in the hearth, the manufacture of comfortable arm chairs, and paper to print books on. But he was also discontented by the waste of old trees and industrial forestry: "Much of Tolkien's attitude to trees reflects a quite different and much older perspective, namely, *woodsmanship*: a sensitive and sustainable use of nature, not for profit but for life, which entails not the conquest of an objectified nature but an ongoing relationship with various subjectivities, many of them nonhuman" (Curry 156). Likewise, in *The Lord of the Rings*, the only cultures to develop woodsmanship are the Elves and the Ents. Tolkien's trees have a point of view, and they are threatening because of it. The trees have long been wronged by the axes and fires of the inhabitants of Middle-earth as they consume them for fuel and timber. Trees, in Tolkien's forests, have long memories of many wrongs. Trees are the Other. How would a tree that is hundreds of years old feel about the other cultures of Middle-earth? If it thought about people at all, it would not be favorably inclined. With the Ents, Tolkien accomplishes something that many environmental activists would like to be able to do: to speak of trees with a language other than that of economic utility as they argue for the rights of forests. With justified indignation, the Ents cry, *"For bole and bough are burning now, the furnace roars – we go to war!"* (*LotR* 474). Unlike in Shakespeare's Birnam Wood, the action is literal.

About the Author

Andrea Denekamp currently lectures at SUNY Oneonta and Hartwick College. She completed her Ph.D., a study of regionalism in Tolkien's works, at Drew University in 2012.

Bibliography

ACKROYD, Peter. *Albion: The Origins of the English Imagination*. New York: Anchor Books, 2002.

BOURASSA, Steven C. *The Aesthetics of Landscape*. New York: Belhaven Press, 1991.

BRISBOIS, Michael J. "Tolkien's Imaginary Nature: An Analysis of the Structure of Middle-earth." *Tolkien Studies* 2 (2005): 197-216.

"Cad Goddeu." *The Mabinogi and Other Medieval Welsh Tales*. Trans. and ed. Patrick K. Ford. Berkeley CA: University of California Press, 1977. 183-187.

COHEN, Cynthia. "The Unique Representation of Trees in *The Lord of the Rings*." *Tolkien Studies* 6 (2009): 91-125.

CRONON, William. "The Trouble with Wilderness; or, Getting Back to the Wrong Nature." *Uncommon Ground: Rethinking the Human Place in Nature*. Ed. William Cronon. New York: W.W. Norton, 1996. 69-90.

CURRY, Patrick. *Defending Middle-earth. Tolkien: Myth and Modernity*. First published 1997. New York: Houghton Mifflin, 2004.

DAVIES, Douglas. "The Evocative Symbolism of Trees." *The Iconography of Landscape*. (Cambridge Studies in Historical Geography). First published 1988. Eds. Denis Cosgrove and Stephen Daniels. New York: Cambridge University Press, 2002. 32-42.

DICKERSON, Matthew and Jonathan Evans. *Ents, Elves, and Eriador: The Environmental Vision of J.R.R. Tolkien*. Lexington KY: University of Kentucky Press, 2006.

EISELEY, Loren. "How Natural is Natural?" *The Firmament of Time*. First published 1960. Lincoln NE: University of Nebraska Press, 1990. 153-181.

FIMI, Dimitra. "Tolkien's 'Celtic Type of Legends': Merging Traditions." *Tolkien Studies* 4 (2007): 51-72.

FLIEGER, Verlyn. "Taking the Part of the Trees: Eco-Conflict in Middle-earth." *J.R.R. Tolkien and His Literary Resonances: Views of Middle-earth*. Eds. George Clark and Daniel Timmons. Westport CT: Greenwood Press, 2000. 145-158.

FORD, Judy Ann. "The White City: *The Lord of the Rings* as an Early Medieval Myth of the Restoration of the Roman Empire." *Tolkien Studies* 2 (2005): 53-73.

HARRISON, Robert Pogue. *Forests: The Shadow of Civilization*. Chicago IL: The University of Chicago Press, 1993.

PETTIT, Edward. "Treebeard's Roots in Medieval European Tradition." *Mallorn* 42 (2004): 11-18.

ROYAL INSTITUTION OF CHARTERED SURVEYORS. *Unemployment after the War. Housing Emergency Schemes. Report of a Special Committee of the Council of the Institution*. London: The Institution, 1916. *Internet Archives*. 13 February 2011.

STEBBING, E. P. *Commercial Forestry in Britain: Its Decline and Revival*. John Murray: London, 1919. *Internet Archive*. 13 February 2011.

SHAKESPEARE, William. *Macbeth. William Shakespeare: The Complete Works*. Eds. Stanley Wells and Gary Taylor. Oxford: Clarendon Press, 1998. 975-999.

SHIPPEY, Tom. *The Road to Middle-earth: How J.R.R. Tolkien Created a New Mythology*. First edition 1982. Third edition. New York: Houghton Mifflin, 2003.

SIMONSON, Martin. *The Lord of the Rings and the Western Narrative Tradition*. Zurich and Jena: Walking Tree Publishers, 2008.

TOLKIEN, J.R.R. *The Lord of the Rings*. First published 1954-55. New York: Houghton Mifflin Company, 1994.

The Letters of J.R.R. Tolkien. First published 1981. Ed. Humphrey Carpenter, with the assistance of Christopher Tolkien. New York: Houghton Mifflin, 2000.

"On Fairy-Stories." *The Monsters and the Critics and Other Essays*. Ed. Christopher Tolkien. First published 1983. London: HarperCollins 1997. 109-161.

The Silmarillion. First published 1977. New York: Houghton Mifflin, 2001.

Jessica Seymour

"As we draw near mountains": Nature and Beauty in the Hearts of Dwarves

Abstract

When discussing the concept of nature in Tolkien's work, there is a tendency among scholars, critics, and even Tolkien himself to privilege the Elvish and Hobbitish love of growing things. This essay argues that the Dwarvish connection to mining and stone represents a celebration of the natural world, and an alternative ideal of beauty which privileges practicality along with aesthetics. This examination will be driven by a textual analysis of the Dwarves' relationship with geology in *The Hobbit*, *The Lord of the Rings*, and *The Silmarillion*. While Tolkien paints a mostly positive picture of Dwarves throughout his works, there remains a thematic connection between the Dwarvish love of gold, jewels and stone, and the negative traits of materialism and greed; but there is a multi-dimensionality to the natural world and the beauty to be found within it. Like their creator Aulë, the Dwarves see the potential of their natural environment, and interact with it in a uniquely utilitarian but nonetheless beautiful manner.

Introduction

Dwarves are known throughout Middle-earth for their craft skills, their extreme fondness for precious metals, and their mines built deep underground. Being carved from stone by their maker Aulë, the Dwarves express this connection to their natural environment through active, practical engagement with the earth, and much of their cultural legacy is entrenched in the treasures which they extract from their environment. Aulë made them "stone-hard" (*S* 39) – able to withstand the ravages inflicted on Middle-earth by the dark powers which dwelt there. Dwarves do not just exist in nature as the Elves and Hobbits do, growing and nurturing what they need to survive, nor do they attempt to suppress it or eradicate it like Orcs; Dwarves express themselves *through* nature, surround themselves with it, and put it to practical use.

Dwarves have a spiritual connection to gold and jewels which stems from their cultural heritage and the practices of their forefathers. Whether by extracting *mithril* to forge armour, or by tending to the Glittering Caves of Helm's Deep and drawing strength from their beauty, Dwarves connect with their geological roots as something living and vulnerable, but also useful and strong. They approach the natural world as a foundation; the stone and earth being the backbone upon which a great fortification can be built. The stronger the geology of an environment, the better the land and the races living there will endure. The Dwarvish connection to mining and stonemasonry represents a celebration of the natural world, and an alternative ideal of beauty which privileges practicality along with aesthetics.

There is a propensity among scholars, critics, and even Tolkien himself, to demonise the connection Dwarves feel to geology. This appears to narrow the focus of the word 'natural' to trees and growing things, and marginalises the Dwarves' culture and heritage. Tolkien, when crafting Middle-earth, reiterates through narration that Dwarves are, as a whole, "pretty bad lots" (*H* 258). He uses metaphors of stone, metal and jewels to indicate the evil aspects of a character, and the worst places in Middle-earth tend to be found deep underground in the darkest mines. While he often paints a rather unflattering image of Dwarves as being possessive, greedy and grasping, they are not the only characters to covet riches and material possessions. There are also several examples throughout Tolkien's œuvre of honourable dwarves who behave in an admirable manner; however, Dwarves remain one of the few races in Middle-earth to be constructed as almost universally untrustworthy by other characters.

It is important to recognise the diversity expressed in Middle-earth, and the different ways that races are portrayed as engaging with the natural environment, because it creates a more inclusive and wide-reaching ideal of 'beauty' which goes beyond simple aesthetics and into the realms of philosophy. While there are many things which could be considered troubling or problematic about the Dwarvish way of life (their excessive secrecy and insularity, their tendency towards greed), their understanding and appreciation of the natural world should not be marginalised simply because it does not conform to the Elvish and Hobbit standard.

I am not arguing in this chapter that Dwarves are perfect, or better than other races at interacting with the natural world. No race in Middle-earth is faultless, and Dwarves have not done themselves any favours by secreting themselves into the mountains and coveting the treasures of other races. Dwarves can, and frequently do, have an unhealthy relationship with the gold and gems they mine from the earth. Diversity in Middle-earth must necessarily lead to a diversity of ideas, and this diversity leads to a more nuanced, deeper understanding of the physical environment where the narratives are based. It is important, then, for different perspectives on nature and beauty to be appreciated for what they are: different, but not necessarily better or worse. If scholars will look beyond the occasional follies of this race to the philosophical justifications behind their love of rock and stone, I am confident they will find something admirable (even desirable) about how Dwarves see the natural world.

The Journey so Far

This chapter is driven by a textual analysis of the Dwarves' relationship with geology in *The Hobbit*, *The Lord of the Rings*, and *The Silmarillion*. This includes analyses of representations of the earth and stone in Middle-earth, how the natural world is portrayed or understood by Dwarves, and the various philosophical implications of races engaging with geology as a way to connect with their spiritual roots and cultural heritage. There is a clear tendency in Tolkien scholarship to glorify and idealise the Elvish and Hobbit relationship with nature – to the detriment of those races in Middle-earth who have carved a different path. By limiting the definition of 'nature' to growing things, Tolkien scholars and ecocritics create a situation where it is almost impossible to analyse how Dwarves interact with the natural world in a positive manner. As a result, most scholars ignore Dwarves entirely when discussing Tolkien and the natural world.

Matthew Dickerson and Jonathan Evans' *Ents, Elves and Eriador: The Environmental Vision of Tolkien* limits the discussion of interactions with the environment to three main methods: agriculture (practiced by Hobbits), horticulture (practiced by Elves and Entwives), and feraculture (practiced by Ents) (31). While Dickerson and Evans' analysis of the various ecocritical themes in Tolkien's work is very thorough, it does necessarily marginalise Dwarvish engagements with the natural world because they do not fit into any of the above categories. In fact, Dwarves are only really mentioned in Dickerson and Evans's work as a negative point of contrast; a way to highlight the goodness of Elves, in particular, by comparing them with Dwarves and their reputed love of treasure: "[...] in terms of aesthetics, the Elves are most sharply contrasted with the Dwarves, who value the environment primarily as a source of fuel, building materials, and precious gems and metals" (Dickerson and Evans 101). Alun Morgan's work on stewardship and Middle-earth also fails to mention Dwarves, despite frequent references in the narratives to Dwarves' desire to protect and manage the natural environment.

It is very easy, when dealing with Tolkien's work, to make the thematic connection between growing things and goodness. There is a clear link between how safe the characters feel, and how many trees and plants happen to be growing nearby. Karen Sullivan writes that "[p]lants sustain life, and the peaceful cultivation of crops is in Tolkien's model the complete antithesis of obtaining incredible objects by force" (93). The obvious exception to this would be the forests; Mirkwood, Fangorn, and the Old Forest on the borders of Buckland, where the trees have become sentient. These forests are portrayed as stifling and dangerous to outsiders, and this is seen as being a direct result of the meddling of other creatures – either the trees have grown angry and dangerous as a response to their mistreatment, or they have been poisoned by dark powers. These forests are sharply contrasted by the realms of Rivendell and Lothlórien, where the inhabitants live in harmony with plants, and the protagonists can rest and recuperate before continuing their quest. As a contrast, the darker, more dangerous places in Middle-earth are described as desolate, gloomy, and devoid of growing things. Mordor has become so poisoned by evil that nothing may ever grow there again, and the lack of green in Gondor is an indication of the sickness which has grown in the city since the days of the King ended.

Interestingly, the most positive discussions of Dwarves and mining are found not among Tolkien scholars or literary theorists, but in the geology discipline. Danièle Barberis, a Natural Resources Lawyer specializing in mineral law and policy, writes a comparative analysis of the portrayal of Dwarves in Tolkien's work and the real-world miners in the 'Fourth Age' (or contemporary times). She aptly points out that the Dwarves in Middle-earth create homes and cities in their mines: "each large mine was more than simply a workplace. They were underground settlements, 'the great city of the dwarrowdelf'. So the dwarves didn't need badges or passwords for access – they were home already" (64). The relationship, then, between Dwarves and the mines they build is less about profit (although that is a significant concern) and more about the construction of a place where Dwarves can feel safe and secure while they develop their crafts and seek their riches.

Barberis also points out the largely ignored Dwarvish desire to preserve natural beauty for future generations:

> It can be said that although modern Men as well as the Dwarves have a common concern for the good of future generations, Men look toward this issue from a purely practical standpoint (roughly, fear of depletion) while Dwarves had a higher ideal (beauty) in mind. Here, Lady Galadriel's words seem appropriate: *"Hear all ye Elves. Let none say again that Dwarves are grasping and ungracious"* and well wonder at our own (human) philosophical concern which has all to do with a fear of lacking in the future and little with a quest for beauty. (61, emphasis in original)

The preservation of the beauty of a mine for future generations is a key part of the Dwarvish identity, as I will discuss later in this chapter. The dynastic nature of Dwarvish mining constructs the mine as a legacy to be cultivated and maintained so that the family may continue to prosper. There is also, among the races of Middle-earth, a distinct stand-offishness towards Dwarves which may well account for their desire to remain down in their mines where they can feel at home. Dennis Knepp writes that Dwarves have a fundamentally different approach to social exchanges and language because they are positioned in the narrative as blue-collar workers; sharply contrasting the upper-class Elves and bourgeois Hobbits (52). Several scholars, as well as Tolkien himself, draw comparisons between Dwarves in Middle-earth and real-world Jews and posit that the narratives are steeped in anti-Semitic stereotypes, but Renée Vink argues that such thinking is problematic because it draws the Dwarves into an unnecessary allegory (141). The fact is, Tolkien drew inspiration from many cultures and traditions when constructing Middle-earth. This paper is focused on how these races are constructed *within* the narratives; in the context of

Tolkien's Middle-earth, the differences between Dwarvish manners and the manners of the rest of the races of Middle-earth separates and marginalizes the Dwarves who are unable to conform to the idealised behaviours of the bourgeoisie or the cultural elite.

Negative Impressions

While the Dwarves enjoy metalwork and stonemasonry, other races such as Elves and Hobbits tend to be associated primarily with growing things; the trees, plants, and flowers native to Middle-earth. Although there are instances, particularly in *The Silmarillion*, where Elves are portrayed as miners and smiths, they are not portrayed as being associated with these trades in the way that Dwarves are. Because the flora of Middle-earth is associated with goodness, and rock and stone associated with evil, it is interesting to note the various comparisons and physical features which separate the races associated with these parts of the natural world.

Throughout Tolkien's works, Dwarves and Elves are consistently portrayed as each other's antithesis. Their physical differences are frequently highlighted in the narration – particularly the Dwarvish beards, which are often used as the Dwarves' defining feature. Dwarves are known throughout Middle-earth for their craftsmanship, but their physical attributes – their beards, grizzled features and size – are just as well-known (*H* 12). Elves, on the other hand, are known for their eerie beauty and ethereal nature; being wise and long-lived, taller than men, and with no beards at all (representing them as cleaner and more refined than the blue-collar mining Dwarves). The antagonistic relationship between Dwarves and Elves is established early in *The Hobbit* when it is pointed out that Dwarves often get annoyed with Elves because they "tease them and laugh at them, and most of all at their beards" (*H* 68).

The antagonism between Elves and Dwarves, arguably born from the Dwarves' theft of the Nauglamir in *The Silmarillion* (*S* 279), has lasted several ages and is portrayed as being integral to their relationship. When the Fellowship reaches Lothlórien in *The Fellowship of the Ring*, Aragorn and Legolas have to vouch for Gimli, who must be blindfolded before he is allowed to enter the Elven realm (*LotR* 362). Likewise, in *The Hobbit*, Thorin is captured by Woodland Elves and dragged "not too gently, for they did not love dwarves, and thought he was an enemy" into their dungeons (*H* 207). Characters frequently note that they are "not over fond of dwarves" (*H* 152) during their dealings with them, particularly in *The Hobbit* where Dwarves are depicted as relying on the kindness and compassion of other races throughout their adventure. Lord Elrond (*H* 72), the Eagles (*H* 140), and Beorn (*H* 152) all offer their assistance to Thorin and Company out of a desire to remove a particular obstacle or inconvenience another race whom they dislike more; not out of any particular regard for the race of Dwarves as a whole. In this way, Dwarves are often depicted as ostracized from the other races of Middle-earth and living on the fringes of society.

The Elves were sung into being by Eru Ilúvatar, the main deity in Middle-earth and the creator of the Valar (or gods), before the world began. They were created, as the first children, to enjoy Eru's unspoiled creation and live a joyous, immortal life. However, after Morgoth's deceit (structured in *The Silmarillion* as a fall from grace similar to that of the Christian Lucifer), the Elves' existence was marred by trouble and discord, and some of them were tortured and warped into the race of Orcs. Aulë, the master of crafts among the Valar, created the Dwarves as a response to Morgoth's rebellion. He built them to be strong and durable, "stone-hard, stubborn, fast in friendship and in enmity, and they suffer toil and hunger and hurt of body more hardily than all other speaking peoples" (*S* 39). This creation myth offers a particularly interesting perspective on the use of Elves and Dwarves to contrast each other in the narratives. Eru adopts the Dwarves as his own children, although he expects them to clash with the Elves, "the children of my adoption and the children of my choice" (*S* 38), and Yavanna, Aulë's spouse, worries that they will not love growing things because her husband made them in his image. Aulë tries to alleviate Yavanna's concerns ("Eru will give them dominion, and they shall use all that they find in Arda: though not, by the purpose of Eru, without respect and without gratitude" (*S* 40)), but Yavanna continues to believe that the Dwarves will disrespect trees and plants because they were not designed to appreciate them as Elves were.

Apart from the obvious connection between gold and the antagonist of *The Lord of the Rings* (Sauron's One Ring), there is a consistent thematic link throughout the narratives between evil, illness, and objects mined from the earth. Sullivan writes that the narratives structure goodness as being synonymous with growing things, while stone, gems and gold are associated almost exclusively with evil (93). When describing the dark, evil creatures in Middle-earth, there is a tendency for Tolkien to use earthy metaphors: describing "their horrible stony voices" (*H* 81) when referring to the Goblins in the Misty Mountains, and transcribing the song of the Barrow-wight in *The Fellowship of the Ring* "[c]old be sleep under stone: never more wake on stony bed" (*LotR* 156). Treebeard uses Saruman's desire to surround himself with stone walls in Isengard as a testament to his shift towards darkness: "[h]e has a mind of metal and wheels; and he does not care for growing things, except as far as they serve him for the moment" (*LotR* 494), and the Men who serve Sauron are separated from Men of other lands by their signifiers of wealth: "[t]hey have [...] gold rings in their ears; yes, lots of beautiful gold" (*LotR* 672). There is a consistent theme in the usage of words and signifiers which remind the reader of earth, stone and mining to indicate that a character is evil.

This theme extends to settings and scenes in the narratives where there is little to no plant-life. There is a stark contrast between the dark, desolate mines of Moria (and the evil which befalls the Fellowship there) and the restful, peaceful, almost spiritual reprieve to be found in Lothlórien. Descriptions of Lothlórien favour the tall Mallorn trees; interestingly using comparisons to precious metals to demonstrate their loveliness:

> There are no trees like the trees of that land. For in the autumn their leaves fall not, but turn to gold. Not till the spring comes and the new green opens do they fall, and then the boughs are laden with yellow flowers; and the floor of the wood is golden, and golden is the roof, and its pillars are of silver, for the bark of the trees is smooth and grey. (*LotR* 353)

It appears that, when described in conjunction with growing things, gold and silver are devoid of their negative connotations. Another illustration of the connection between growing things and goodness can be found in the minor reprieve Frodo and Sam find in Ithilien, before beginning the final leg of their journey into Mordor: "After they had passed the passages and stairs they felt the cool morning air, fresh and sweet, about them [...] To the west they could see light through the trees, as if the world came there to a sudden end" (*LotR* 722). Descriptions of Moria, however, tend to focus on the lack of light (almost oppressive), the foul smell of the air (*LotR* 328), and the knowledge that Moria is actually the tomb of Balin, Oin and Ori; further solidifying the mine's relationship to darkness and death. There is also the Dwarvish desire for *mithril*, which awakes the Balrog when the Dwarves of Moria "delved too greedily and too deep" (*LotR* 308) in search of it.

Dwarves are often portrayed as being particularly susceptible to greed, and as having an unhealthy desire for wealth and riches. This is seen by Tolkien scholars and the other characters in the narratives as at best a personality flaw, and at worst a crippling illness. The most obvious narrative example of gold-sickness can be found in *The Hobbit*, when Thorin Oakenshield attempts to cast Bilbo off the gates of Erebor in a fit of madness (*H* 331). Thorin's madness is structured in the narrative to directly follow his over-exposure to Smaug's hoard – establishing a causality between the two: "Long hours in the past days Thorin had spent in the treasury, and the lust of it was heavy on him. Though he had hunted chiefly for the Arkenstone, yet he had an eye for many another wonderful thing that was lying there" (*H* 318). His violent altercation with Bilbo after the theft of the Arkenstone is represented as a culmination of his gold-sickness.

Although it can be said that many other characters are considered greedy and needlessly concerned with treasure and material possessions, it is only the Dwarves, as a collective, who are perceived to be universally untrustworthy. One of the first descriptions of the Elevenking Thranduil in *The Hobbit* emphasises his love of treasure and his jealousy of others who have more than him: "If the elf-king had a weakness it was for treasure, especially for silver and white gems; and though his hoard was rich, he was ever eager for more, since he had not yet as great a treasure as other elf-lords of old" (*H* 208). Later, this description of Thranduil is juxtaposed and softened by his generous treatment of the Lake Town refugees (*H* 306).

There are also examples of greed and envy in one of Tolkien's most idealised races: the Hobbits. Bilbo's spoon-stealing relatives, the Sackville-Bagginses, are portrayed throughout the narratives as jealous of Bilbo and covetous of his possessions: "On their side they never admitted that the returned Baggins was genuine, and they were not on friendly terms with Bilbo after. They really had wanted to live in his nice hobbit-hole so very much" (*H* 363). Their son, Lotho, is also credited with allowing Saruman enough trade power to eventually take over the Shire in *The Return of the King* (*LotR* 1051). Nevertheless, it is the Dwarves who are consistently described as almost irredeemably greedy and grasping, and these descriptions often refer to the entire race:

> There it is: dwarves are not heroes, but calculating folk with a great idea of the value of money; some are tricky and treacherous and pretty bad lots; some are not, but are decent people like Thorin and Company, if you don't expect too much. (*H* 258-259)

While *The Hobbit* is considered by many to be an exceptional narrative as part of the legendarium (with its references to Goblins instead of Orcs, and the more fantastical style of storytelling), the above description echoes through the tales and colours many of the interactions between races. As noted previously, many characters and races "have no great love" of Dwarves based on the cultural assumption that Dwarves are untrustworthy or disinterested in things not representing material wealth. *The Hobbit*, as the first published of the legendarium, and the book to deal most heavily with Dwarves and the relationship Dwarves have with other races, becomes the catalyst for the reader's understanding of the social affairs of Middle-earth.

Dwarvish Connections with Nature

In Tolkien's works, Dwarves are generally portrayed as engaging with the geology of Middle-earth as craftsmen; imagining and appropriating the materials around them, crafting new and beautiful objects from the stone and gems they liberate from the earth, and protecting and admiring those rock and stone formations which are considered particularly aesthetically pleasing.

G. Seddon's 1996 Mawson Lecture on "Thinking like a geologist" notes the importance of geology for tracing the history of a place and understanding the people who live there: "the discipline of geology affect[s] the case of mind, the way one thinks and perceives and behaves" (487). During *The Lord of the Rings* trilogy, Gimli frequently makes note of the natural rock formations around him, and often judges the durability and beauty of an area by how it is formed: "There is good rock here. This country has tough bones […] Give me a year and a hundred of my kin and I would make this a place that armies would break upon like water" (*LotR* 555). In *The Return of the King*, Gimli notes that Minas Tirith appears to have had some good stonemasons working on its construction, but that he can see areas of improvement and would be happy to render his assistance in this endeavour (*LotR* 906). These moments clearly indicate the Dwarvish relationship with rock and stone as one of mutual benefit; Dwarves approach the natural world with a desire to improve and make use of it, while noting that a good natural foundation is the best basis for their labours.

While Dwarves are portrayed as enjoying working with gems and jewellery, they have a particular affinity with steel and iron which is reminiscent of the relationship between potters and clay. When the Fellowship is ploughing through the depths of Moria, Gandalf recounts how the Dwarves interact with the various substances they pull from the earth: "[t]he wealth of Moria was not in gold and jewels, the toys of the Dwarves; nor in iron, their servant" (*LotR* 335). This is an interesting choice of words, and it implies that the Dwarvish connection with iron is very much linked with purpose and applicability. Dwarves *use* the iron they draw from the earth – fashioning useful things like armour, helmets and weapons which can be used to defend themselves and their mines. *The Silmarillion* also makes it a point to explain the craft of Dwarves as it relies on the natural environment where they get their tools: "for even from the first days of their Fathers they had marvellous skill with metals and with stone; but in that ancient time iron and copper they loved to work, rather than silver or gold" (*S* 103). It appears that the usefulness of metals is as important to Dwarves as their beauty – although in some cases when a metal is as beautiful as it is useful it is doubly valuable, as in the case of *mithril*.

Dwarves tend to be portrayed as gaining the most satisfaction from working directly with the tools and materials of the earth to create something new and exciting. Many of their most beautiful pieces are designed with some practical element or use. The Nauglamir, or the Necklace of the Dwarves, was designed to be so light that the wearer would barely notice it, and the *mithril* shirt gifted to Bilbo by Thorin Oakenshield is both beautiful and wonderfully useful. Dwarvish smiths appropriated designs from the Elves to enhance the beauty of the piece, but made sure that the mail was practical by working it from one of the toughest materials they had. *Mithril* looks like silver, which appeals aesthetically to Elves and Hobbits (without the negative connotations attributed to gold), and even the Orcs of Mordor start a brawl over who can keep the shirt once they have stripped Frodo: "It was Gorbad started it, trying to pinch that pretty shirt" (*LotR* 940). The incredible wealth represented in a shirt of pure *mithril*, a "kingly gift" as Gimli puts it (*LotR* 335), is also a status symbol. The Dwarves appropriated these ideals (presumably working to a brief, since it was originally a gift) to create a piece of clothing which appeals aesthetically to every race, but which proves practically invaluable in the War of the Ring by protecting the Ringbearer.

As craftsmen, the Dwarves primarily enjoy the natural world as it provides raw material for their works. There is also a sense of place and connection with the natural environment demonstrated when the Dwarves consistently choose to surround themselves with rock and stone. As mentioned above, Dwarves frequently turn their mines into homes and settlements. They create elaborate cities beneath the surface, and these cities demonstrate the pride Dwarves take in their craft and the feats of engineering required to construct them. In *The Hobbit*, the narration describes Erebor's beautiful architecture as a link to Dwarvish pride and skill: "[i]t was a passage made by dwarves, at the height of their wealth and skill: straight as a ruler, smooth-floored and smooth-sided, going with a gentle never-varying slope direct" (*H* 259). The aesthetics of Dwarvish architecture may not align with the elegance of the Elves or the simplicity of the Hobbits, but there is something admirable in the skill and execution of the Dwarvish architects; especially when compared to the ugly, ill-thought-out structures of other earth-dwelling creatures like Goblins and Orcs (*H* 67).

When Dwarves come across a particularly beautiful natural structure, such as the Glittering Caves at Helm's Deep, they are compelled to preserve it. During *The Two Towers*, when Legolas jokingly tells Gimli to keep the Glittering Caves a secret to protect them from the ravages of his race, Gimli replies indignantly:

> No dwarf could be unmoved by such loveliness. None of Durin's race would mine those caves for stones or ore, not if diamonds and gold could be got

there. Do you cut down groves of blossoming trees in the spring-time for firewood? We would tend these glades of flowering stone, not quarry them. With cautious skill, tap by tap – a small chip of rock no more, perhaps, in a whole anxious day – so we could work, and as years went by, we should open new ways, and display far chambers that are still dark, glimpsed only as a void beyond fissures in the rock. And lights, Legolas! We should make lights, such lamps as once shone in Khazad-dûm; and when we wished we would drive away the night that has lain there since the hills were made; and when we desired rest, we would let the night return. (*LotR* 571)

Although Dwarves are not known for their poetry and prose, it must be said that the natural beauty of geology is one of the few things which can inspire a Dwarf towards rhetoric. It is important to note that, in the above passage, Gimli does not rule out Dwarvish interference with the Caves – in fact, he makes a point of explaining how a group of Dwarves could go about carving and mining the Caves to enhance the natural beauty which is already there. Here, the relationship Dwarves have with the natural world is made particularly clear. While no Dwarf would dare to sully the Caves with unnecessary mining, they would be remiss if they did not cultivate and develop the Caves to showcase the best rock. Dwarves immerse themselves in natural beauty by identifying ways in which it can be improved, and then going about the necessary improvements using their skills as craftsmen; building on the natural aesthetic, but putting a part of themselves into the stone.

It must also be said, for it is not said often enough, that there is a clear narrative separation between the Dwarvish love of stone and the practices of evil characters such as Saruman and the Orcs. While the Dwarves are most often associated with mining and stonemasonry, the use of industrial practices is not typical of their race; they use neither big machinery nor mass-production when working their crafts. Although Aulë notes in *The Silmarillion* that "they will have need of wood" (*S* 42), referring to smelting practices which require intense heat, they are very rarely referenced in the narratives as clearing trees or unnecessarily burning them. This is a sharp contrast to the practices of Saruman during *The Lord of the Rings*, when he begins cutting down the trees of Fangorn forest "to feed the fires of Orthanc. There is always smoke rising from Isengard these days" (*LotR* 495).

Saruman's destructive industrial expansion is seen later, towards the conclusion of *The Return of the King*, when the Hobbits return to the Shire and find that it has been swept up in a tide of 'progress'. The mill has been knocked down and replaced with a much larger one "full o' wheels and outlandish contraptions [...] They're always a-hammering and a-letting out a smoke and a stench [...] And they pour out filth a purpose; they've fouled all the lower Water" (*LotR* 1050-1051). While it could be said that some Dwarvish practices are not ideal in a world which privileges the love of growing things over all others, Dwarves are never depicted as engaging in the destructive, 'progressive' practices of Saruman and his followers.

Because of the underground cities and mining practices employed by both species, there is occasionally a narrative link between Dwarves and Goblins (or Orcs, as they are known in *The Lord of the Rings* and *The Silmarillion*). When Goblins are first introduced to the reader in *The Hobbit*, the narration explains the Goblins' affinity with building apparatuses and caves which are designed to be unpleasant to outsiders:

> Now goblins are cruel, wicked, and bad-hearted. They make no beautiful things, but they make many clever ones. They tunnel and mine as well as any but the most skilled dwarves, when they take the trouble, though they are usually untidy and dirty [...] It is not unlikely that they invented some of the machines that have since troubled the world, especially the ingenious devices for killing large numbers of people at once, for wheels and engines and explosions always delighted them, and also not working with their own hands more than they could help. (*H* 83-84)

Goblins are particularly noteworthy because they are the only race which is not described as actively ostracising Dwarves; in fact, they are described as working alongside the most wicked of the Dwarves on odd occasions, and as not having any particular hatred for the race as a whole. As discussed above, most races in Middle-earth treat Dwarves comparatively harshly.

This could lead some readers to make a connection between the Dwarves and Goblins, although this connection is very shallow when the numerous differences between the philosophical and moral practices of the two races are explored. For example, the above quote notes that Goblins never work with their hands if they can help it, preferring instead to make "prisoners and slaves that have to work till they die for want of air and light" (*H* 83) to do most of their building for them. This is a sharp contrast to the joy and purpose which Dwarves find in craftsmanship. There is also a clear abhorrence among Goblins towards beautiful objects of no value, whereas Dwarves, as discussed previously, enjoy making beautiful things with a practical element to them. The Goblins and Orcs are also described as revelling in the destruction of trees and growing things. In *The Two Towers*, when Gimli is introduced to Fangorn, he tries not to offend the trees there because he recognises and respects their power: "'[...] I will keep my axe loose in my belt. Not for use on trees,' he added hastily, looking up at the tree under which they stood" (*LotR* 512). The narrative sets up the two races as similar in their approach, but radically different in their philosophy.

Dwarves, being mythically associated with Aulë's love of rock and stone, express their family connections and heritage through artefacts drawn from the earth and passed through the generations. In *The Silmarillion*, the Men of Númenor are described as long-lived, but not immortal, in a similar manner to the Dwarves (*S* 315). As a result, the Númenóreans become obsessed with the gathering of knowledge and possessions, and eventually rebel against the Valar because they want more time to enjoy them. The Dwarves seem to have compensated for their long-lived mortality by valuing the artefacts created by their forefathers: "Memory is not what the heart desires. That is only a mirror, be it clear as Kheled-zâram [...] Elves may see things otherwise [...] Not so for Dwarves" (*LotR* 399). Gimli, upon receiving his gift from the Lady Galadriel of three strands of her hair, plans to treasure it to the end of his days and beyond: "And if ever I return to the smithies of my home, it shall be set in imperishable crystal to be an heirloom of my house, and a pledge of good will between the Mountain and the Wood until the end of days" (*LotR* 396). This is the highest honour he can afford to the gift of Galadriel, hoping he will live long enough to enjoy and preserve it for future generations, so they also can get to appreciate it after his demise.

Unlike Smaug and the Trolls described in *The Hobbit*, Dwarves are not depicted as collecting gold in large quantities for the sake of having lots of gold – they tend to collect beautiful things and make use of them; for pleasure, development of craft, or to use in trade. They use gold to improve their quality of life and enjoy the pleasures their trades afford them: "[...] the poorest of us had money to spend and to lend, and leisure to make beautiful things just for the fun of it, not to speak of the most marvellous and magical toys" (*H* 37). Thorin Oakenshield describes the treasure of Erebor as his heritage, indicating a personal relationship with the gold, silver and jewels owned by the Dwarves living there:

> From there the talk turned to the great hoard itself and to the things that Thorin and Balin remembered. They wondered if they were still lying there unharmed in the hall below: the spears that were made for the armies of the great King Bladorthin (long since dead) each had a thrice-forged head and their shafts were inlaid with cunning gold, but they were never delivered or paid for; shields made for warriors long dead; the great golden cup of Thror, two-handed, hammered and carven with birds and flowers whose eyes and petals were of jewels; coats of mail gilded and silvered and impenetrable. (*H* 279)

When Bard and the Lake Men approach Thorin at the climax of *The Hobbit* and demand one twelfth of Smaug's hoard, Thorin refuses because, not only is he suffering from gold-sickness, but he also considers the request particularly threatening: "none of our gold shall thieves take or the violent carry off while we are alive" (*H* 312). The treasure, as representative of Thorin's kin, has far too much sentimental value to be bartered over by greedy Men. Despite the Lake Men's claim to *some* of the treasure (being the descendants of Dale, which was frequently sacked by Smaug when it was inhabited), a twelfth share is alarmingly high considering each member of Thorin's company would only have been entitled to one fourteenth of the *profits* of their venture.

While Dwarves rarely come up in the discussions of ecocritical themes in Tolkien's work, I would argue that the ecocritical concerns gleaned by critics can apply to the Dwarvish relationship with nature – just not in the traditional manner. For example, the Dwarvish approach to the natural world could be considered a geological appropriation of the agricultural lifestyle favoured by Hobbits. Dickerson and Evans describe the Hobbits' use of agriculture as the cultivation of the natural environment for food and useful materials. While they write that "[o]ne possible criticism of Tolkien is that these images are purely romantic, giving an idealized and unrealistic vision of a pastoral landscape" (73), the fact remains that the idealisation of the Hobbit lifestyle is a key factor in its continued presence in ecocritical scholarship. The instrumental value which Hobbits find in their plants and trees is similar in many ways to the instrumental value Dwarves find in geology. Hobbits also enjoy decorative plants, as demonstrated in Bilbo's apparent love of flowers in *The Hobbit* (*H* 16), and the use of flower names for their female offspring. This indicates a relationship with the natural world which is based on reciprocity. Hobbits till the earth and tend their gardens, and in return they obtain food and pleasant views for their leisure time. Dwarves approach mines, rock and precious metals in a similar way: they either use the natural resources available to them, or cultivate them for their aesthetic quality.

Dwarves occupy the fringes of Middle-earth because they are considered neither wholly evil nor wholly good. As discussed previously, Dwarves were created by Aulë out of the stone taken from Middle-earth. They were created as a response to the dangers of their world, but were instilled with an appreciation and love of all things which are born from the earth: "For it seemed to me that there is great room in Arda for many things that might rejoice in it" (*S* 37). They express this love, and their connection with their maker, through their craftsmanship; creating as many beautiful, practical things as they can. They also keep a watchful eye out for natural rock-formations and well-executed masonry. Their connection with geology is an extension of their creation myth which draws a direct link between the Dwarves and Aulë's love of stone. The relationship they have with the natural world likewise occupies its own space separate from the Elves, Hobbits and Orcs of Middle-earth. They occupy the hazy philosophical gap between preservationism and exploitation; between nostalgia and progress. They are not depicted as enjoying the building of machines and engines, but they are not particularly appreciative of untouched, unassisted natural formations either. The Dwarves are portrayed more frequently than other races as connecting with the natural world through their bare hands. They are, at heart, creatures of tradition and heredity, and rarely learn to use new skills or tools unless they are addressing a gap in knowledge which needs to be filled.

Conclusion

While representations of the Dwarvish connection with geology in Tolkien scholarship tend to err on the side of negativity, the way Dwarves interact with the natural world is beautiful in its own way. When a fictional world has been constructed with such attention to detail – such intense scrutiny to the development and execution of a mythology – it makes sense that different races would respond to their geography in different ways. The representation of certain ideals of beauty and nature in scholarship as being somehow 'better' is troubling, because it marginalises diverse portrayals of the natural world and the connection different races have with it. The Dwarvish ideal of beauty celebrates practicality along with aesthetics, and this creates an alternative relationship with the natural world which is based on mutual benefit.

Dwarves are depicted as reacting to the natural world differently to the other races of Middle-earth, and this difference is often portrayed as reflecting negatively on their race as a whole. The assumption of goodness which is associated with growing things in Tolkien's works marginalises the parts of the natural world which, while not associated with plant or animal life, are nonetheless crucial to the development of the fictional world. As Seddon notes, the geography of a place, the foundations which the plant life develops from, speaks to the world and creates a sense of tone which can translate to the characterisation of the races living there (495).

Hobbits respond to the rolling hills of the Shire by building homes just beneath the surface; taking advantage of the natural volume of hills to build large, safe holes, which are shallow enough that they are never too far from trees and plants. The Rohirrim come from a land of wide pastures and lush grassland, which accounts for their deep connection with horses as both companions and transport. The Men of Gondor, by contrast, are superstitious and defensive – which connects them symbolically with their many powerful fortifications: these are easily protected, but consequently isolated. The multi-dimensionality of nature in Middle-earth allows for alternative interpretations of beauty and goodness, and this can lead to intriguing examinations of difference and philosophy – but the reader or scholar must be open to these alternative portrayals of natural beauty in order to best appreciate them.

About the Author

Jessica Seymour is an early-career researcher at Southern Cross University and a recipient of the Australian Postgraduate Award. Her research interests include children's and young adult literature, genre theory and textual analysis, speculative fiction and transmedia storytelling.

Bibliography

BARBERIS, Danièle. "Tolkien: The Lord of The Mines – Or A Comparative Study Between Mining During the Third Age of Middle-earth by Dwarves and Mining During Our Age by Men (or Big-People)." *Minerals & Energy* 20.3-4 (2006): 60-68.

DICKERSON, Matthew and Evans, Jonathan. *Ents, Elves, and Eriador: The Environmental Vision of J.R.R. Tolkien*. Lexington KY: The University Press of Kentucky, 2006.

KNEPP, Dennis. "Bilbo Baggins: The Cosmopolitan Hobbit." *The Hobbit and Philosophy*. Ed. Gregory Bassham and Eric Bronson. Hoboken NJ: John Wiley & Sons, 2012. 45-60.

MORGAN, Alun. "The Lord of the Rings – A Mythos Applicable in Unsustainable Times?" *Environmental Education Research* 16.3-4 (2010): 383-399.

SEDDON, G. "Thinking like a Geologist: The Culture of Geology Mawson Lecture 1996." *Australian Journal of Earth Sciences: An International Geoscience Journal of the Geological Society of Australia* 43.5 (1997): 487-495.

SULLIVAN, Karen. "One Metaphor to Rule Them All? 'Objects' as Tests of Character in *The Lord of the Rings*." *Language and Literature* 22.1 (2013): 77-94.

TOLKIEN, J.R.R. *The Hobbit*. First published 1937. London: Grafton, 1991.

The Lord of the Rings. First published 1954-55. London: HarperCollins, 2002 (Film Tie-In Edition).

The Silmarillion. First published 1977. London: HarperCollins, 1999.

VINK, Renée. "'Jewish' Dwarves: Tolkien and Anti-Semitic Stereotyping." *Tolkien Studies* 10 (2013): 123-145.

Gabriela Silva Rivero

"Behind a grey rain-curtain": Water, Melancholy, and Healing in *The Lord of the Rings*

Abstract

Water has traditionally been a symbol of healing and rebirth, from baptism and ritual ablutions to straight-out water deities. In Tolkien's mythology, I will argue, water serves more as a vehicle *towards* healing, not of the body but of the world-weariness that affects many of his characters. In my paper I will explore this by examining how the people of Middle-earth, in particular Elves and Hobbits, relate to water and healing, as well as the melancholia that this healing often brings.

The day before they reach Mount Doom, as night falls over Mordor, Frodo Baggins collapses with just a few words – "I'm thirsty, Sam." Samwise Gamgee's answer is to give him all of their remaining drinking water, fully knowing that he will find none for himself for the remainder of the journey.

What follows is a poignant, evocative passage in which Sam remembers water: "through all his thoughts there came the memory of water; and every brook or stream [...] that he had ever seen, under green willow-shades or twinkling in the sun, danced and rippled for his torment behind the blindness of his eyes." The discussion that follows, Sam Gamgee versus Sam Gamgee, culminates with him fully realizing – perhaps for the first time in the book – how desperate their quest is, and how likely it is that both will die. Still he finds the tenacity to go "if it breaks [his] back and heart" (*RK* 939).

Nature, as space, description, and character, plays a foremost role in *The Lord of the Rings*. It can be found wounded, like Nan Curunír after Saruman has it ravaged, or else it can be an aggressor, like the Old Forest bordering on the Shire. Much has been written on trees and Tolkien's seeming preference for 'natural' landscapes, and whether this betrays him as an early environmentalist. But water, if more understated, is the more abundant of nature's elements, in the form of rivers, marshes, and the Great Sea that is at the heart of *The*

Lord of the Rings. In this paper I will focus on how water represents both the loss and melancholy that is prevalent in Middle-earth, as well as the potential healing it brings.

In the first part of this paper I will concentrate on the relationship the different races of Middle-earth keep with water; then focus on the Sea-longing or "the Unquiet of Ulmo" that affects the Elves, and finally I will examine the healing properties of water, particularly in the hobbits' experience in Tom Bombadil's house and how it reflects on Frodo's ultimate departure from Middle-earth. This analysis will be restricted to *The Lord of the Rings*, though references to *The Hobbit* and *The Silmarillion* will be made when relevant to the topic.

A Fainéant Melancholy

What is melancholy? The term, in use since Classical Greece, is so slippery that I find it necessary to stop and define the meaning I will attribute to it in this paper. I'm not going to use Robert Burton's famous definition of it in his colossal *Anatomy of Melancholy*, as a "malady that goes and comes upon every small occasion of sorrow, need, sickness, trouble, fear, grief, passion, or perturbation of the mind" (15), an affliction brought even more famously by causes as varied as idleness, loneliness, flights of fancy, and demonic possession. Neither will I use it as a synonym of "clinical depression", as some modern psychology does.

Melancholy, I argue, is less a disease but a mood that affects Middle-earth and its inhabitants. It is closer to how Johan Huizinga describes the Middle Ages in his famous 1929 book, *The Waning of the Middle Ages*: there was "a sombre melancholy [weighing] on people's souls" (30). Despair was a fashionable emotion; the age was to be condemned and the fact that the end of times approached was something to be celebrated. The dwellers of Middle-earth too await the ending of an era while condemning the times they were born to, and there is certainly a melancholy weighing on their souls – it is only in its tonality that Tolkien differs.

As a word or expression, "melancholy" is in fact nearly absent from *The Lord of the Rings*. It appears only once in *The Fellowship of the Ring*, as dusk falls on the hobbits and Strider as they approach Weathertop and "a few melancholy birds were piping and wailing" (*FR* 184). In Tolkien's collected letters the word is used four times, though only once applied to the legendarium, describing the Elves' tendency to "a fainéant melancholy, burdened with Memory" (*L* no. 208). Where Huizinga talks of sombre shadows and despair, Tolkien's melancholy is the golden light of longing for a past that lives in the memories of Elves.

I find one description in psychoanalytic theory that I believe is fitting. In her 1989 book, *Black Sun: Depression and Melancholia*, Julia Kristeva breaks from the Freudian tradition that sees melancholy as a reaction attack by a diminished ego and instead considers it a sadness that points to "a primitive self – wounded, incomplete, empty. [...] [This] sadness would be rather the most archaic expression of an unsymbolizable, unnameable narcissistic wound" (12). Furthermore, she says, this sadness can appear in individuals without need for a previous reference – loss does not have to occur for the subject to feel it. "The Thing is inscribed within us without memory, the buried accomplice of our unspeakable anguishes" (Kristeva 14).

Does this not seem closer to the reigning mood in Tolkien's work, both in land and characters? The land itself is incomplete, a Middle of the Earth, and wounded so much that parts of it will remain barren until they are washed by the sea into oblivion (*TT* 362). And while there are some characters, like Galadriel, that are in fact able to remember the loss of Aman, there are others, like Legolas and Frodo, who could possibly have no memory of that original loss and yet have it inscribed within, ready to awaken – at the sound of water that calls, in fact, to guide them to healing. For crossing to the Immaculate Lands is not to achieve immortality or escape time, but a chance to heal before reaching death, and therefore only those that carry a great hurt (innate, like all Elves, or acquired) are "sent or allowed to pass over the Sea to heal" (*L* no. 246).

Boating, Sailing, Divining: Uses of Water

All the goodly races of Tolkien's legendarium share a deep connection with nature, one that translates not only in their ways of life but in their dwellings. Created underground, Dwarves still carve their kingdoms under the mountains. The Ents, both in male and female form, protect and raise the forests, and while the Hobbits are the least 'natural' of the races, they live in harmony with their surroundings, keeping the countryside "well ordered and well-farmed," taking no more than what they need and not using machines more complicated than forge-bellows (*FR* 1).[1] And Elves shape the world to their need: like Dwarves they can live in caves (like Thranduil's Halls in *The Hobbit*), in man-like dwellings like Rivendell, or like the Ents, shape forests to become their cities, as happens in Lothlórien and Ithilien at the beginning of the Fourth Age.

In this section I will try and examine how each of these races relates to water. I will start with the races of Men and Hobbits, as the way they relate to water is similar, and then go on with Dwarves and Elves, as again I find similarities between them.

The narration in *The Lord of the Rings*, if we are to believe Tolkien himself, is anthropocentric. "As the earliest Tales are seen through Elvish eyes," wrote the professor in a letter to Milton Waldman, possibly in 1951, "this last great Tale, coming down from myth and legend to the earth, is seen mainly through the eyes of Hobbits: it thus becomes in fact anthropocentric" (*L* no. 131). Even then, there is by far less information on Men and Hobbits than there is on Elves.

Famously, Hobbits do not like bodies of water bigger than a bathtub. Indeed, when the first Hobbits came to occupy the territory that came to be the Shire they were limited by water: the Baranduin River on the East, and the Shirebourne and its marshes in the South (even if they had conquered the mountains to the North, the lake Evendim would have blocked their passage once again). Even once the Baranduin had been crossed and Buckland had been established, "decent" Hobbits would stay well away from the river, and those that lived "on the wrong side" of it were considered queer by those that remained in Hobbiton (*FR* 22).

---

1 I leave the race of Men aside not because they have no connection to nature at all, or indeed to imply that the only one they have is based on destruction (as is the case of the Orcs). Men too enjoy the landscape and read history and poetry of fields and rivers, but their dwellings are a far cry from the organic dwellings of the other races. There simply is not a lot of emphasis in mankind's relation to nature, with perhaps the exception of the Rohirrim and the bond they have with their horses.

This was not always the case: the Stoors, one of the three original hobbit families, liked rivers enough to live by them, and enjoyed fishing, swimming and boating. Though the Stoors might be extinct or their blood diluted by the Third Age (*UT* 457) some brave (or reckless) Hobbits maintained this view of rivers as a source of adventure and fun. Bilbo is quoted using the image of roads as rivers, saying:

> There was only one Road; that was like a great river: its springs were at every doorstep, and every path was its tributary. [...] 'You step into the Road, and if you don't keep your feet, there is no knowing where you might be swept off to.' (*FR* 74)

The Took and Brandybuck families, too, enjoyed water and its sports: boating, principally, which they practised after dinner, with sometimes tragic results: Frodo Baggins's parents died in one such accident, for example, though the news caused more condemnation than pity (*FR* 23).

It is strange that, of all the races in Middle-earth, the Hobbits lived the closest to the Great Sea, not more than a day's ride away from the Grey Havens and even closer to Tower Hills, where three elf-towers overlooked the sea. We know, thanks to the prologue, that at least a few adventurous hobbits ventured beyond the towers and maybe sailed the sea. But fewer returned to tell the tale, and as the Shire's inhabitants became more reclusive and began to avoid outsiders, "the Sea became a word of fear among them, and a token of death, and they turned their faces away from the hills in the west" (*FR* 7). By the time the narration starts, some hobbits seem to believe that not only the sea, but even the Elves, are a sort of fairy tale or oral tradition remote and unconnected to life in the Shire (*FR* 45).

Like the Hobbits, Men in Tolkien's works do not seem to have a wildly different relationship with water. There is virtually no mention of it during the hunt of Aragorn, Gimli and Legolas, nor any during the time they spend with the Rohirrim. Water has a rather utilitarian role: for drinking, and in Gondor at least, for the beautification of the city.[2] But there are two incidents of interest,

---

[2] It could be argued that the fact that the White Tree of Gondor is planted *within* a fountain is proof of the symbolic importance of water among Gondorians. On two occasions Tolkien makes reference to water droplets falling off the dead branches and into the pool, a remembrance of the absent king, though melancholy in this case is brought forth by the tree and not the water. The tree, the third sapling to be planted in Middle-earth, served as a memory of Númenor before it was drowned by the sea. The White Tree then could be said to stand not only for the lineage of the kings, but for land itself while the fountain represents the sea itself: the fountain then becomes an image of the loss of the original land and the pride that brought about the destruction of Númenor. However, there is not much in the text to confirm this reading.

the two relating to the men of Gondor: Boromir's ship-burial, first of all, and Henneth Annûn, the "Window of the Sunset" that Frodo and Sam witness with Faramir.

Though Tolkien does not dwell too much on the funerary rites of the different people, there is enough for us to know that Boromir's boat-burial is not usual. In Middle-earth people are buried in graves, under tumuli, or burial mounds often marked by cairns. This is true for Men and Hobbits, though we can assume that Dwarves have similar traditions – both Balin and Thorin are said to have stone tombs. And finally, Denethor states that, before the Númenóreans sailed from the West into Middle-earth, "heathens" would burn the bodies of their dead on funeral pyres (*RK* 825).

But Boromir dies when his companions have little time to bury him or construct a cairn. The river Anduin becomes the best option: "'Let us lay him in a boat with his weapons, and the weapons of his vanquished foes,' said Aragorn. 'We will send him to the Falls of Rauros and give him to Anduin. The River of Gondor will take care at least that no evil creature dishonours his bones'" (*TT* 415). There is, then, a relationship between Anduin and Gondor – or at least Anduin and Men of Númenórean descent.

In her essay for the Tolkien Society "Death and Funerary Practices in Middle-earth", Pat Reynolds rightly points out that Boromir's death rites draw from the Northern traditions of boat-burials, comparing it to the ones seen in *Beowulf* (4). More importantly, she touches on the idea of death as a journey that will eventually lead the deceased to the land of the dead across the sea. This too would explain Aragorn's trust in the course of the river: the Anduin empties into the Great Sea, which in turn extends westwards all the way to Aman.[3]

Another proof of the goodliness of Anduin is that it delivers Boromir, untouched, to his land and his brother:

> Then the boat turned towards me, and stayed its pace, and floated slowly by within my hand's reach [...] It waded deep, as if it were heavily burdened, and it seemed to me as it passed under my gaze that it was almost filled with

---

3 Which is not to say that Boromir travelled across the Sea into the Undying Realms, as that privilege is reserved for very few. Given the importance of the East/West distinctions in Tolkien, however, I would insist that being carried westward is a blessed end to life.

clear water, from which came the light; and lapped in the water a warrior lay asleep. [...] Dreamlike it was, and yet no dream, for there was no waking. And I do not doubt that he is dead and had passed down the River into the Sea. (*TT* 666)

Water, in this scene, both transports and sanctifies the man lying in the boat. If Faramir had any doubt about his brother's death he needed only think of the way the water reacted, and how it protected the body (something at which even Frodo expresses surprise).

Faramir is my second example of the relationship between Men and water. He is presented as a particularly sensitive man, "touched with the wisdom and sadness of the Elder Race" (*RK* 810), one constantly visited by dreams and visions. It is almost no wonder that his base of operations, Henneth Annûn or "the Sunset Window", also has touches of the elder race. Frodo and Sam's visit as both guests and prisoners reveal several things about the day-to-day routine of Men – most importantly how they keep a moment of silence before eating to look West, in remembrance of "Númenor that was, and beyond to Elvenhome that is, and to that which is beyond Elvenhome and will ever be" (*TT* 676).

Water plays a strangely important role here. It created the refuge itself, hollowing the stone until men blocked and diverted the path of the stream to open the cave and doubled the height of the waterfall. Water also constitutes the first line of defence, as the only two entrances into Henneth Annûn are hidden by water: the first a passage concealed by a waterfall, and the second one through a tunnel "into a deep bowl" where the water pools, "filled with knives of stone" (*TT* 674). The waterfall, which faces the West, shimmers with the colours of the sky behind it. To the hobbits it is intrinsically Elvish: "as if they stood at the window of some elven-tower, curtained with threaded jewels of silver and gold, and ruby, sapphire and amethyst, all kindled with an unconsuming fire" (*TT* 674). When Gollum comes to the pool where the falls gather, he is threatened with death – not for stealing the fish, but simply because he has "come here and looked on the pool" (*TT* 689).

It is not clear, I feel, whether Faramir is concerned because Gollum has discovered the refuge itself or because he breached a taboo by visiting the waters. A practical reading would suggest that Faramir worries that Gollum would disclose the location of the refuge to orcs or other enemies. But for a man like Faramir, laden with melancholy and aware of the end of times, it could be just as important that this pool – infused with western light – was polluted by Gollum's presence.

There is less information on the Dwarves and their relationship with water. It is almost null, in fact: Tolkien based them on Norse and Germanic myths, and retains their association with the mountains and the earth, as well as the perceived characteristic of stone: resilience, loyalty, solidity. There is only one instance in *The Lord of the Rings* when we see Dwarves interact with water: when the Fellowship leaves Moria and advances towards the woods of Lothlórien. As they pass the Mirrormere Gimli takes Frodo aside, saying he would not allow him to go without seeing the lake of Kheled-zâram. In the waters they see, in spite of it being broad daylight, stars reflected in the waters "like jewels sunk in the deep" (*FR* 334). Two things I find interesting about this passage: first, that even things seen in water are treated like things that come from the earth, the stars are not stars but jewels untouched in the deep. Secondly, that the lake reflects the stars in spite of the sunlight and, furthermore, that "of [Gimli and the hobbits'] stooping forms no shadow could be seen."

The lake, I position, literally reflects memory – the lake's own memory perhaps, of things long in the past, perhaps as far removed as the night Durin first saw his own reflection crowned by stars.

I find this very similar to how the Elves seem to relate to water – and taking into account that Dwarves and Elves are the elder races of the world, it is no coincidence. Unlike the Dwarves and the mountains, or the Hobbits and their farmland, Elves are not tied down or associated with a single facet of nature. If there is any particular element with which Elves are associated more strongly, it is light – moonlight and starlight, predominantly, though standing in Cerin Amroth, Sam exclaims of the sunlight: "I thought that Elves were all for moon and stars: but this is more elvish than anything I ever heard tell of" (*FR* 351). He is not wrong, of course. Lothlórien, and Cerin Amroth in particular, is "the heart of Elvendom on earth" (*FR* 352), and Elves, no matter of what generation, carry starlight within, for it was the first thing they beheld when they awoke:

By the starlit mere of Cuiviénen, Water of Awakening, they rose from the sleep of Ilúvatar; and while they dwelt yet silent by Cuiviénen their eyes beheld first of all things the stars of heaven. Therefore they have ever loved the starlight [...] (*S* 48)

But it is not only starlight that the Elves love, for as starlight is the first thing they see, "the sound of water flowing, and the sound of water falling over stone" was the first they ever heard. Water, by association, is as Elvish as starlight, and thus Elves should be associated with it.

There are many instances in *The Lord of the Rings* when this association is touched upon, though never as overtly as with light. There is, of course, the deep link between Elves and the Sea – but I will start with rivers, and the water used for divining purposes, and leave the greatest body of water till last.

I have already touched upon rivers several times in this paper. They are an expected feature of the fictional landscape, serve as natural boundaries and defences, metaphors for both life and death, and in many instances come to reflect or resemble the landscape and the changes around it. Such is the case of the Bruinen river running through the valley of Rivendell, the Nimrodel that leads into Lothlórien, and – to a lesser degree – the dark forest river that crosses northern Mirkwood. On this one I won't dwell too much, as it appears very briefly in *The Hobbit*: by this time Mirkwood has been corrupted by the power of the "Necromancer" in Dol Guldur. Bilbo and his fellow travellers are warned by Beorn not to trust it, and most of all warns them against either drinking or bathing in the river that crosses the path, "for I have heard that it carries an enchantment and a great drowsiness and forgetfulness" (*H* 155). When Bombur falls into the river he falls into a four-day slumber from which he wakes up with no memory of the previous days (*H* 170-176). There is no explanation given for this, neither for the origin of the "enchantment" nor its effects (Bombur's lack of memory is never touched upon again after their capture by the elves) and it is also a unique event in most of Tolkien's writing, as magic often takes the shape of objects rather than charms or spells.[4]

---

[4] It could be argued that Gandalf casts several spells throughout the narrative to create fire (and fireworks), light, and to bless creatures or communicate with them. However this should be read as an extension of his nature, in the same way that Galadriel rejects the word 'magic' for her mirror and her gifts. On 'magic' and related terms and concepts, see Bachmann and Shippey (2007).

I would venture to say that the effect the river has on Bombur is but a reflection of what the land itself is going through: Mirkwood, under the influence of Sauron, is *forgetting* what it used to be, and the Silvan Elves that shaped it before. It therefore inflicts forgetfulness on whoever drinks from its waters – though it also gives them good dreams. The forest stream, perhaps like Kheled-zâram, remembers times past.

This is perhaps similar to the river Bruinen that protects Rivendell. It is never described as unfriendly, and Thorin and company are able to cross both the river and the ford into Rivendell without problems. It is a different story when the Black Riders try to cross the ford to capture Frodo:

> At that moment there came a roaring and a rushing: a noise of loud waters rolling many stones. Dimly Frodo saw the river below him rise, and down along its course there came a plumed cavalry of waves. White flames seemed to Frodo to flicker on their crests [...] The three Riders that were still in the midst of the Ford were overwhelmed: they disappeared, buried suddenly under angry foam. (*FR* 214)

The sudden flood is explained later as a last-resource protective measure: Elrond commanded it, we are told, as the river in the valley is under his command, and Gandalf added a few touches (*FR* 224). It is interesting enough that Elrond commands the river itself – not through spells or "magic", but due to the connection between the Eldar and nature – but I find two points even more interesting. First, Frodo sees "white flames" flickering atop the waves, which is also how he perceives Glorfindel across the river, "a shining figure of white light." (*FR* 214). Second, Gandalf fears that the flood would get out of control and wash Frodo away along with the Ringwraiths. This implies, I believe, that the waters have greater autonomy than is stated by the narration, that neither Elrond nor Gandalf fully control them. The wizard perhaps explains it by saying that "there is great vigour in the waters that come down from the snows of the Misty Mountains" (*FR* 224), and I would also focus on the use of the adjective "angry" in the paragraph above, which again grants some autonomy to the waters.

Finally, and most importantly, the white flames that Frodo sees in both the waters and Glorfindel. This white light is the purest expression the *fëa*, the spirit or soul that comes from the Creator. Why would the water in the river sport this white light, when it is not a living being *per se*? The light could be one of Gandalf's touches, adorning the white riders he creates in the water to make them seem more Elvish. I am inclined to read this as once more the water taking part of the attributes of the land around it and its inhabitants: crossing Rivendell, the Bruinen has also become like the "lords of the Eldar from beyond the furthest seas." These lords, Elrond and Glorfindel, do not fear the Ringwraiths (*FR* 222), and neither does the river.

Finally, we come to Lothlórien, a place connected to water in many different ways. There are at least two rivers crossing it, as well as at least one fountain whose water Galadriel uses for divinatory purposes, and at the very centre of it lays the sea.

I start again with a river, Nimrodel, that flows through Lothlórien before joining the Anduin.[5] This is the second body of water that the Fellowship comes across after leaving Moria, and as Gimli led Frodo, this time Legolas takes the reins. He invites the Fellowship to bathe their feet, as the waters are said to be healing to the weary, and then sings of the river's namesake, an Elvish woman who died attempting to reach the harbour and leave Middle-earth. Of this river, and of the maiden, Legolas says "the Silvan Elves made many songs long ago, and still [they] sing them in the North, remembering the rainbow on its falls […]'" (*FR* 339).

Again, I argue that water takes on the properties of the land that it crosses. If the black stream of Mirkwood causes forgetfulness, Nimrodel makes memory come alive, and while the Bruinen shares the anger of the "lords of the Eldar" at the Black Riders, the river that crosses Lothlórien, erstwhile known as *Laurelindórenan* or "Valley of the Singing Gold", sings:

> At length silence fell, and they heard the music of the waterfall running sweetly in the shadows. Almost Frodo fancied that he could hear a voice singing, mingled with the sound of the water. (*FR* 339)

Legolas identifies this voice as simply "the voice of Nimrodel", without specifying if it is the maiden or the river. Whichever it is, it moves him to song – and works the same influence on Frodo, later when the company

---

5 The Nimrodel joins the Silverlode or Celebrant before reaching Lórien. This other stream, which runs from the Misty Mountains, is too cold to be touched or to be drunk from until it meets the Nimrodel.

rests in Caras Galadhon. Upon resting by a fountain, thinking of Gandalf, "his thoughts took shape in a song" that seemed fair but fades quickly. To a lesser degree Sam is affected too, and completes the song with a short stanza on Gandalf's fireworks.

It is while they stay in Caras Galadhon that Frodo and Sam are invited to look into the Mirror of Galadriel. The basin that forms the Mirror is filled with water from a silver stream running at the bottom of her private garden. She fills the basin to the brim, and breathes on it, and when the water is still again she speaks.

> 'Here is the Mirror of Galadriel,' she said. 'I have brought you here so that you may look in it, if you will. [...] the Mirror will show things unbidden, and those are often stranger and more profitable than things which we wish to behold [...]' (*FR* 361-362)

In Tolkien's writing, divination – even when it comes from benign sources – never brings positive results. Typically it will bring about fragmented scenes that often lead the viewer to draw the wrong conclusion (Shippey 2005, 423-426). The Mirror of Galadriel is no exception, and in fact its appearance endangers the Quest inasmuch as it makes Sam feel doubt about his path. However, it is a quintessential expression of Elvishness, a re-imagination of Cuiviénen itself: still water with stars reflecting off its still surface. Furthermore, it is the Mirror and the stars that allow Frodo to see, on Galadriel's finger, Nenya – the Ring of Water. It is this ring that allows Galadriel to keep Lothlórien unchanged or without decay (*S* xix) as the embodiment of the *fainéant* melancholy that Elves are destined to suffer from. This land is the Eldar's most accomplished effort in fighting the "long defeat" against time, where "the wearing is slow" and hours and days blend together (*FR* 388). And what do we find, at the Heart of Elvendom, the closest in Middle-earth to the Undying Lands?

> Frodo stood still, hearing far off great seas upon beaches that had long ago been washed away, and sea-birds crying whose race had perished from the earth. (*FR* 351).

Water – neither the river nor the divinatory liquid imbued with starlight, but the ocean – runs through Lothlórien. Old, not to be found in Middle-earth anymore, more present than reality itself and always calling.

The Unquiet of Ulmo: Longing and Melancholy

> Legolas Greenleaf long under tree
> In joy thou hast lived. Beware the Sea!
> If thou hearest the cry of the gull on the shore,
> Thy heart shall rest then in the forest no more. (*TT* 503)

It is with this message that Gandalf greets Legolas upon meeting with the Three Hunters in the outskirts of Fangorn. Legolas reacts grimly to this announcement, originally spoken by Galadriel, thinking it forecasts his death. Much later we find that the poem was meant to be taken more literally: the cry of the gulls does not herald death but instead awakens the "Unquiet of Ulmo", the feeling of longing for the sea and for the land on the other end. The rousing of this feeling is often talked of by Tolkien as a landmark in the sufferer's life, the moment from which the ultimate goal of life is to cross the sea. This is not to say that sea-longing becomes a consuming mania,[6] it is a melancholia that from then on makes it impossible to ignore the fact that life, as one knows it, will come to an end. "No peace shall I have again under beech or under elm" (*RK* 873) is how Legolas explains it: being a sylvan elf, few things make him happier than forests and trees, and yet the sight of gulls and the ocean have the power to change that.

There are many reasons why the sea-longing is so powerful. It can be read as the moment when the illusion of immortality is broken, even for those immortal because it represents a definite break from the life they had led until then. Meeting the sea for the first time is, for the Elves, to realise they love the world while at the same time they realise they will have to leave it. It is the clear enactment of what Tolkien calls the greatest theme in *The Lord of the Rings*, "the love of the world in the hearts of a race 'doomed' to leave it and seemingly lose it" (*L* no.186)

There is also a more direct explanation: longing for the sea is a home-longing, for the home that was lost or else never reached in the first place. This home is of course the Undying Lands, lost to the world after the Númenóreans tried to

---

[6] That said, Legolas does seem rather distracted when he and Gimli reunite with the hobbits during the Last Debate. He falls silent while others chat and a couple of times interrupts the conversation to talk about his complex feelings regarding the gulls and the ocean. It might not be a mania, but the shock is apparently rather strong.

attack it, and lost to different kinds of Elves for various reasons. The Noldor, for instance, were expelled after the First Kinslaying, while the Sindar (and other "dark" Elves) never reached it in the first place. This kind of longing can also be found in chosen individuals from other races: Tuor had an unquiet placed on him by Ulmo – first to leave the land of his fathers, and then to eventually travel across the sea (S 238). It is as a home that Legolas identifies in song:

> Grey ship, grey ship, do you hear them calling,
> The voices of my people that have gone before me?
> [...]
> Sweet are the voices in the Lost Isle calling,
> In Eressëa, in Elvenhome that no man can discover,
> Where the leaves fall not: land of my people forever! (*RK* 956)

But why would an elf that had never seen the sea feel the sea longing? How can a place that has never been known be called home? There is the familiarity of knowing that part of the Undying Lands was designated as Elvenhome from times beyond Legolas's own memory, and that his kin live there and call for him to join. But I think there is a second possible reading in the "voices" that Legolas mentions, one that he himself might not realise. For if in the Ainulindalë we are told that

> [in] the roaring of the sea [...] there lives yet the echo of the Music of the Ainur more than in any substance else that is in this Earth; and many of the Children of Ilúvatar hearken still unsated to the voices of the Sea, and yet know not for what they listen. (*S* 19)

The voices that Legolas hears – that he attributes to his people on the far shore – could in fact be the unspoiled echo of the music of creation. In water there is an expression of perfection, of completeness. Even the Valar are moved by it, and when they first behold the ocean they are awed, for they themselves are incomplete when the unity of the song breaks.

In longing for the Sea these characters in fact long for a state of perfection or completeness, and a realisation of the incompleteness of their own being. At the beginning of this paper I commented on Julia Kristeva's definition of melancholy as that which is "inscribed within us without memory," and once more I would like to stress how fitting this is to the sadness that arises at the sound and sight of water. The sounds of creation, resonant within each living being, might be forgotten or else sundered from the Creator, but the music lives there and the sea awakens the promise of completion.

Furthermore, I would argue that this effect is not limited to the sea but can be found (if to a lesser degree) in all bodies of water. This is easiest to observe in Legolas and Frodo, though there are instances in which other characters exhibit this melancholia – from Gimli's remembrance in front of Kheled-zâram to Merry's anxiety in Tom Bombadil's house that he will drown in his sleep.

The visit the four hobbits pay to Bombadil's house at the beginning of the novel is drastically different in tone from the rest of the quest. There is a certain playfulness here that invades everything, nightmares and death vanish with a song. Even the One Ring is diminished in Bombadil's hand! Quite literally it seems to become an ordinary knick-knack, as it neither turns him invisible nor tempts him at all. When Bombadil takes it up to his face, his "bright blue eye" gleaming through the Ring creates an odd pastiche of the Eye of Sauron (*FR* 133). Tom Bombadil is the topic of much discussion – who is he, what is he, what role does he play in the text. The internet fandom has theorized that he is a Maia or a Valar, a representation of Tolkien himself, the Witch-King, and a intradiegetic reader. In *The Road to Middle-earth*, Tom Shippey compares him to mythical figures such as Adam and the Green Man, because he is fatherless and able to understand all languages and Master of nature: the uncreated man (Shippey 2005, 122-123).

However, I find more relevant to my paper that Shippey describes Bombadil as "fearless [...] he antedates the corruption of Art" (Shippey 2005, 122). I would take this to mean that Bombadil is complete: even more so than the Ainur, definitely more so than the Elves. Goldberry is not lying or misrepresenting him when she says that "He is" (*FR* 124) because in his completeness he needs not specify anything beyond his existence. It makes sense to me then that his house is full of water (he is married to the embodiment of a river!), and that water reflects his own completeness. Water in Bombadil's house is "glad water flowing down into the night from a bright morning in the hills" (*FR* 122), it falls like Goldberry's voice out of the sky in a song that the hobbits understand without any effort (*FR* 129), goes to the heart like wine and makes the hobbits break into song. I won't propose that this means the hobbits have re-joined the

Song of the Ainur – more likely they are tipsy – but the peace they enjoy in Bombadil's house is greater than any they will encounter from then on. Greater than in Rivendell and Lothlórien, greater than in the Houses of Healing.

This is because the need for healing is not yet there. The hobbits are unharmed, and Frodo has not yet begun to fully feel the influence of the One Ring – in their own Hobbit way, they are complete and rather attuned to the world around them. In his essay "Death, Immortality, and their Escapes", Andrea Monda suggests that Hobbits are in fact closer to Elves than any of the other races. Like the *fainéant* melancholy of the Elves that leads them to try and stop change (or "decay"), Hobbits "are also driven by their nature to 'embalm' life [...] Their whole existence is marked by birthday parties accompanied by intricate genealogical trees and stuck in the cult of tradition" (Monda 162). Both the Hobbits and the Elves have a set idea of how the world should be and fight to shape the world around that idea – the Elves by creating their homely houses with the power of the Three Rings, the Hobbits by abiding to tradition and genealogy. The greater difference, Monda goes on to say, is that the nostalgia a hobbit might feel for the good old days is expressed through bad gossip, while in the Elves it is expressed through an "almost existentialist and ontological"[7] melancholy (162).

I agree almost completely with this, though I would say that the divide between both races is bridged by both Sam and Frodo; by Sam just a little, but by Frodo almost completely. Both of them seem more conscious of the fading of the world, of the "long defeat" that Galadriel talks about. Initially it is due to different factors: Sam's love for all things "Elvish" makes him more attuned to this melancholia, Frodo's education and knowledge make him able to notice it. But whatever melancholia or potential for melancholia there was, it is exacerbated when the characters become Ring-bearers, and in Frodo's case, by the wounds he receives during the Quest.

---

7 I believe the "almost" is unnecessary, given my above argument regarding the longing for completeness of being.

To the Havens: Water and Healing

Upon returning to the Shire, there is not one year that Frodo does not take ill on at least two occasions, March 13th and September 6th, the anniversaries of his poisoning by Shelob and the Nâzgul attack at Whethertop, respectively. He conceals his pain from the people around him, especially from Sam, who is starting both a family and the first of several tenures as mayor in the Shire. But not two years after returning to the Shire, he takes the road to the Grey Havens and, together with Bilbo, undertakes the last journey into the West. When Sam expresses perplexity at this, Frodo explains that "it must be often so [...] when things are in danger: some one has to give them up, lose them, so that others may keep them" (*RK* 1029). And so Frodo has given up his health, both physical and mental, and his wounds and experience haunt him. If he started the quest closer to completion of being, relatively attuned to his nature as a Hobbit, he has now lost this and much more.

It is this loss that brings him closer to the Elven worldview, that fully brings him out of the Hobbit nostalgia for the landscape and traditions and into the *fainéant* memory of the Elves. Already in Rivendell, after being cured by Elrond of the Nâzgul wound, Gandalf observes him fading:

> But to the wizard's eye there was a faint change, just a hint as it were of transparency, about him, and especially about the left hand that lay outside upon the coverlet.
>
> '[...] To what he will come in the end not even Elrond can foretell. Not to evil, I think. He might become like a glass filled with a clear light for eyes to see that can.' (FR 223)

This transparency, this being filled with light reflects not only the way Elves are often described from the Hobbits' point of view, but the same kind of stretching that Bilbo mentions in the first chapters of the novel. Frodo's wounds exacerbate the world-weariness that the Ring brings; the comparison to a glass filled with a clear light brings to mind the phial that Galadriel gives him, filled with water that becomes light just as much. Frodo is becoming perhaps the distillation of Elvish values, more Elvish than many Elves, too pure for this world: he is in constant need of the promise of healing that water brings.

This is relatively easy to see in the narration: from the moment he crosses the fords of Rivendell, almost every time the Fellowship stops by a body of water there is for Frodo a moment of respite and reflection. It also tends to mirror any losses the Fellowship has experienced: Gandalf's death is followed by the short stop by the shores of Kheled-zâram, as well as a rest by Nimrodel, where Frodo feels "the stain of travel and all weariness" being washed away. This is followed by the Farewell to Lórien, which at least Frodo and Aragorn will never again visit,[8] and then by the journey down the Anduin, where Boromir passes away and the Fellowship is broken and lost. In the second volume we come across Ithilien and the Window of the Sunset, the last respite Frodo enjoys before heading into Mordor, where there is no water – and, as I will argue in my conclusions, simply no possibility of healing.

There are only two sections I can recall where the characters come to large bodies of water that do not foretell healing or offer an opportunity of reflection: one is the Watcher in the Water outside of Moria, and the second are the Dead Marshes through which Gollum leads them. The Watcher in the Water seems more than anything to indicate the stagnancy into which the dwarf kingdom of Moria had fallen, but the Dead Marshes seem to me far more interesting: they mark the transition into Mordor as a liminal space where time, along with several natural laws, seems to be suspended.[9]

Nothing in the marshes is fully what it seems to be: solid land may give way and send the travellers into the swamp, and water itself might prove more solid than at first sight. Similarly, the marshes seem to be a mass grave, where the corpses of Elves, Orcs, and Men alike rest forever after the battle. At first sight it might strike us as death being the great equalizer, perhaps even Tolkien's greatest statement on war: creatures foul and fair resting together, victims of the same carnage. But as Sam points out, "that [was] an age and more ago. […] The Dead can't be really there! Is this some devilry hatched in the Dark Land?" (*TT* 628)

---

8 And, given that Galadriel leaves Middle-earth soon after the War of the Ring, Lothlórien, as we first get to know it, is lost to every living being as well.
9 See also Michaël Devaux's "The Dead Marshes and Oikoumene: The Limits of a Landscape in Middle-earth."

Sam is right: the corpses surely cannot be there anymore. For one thing, more than two thousand years ago, and as I argued above, it would be unthinkable for the Elves (victors, to a degree, of that battle) to leave the corpses of their fallen forgotten and abandoned. But I would argue it is no devilry, but nature itself coming forth to create a tomb. It would not be the first time: the first "war memorial" of Middle-earth can be traced down to the Hill of Tears, that Morgoth made after the Nirnaeth Arnoediad. Originally meant to inspire fear and establish his dominion, it was transformed by Nature into "a symbol of grief, but also of unyielding hope" (Bonechi 143). I find the Dead Marshes to be doing something similar though not as deliberately: they preserve the memory of the battle, and the memory of death, but without any intention of glorification. Water, as I have argued before, shapes itself after the land it is in, but the land where the Dead Marshes grew is an unclaimed no man's land. The only thing there to reflect is death, and that is what the water does.

And yet the mere presence of water promises new life: "Even to the Mere of Dead Faces some haggard phantom of green spring would come," we are told. There is water; though stagnant it still represents the potential of the land to heal. Not so with the desolation before Mordor and the Dark Land itself. "Here nothing lived, not even the leprous growths that feed on rottenness" goes the description, and what little water there is, is "choked with ash and crawling muds, sickly white and grey, as if the mountains had vomited the filth of their entrails upon the lands about" (*TT* 631). The shock is so great that, even after passing unaffected by the faces of the dead, on seeing this desolation Sam declares he is going to be sick (*TT* 632).

It seems almost redundant to state that there is near to no water at all in Mordor. Orcs do not seem to drink any, the only time we see them imbibe something is when the Uruk-hai take Merry and Pippin, and then they seem to only drink a kind of alcoholic cordial. Frodo insist that Orcs are bound to drink and eat like all other creatures, and Sam does mention seeing a couple of dirty cisterns along their way. But as a natural source for water they find only two very small, oily streams. Just as there is water in Mordor there is life, but it is bitter, twisted. And as Sam and Frodo push onwards to Mount Doom, water is the first thing they run out of, and it is water that haunts Sam's waking nightmares: "every brook or stream or fount that he had ever seen, under green willow-shades or twinkling in the sun, danced and rippled for his torment behind the blindness of his eyes" (*RK* 938). But even that torment is consolation: Sam remembers life in the Shire, playing with the Cotton family at Bywater, and he remembers Ithilien, and the rabbit he stewed for them to eat.

This is all already beyond Frodo's ability: he cannot remember the taste or the feel of the things that used to be his life, he describes himself as "naked in the dark," with no veil between him and the eye of Sauron. This is perhaps how Frodo articulates the same transparency that Gandalf first notices, and that is destined to never fade. Upon returning to the Shire Sam is the one who best re-adapts to the life they had left before, while Frodo struggles with his repeating illnesses, becomes reclusive, and is forgotten by his own countrymen. This alienation is reflected in one of Tolkien's most mysterious texts, "The Sea Bell". Included in the 1962 collection of poetry *The Adventures of Tom Bombadil*, we are told in the introduction that "someone" has subtitled the poem "Frodos Dreme". The poem is a dark story about a traveller who abandons his home in search of a land across the sea, and while the land he finds is beautiful its inhabitants refuse to talk to him. Upon returning to his home, the traveller finds it changed too, and once more there is no one he can talk to.

I read this as the introduction to *ATB* suggests: dark dreams plaguing Frodo before he takes the Last Journey. He knows himself too wounded, but that could be bearable if it was not for the fact that he has begun to doubt that he could ever be healed. This is the anxiety in "The Sea Bell", the fear that the melancholia will never be assuaged and he will be forever broken. In the dream the Sea Bell itself works as a synecdoche for the sea itself, there to guide the traveller into an unknown land, where he will be understood and made complete – but offering no certainty, only the possibility of further alienation.

All to Silver Glass

There is much more on this topic, limited as it is, of water, healing, and melancholia, that I won't be able to touch on. The Ents, first of all, with Treebeard's drink that make Merry and Pippin grow, the cleansing of Isengard and their own melancholy outlook on life. In destroying the Shire Saruman too targets the water sources, polluting the rivers and controlling their flow.

Beyond that, I believe another very interesting topic has emerged from this short study: the relationship between water, memory, and lack. Water seems to reflect what is lacking from the land, and that which is lacking can usually be found in memories. So it is that the lake of Kheled-zâram reflects a crown and the lack of a king of legends, the Dead Marshes reflect the life that once existed, and the river coursing through Lothlórien reflects the Elvenhome that the Noldor knew but had lost.

And in Mordor the lack of water, to me, speaks of the memory of the pride displayed both by Morgoth and Sauron. If melancholia reflects, as I have argued, the realisation of one's own incomplete being, then lack of melancholia is pride: a negation of our incompleteness, and in the terms of the legendarium, a negation to accept our part in the Music of Creation. Without that realisation – without melancholia – there is no possibility of healing, and indeed the land of Mordor will remain a prideful "void; a land defiled, diseased beyond all healing – unless the Great Sea should enter in and wash it with oblivion" (*TT* 632), and bring with it once more the yearning to be at one with creation.

And as for Frodo and his Sea Bell, Tom Shippey has proposed a dark interpretation of the poem: that it is in fact a sort of epilogue where Frodo finds his fears validated, and even after reaching Valinor finds no healing and no rest (Shippey 2000, 282). But I would insist in reading it only as an anxious dream born from Frodo's own fear. Frodo finds healing in the Undying Lands, and we know this because as he passes into the West, on a night of rain he hears singing over the water and "it seemed to him that as in his dream in the house of Tom Bombadil, the grey rain-curtain turned all to silver glass and was rolled back" (*RK* 1030). Bombadil's house, the place that like its master *is*, where nothing passes through the door and window save the starlight, is the last place of rest that Frodo knows before his fading begins. That the feelings of the nights he spent there are being revived – that he is literally regaining the ability to feel and remember, which seemed lost in Mordor – can only indicate that Frodo's healing has already begun, and the process shall continue on the shores of the Undying Lands.

About the Author

Gabriela Silva Rivero (Mexico City, 1985) studied English Literature at the National Autonomous University of Mexico, and is currently doing a PhD in Creative Writing and Literature at the University of Essex. Her first novel, a slow fantasy called *Los doce sellos*, was published in Mexico in 2009. She is currently working on her second novel and a collection of short stories that look to mythologize the female body.

Bibliography

BACHMANN, Dieter. "Words for Magic: *goetia*, *gúl* and *lûth*." *Myth and Magic. Art According to the Inklings*. Eds. Eduardo Segura and Thomas Honegger. Zurich and Jena: Walking Tree Publishers, 2007. 47-55.

BURTON, Robert. *The Essential Anatomy of Melancholy*. First published 1621. New York: Dover Publications, 2002.

DEVAUX, Michaël. "The Dead Marshes and Oikoumene: The Limits of a Landscape in Middle-earth." *Hither Shore* 11 (2014): 116-128.

HUIZINGA, Johan. *The Waning of the Middle Ages*. First published 1919. New York: Penguin, 1987.

KRISTEVA, Julia. *Black Sun: Depression and Melancholia*. Trans. Leon S. Roudiez. New York: Columbia University Press, 1989.

MONDA, Andrea. "Death, Immortality and their Escapes: Memory and Longevity." *The Broken Scythe: Death and Immortality in the Works of J.R.R. Tolkien*. Eds. Roberto Arduini and Claudio A. Testi. Zurich and Jena: Walking Tree Publishers, 2012. 155-173.

"One Wiki to Rule Them All: Theories about Tom Bombadil." 17 Jul. 2012. http://lotr.wikia.com/wiki/Theories_about_Tom_Bombadil

REYNOLDS, Patricia. "Death and Funerary practices in Middle-earth." *The Tolkien Society Essays*. 17 Jul 2012. http://www.tolkiensociety.org/wp-content/uploads/2014/03/Death-and-funerary-practices-in-Middle-earth.pdf

SHIPPEY, Tom. *J.R.R. Tolkien: Author of the Century*. London: HarperCollins, 2000.

The Road to Middle-earth. First published 1982. London: HarperCollins, 2005.

"New Learning and New Ignorance: Magia, Goeteia, and the Inklings." *Myth and Magic. Art According to the Inklings*. Eds. Eduardo Segura and Thomas Honegger. Zurich and Jena: Walking Tree Publishers, 2007. 21-46.

TOLKIEN, J.R.R. *The Fellowship of the Ring.* First published 1954. London: HarperCollins, 2013.

The Two Towers. First published 1954. London: HarperCollins, 2013.

The Return of the King. First published 1955. London: HarperCollins, 2013.

The Silmarillion. First published 1977. London: HarperCollins, 2011.

The Hobbit. First published 1937. London: HarperCollins, 2006.

The Adventures of Tom Bombadil. First published 1962. London: George Allen & Unwin, 1971.

The Letters of J.R.R. Tolkien. Ed. Humphrey Carpenter, with the assistance of Christopher Tolkien. First published 1981. New York: Houghton Mifflin, 1999.

Yannick Imbert

Eru Will Enter Ëa: The Creational-Eschatological Hope of J.R.R. Tolkien

Abstract

As Tolkien readers and scholars have long noted, nature holds a special place in Tokien's primary and secondary worlds. As such, nature is constantly on the central stage, even when it is not the primary narrative plot. Intertwined with the centrality of the natural world, brought to life on numerous occasion by Tolkien, we find an ever-present but veiled hope for a renewed natural environment. The thesis of this paper is that this very hope is central to Tolkien's works, as particularly seen in *The Lord of the Rings* and *The Hobbit*, but also in *The Silmarillion* and other lesser works. However, hope for such a renewal of nature always seems so distant as to be merely a dream. Songs and stories assume this, but only on rare occasions is this hope clearly expressed.

This paper aims to demonstrate that Tolkien's hope for a future restoration of nature rests upon a fundamentally Catholic understanding of nature and history, and more precisely Thomistic. To do so, the paper will first look at central aspects of this future 'natural hope' in Tolkien's works. References to Christopher Tolkien's *History of Middle-earth* will serve to underline Tolkien's conception of what theologians call "eschatological hope." References to other mythological works, particularly those well-known to Tolkien, will serve to enhance the specifics of Tolkien's mythopoeic vision. Secondly, this paper will argue that the future dignity, integrity, and beauty of nature is determined by a specific vision of time and history. Only because history moves towards its fulfillment, can hope in a final and glorious restoration of nature be truly held.

Tolkien and the Environment

Nature, earth, trees, creation: all are themes crucial to Tolkien's vision, not only to his mythological corpus, but to all his works, including "Farmer Giles of Ham" and "Leaf by Niggle." In fact, as Tolkien readers and scholars have long noted, nature holds a special place in both Tolkien's primary *and* secondary worlds. Some academics have argued that Middle-earth might be the main character of Tolkien's mythology. We know of the beauty of Arda and Valinor, of Lothlórien and the Shire – and Tolkien also knew of the beauty of the English countryside. As Tolkien recounts:

> My earliest memories are of Africa, but it was alien to me, and when I came home, therefore, I had for the countryside of England both the native feeling and the personal wonder of somebody who comes to it. I came to the English countryside when I was about 3 ½ or 4 – it seemed to me wonderful. If you really want to know what Middle-earth is based on, it's my wonder and delight in the earth as it is, particularly with the natural earth. (Birzer 42)

As such, nature is constantly on the central stage of Tolkien's work, even when it is not the primary narrative plot. This has led to the linguistic anachronistic conclusion that Tolkien is, properly speaking, an ecologist. However, this is, at best, a confusion of categories. Tolkien's love of nature did not spring only from a necessity of opposing and reacting to the destruction of nature, but from a profound love of nature in and for itself. This can be seen in the different races' relation to nature. One thinks of the Elves or the Ents, but we might also well think of the Hobbits' love for a "well-tilled earth" (*FR* 1), as well as the significance of their names. Indeed, Hobbit names reflect their love of nature, or even more accurately, the fact that they *inhabit* nature, in a most profound sense. Since names, for Tolkien, are not arbitrary words given to people or individuals but in many ways represent their *nature* (their *essence*), it might well be that Hobbit names are of great significance to the value of nature in Tolkien's *mythological corpus*.

Hence, *contra* Kocher who calls Tolkien an "ecologist" (26), Dickerson and Evans are certainly right in concluding that Tolkien is not an environmentalist but that he has definitely brought forth an environmental *vision* (Dickerson and Evans xvi-xvii). That is not all: Tolkien was no environmentalist in the modern sense, but in a way, he is more profound than most modern environmentalists. This is so for one particular reason that stands at the heart of this paper. Tolkien's love of the environment arises from metaphysics. His loving relation to the natural world was grounded in the nature of reality. Because things *are* (they exist) and because they have an *origin*, they can be loved for themselves.

Tolkien and Thomism

The primary methodological approach taken in this paper is that Tolkien's profoundly felt love of creation (natural and non natural) is deeply rooted, albeit implicitly, in a metaphysics of creation. This starting point might, in and of itself, be a matter open for debate, that will not be discussed here. However, if this assumption is correct, we must consider more precisely what these metaphysical considerations are. Considering Tolkien's religious convictions, scholars have seen in the Neoplatonist tradition of early Christianity, as represented in Augustine and Boethius, the obvious source of Tolkien's metaphysics.[1] However, we will not consider this philosophical-theological point of view as the most fundamental component of Tolkien's metaphysical outlook. Rather, it is Thomas Aquinas who will stand at the heart of our metaphysical investigations. Of course, the role of Thomism in Tolkienian scholarship is also a topic for debate.[2] Among Tolkien's theological influences, Thomas is not yet widely acknowledged as a primary source,[3] and even though we have seen more of a distinctive Thomistic approach in recent years, the 'Platonist' interpretation of Tolkien has been much more important.[4] However, Thomas seems a more obvious theological path to understanding Tolkien.[5] In a few words, McIntosh summarizes the main reasons supporting the centrality of Thomas for Tolkien:

> As for our present interest in St. Thomas in particular as an ideal dialogue partner for understanding the metaphysics of Tolkien, the rationale behind this may be broadly divided into two parts, the first of which [...] has to do with the real-life, religious, theological, historical, and cultural connection we

---

1 The current consensus, if such a thing is even possible in any scholarship, tends towards a Neoplatonist reading of Tolkien, whether in his politics or in the use of the "ring" symbol (Morse 1980).
2 As McIntosh indicates: "It is in similar terms, finally, that I want to suggest that Tolkien's own Thomism is to be understood, for regardless of what might be conjectured about Tolkien's direct or indirect exposure to the writings of Thomas or other Thomists, in the end the thing calling for analysis and comment is the undeniable fact of just such an 'innate philosophical affinity' and 'intellectual sympathy' between Tolkien and St. Thomas, whatever the historical causes might have been in producing it" (33).
3 In the *J.R.R. Tolkien Encyclopedia*, Thomas receives his own article by Birzer, who speaks of an "implicit rather than explicit Thomism" (Drout 22).
4 See the following articles: Cox, "Tolkien's Platonic Fantasy"; Houghton, "Augustine in the Cottage of Lost Play: The Ainulindale as Asterisk Cosmology"; Fisher, "Working at the Crossroads: Tolkien, St. Augustine, and the Beowulf-poet"; Dubs, "Providence, Fate, and Chance: Boethian Philosophy in The Lord of the Rings," Mary Carman Rose, "The Christian Platonism of C.S. Lewis, J.R.R. Tolkien, and Charles Williams," and more importantly Flieger, "Naming the Unnameable."
5 Even though, as McIntosh reminds us, "thirty-five years later, the question of Tolkien's Thomism has progressed very little beyond the state in which Kocher left it" (11).

may suppose to have existed between these two individuals. The second basis for our comparison, of course, has to do with the discernible theological and philosophical affinities between St. Thomas and Tolkien […]. (21)

We share the same conviction about the importance of Thomas's theology for understanding Tolkien's vision. While not a Thomist in the sense of being a student of the great medieval theologian, "Tolkien, while not straightforwardly 'Thomist', is quite clearly, like Flannery O'Connor, at least 'a Thomist thrice-removed'" (Candler 7).

Hope for Nature

The second main thesis of this paper is that Tolkien's love of nature is nourished by a profound hope for the restoration of the natural world. This very hope is central to Tolkien's works, as particularly seen in *The Lord of the Rings* and *The Hobbit*, but also in *The Silmarilion* and other lesser works. Entwined with the centrality of the natural world, and brought to life on numerous occasions by Tolkien, we find an ever-present but veiled hope for a renewed natural environment; yet, hope for such a renewal of nature always seems so distant as to be merely a dream. Songs and stories assume this hope, but only on rare occasions is it clearly expressed. This paper aims to demonstrate that Tolkien's hope for a future restoration of nature rests upon a fundamentally Catholic, and more precisely Thomistic, understanding of nature and history.

To demonstrate such a hope for the restoration of creation, which itself springs from a metaphysical perspective of creation, we will first explore the grounding of the value and integrity of creation, taking into account the debate over the nature of Middle-earth's history. Indeed, if hope is dependent upon an unfolding history, history is dependent for its course upon its general direction given at its origin. The question of the origin of Arda is thus crucial to our investigation. Only then will we be able to consider more closely what we could call "creational hope."

History and the Integrity of Creation

The first lines of the Ainulindalë, that all remember quite well, are telling: "There was Eru, the One, who in Arda is called Ilúvatar; and he made first the Ainur, the Holy Ones, that were the offspring of his thought, and they were with him before aught else was made" (*S* 3).[6] Consistent with this, Tolkien also referred to God as the "supreme Artist and the Author of Reality" (*L* 101). At first then, it would seem that there is nothing much to be said about the origin and nature of the natural creation: there is a creator, there is a creation. However, this would certainly be over-simplistic. For, if creation comes from a creator, there is little doubt that the nature of the creation will entertain a profound relationship with its creator – it will, in an analogical way, resemble it.[7] This first observation is more important than it seems. In fact, it has given rise to an important debate over the nature of Eru, the nature of his creation, and then, the nature of history. So far, we can only conclude that the value and integrity of nature is grounded in an original creative act. But what of the author of this archetypal act? Is the presence of an original supreme deity who evidences power to bring lesser divinities into being enough to explain creation? We might even wonder if the presence of such a remote creator can really sustain the beauty and integrity of the natural environment. In fact, if Eru is such a disengaged creator, what hope is there for nature within Tolkien's mythological history? Let us now consider two different options.

The Long Defeat as a History of Decay?

Noting that Eru is described by Tolkien himself as "immensely remote" (*L* 204), many commentators have concluded that Tolkien's creation is a "perfectly good Neoplatonist Christian cosmos" even resulting in a "full-blown *pagan* Neoplatonism" (Hutton 63). The Neoplatonist description of Tolkien's creation-drama was further highlighted by Flieger's conclusion that Eru was

---

6 This is of course reminiscent of the creation account found in the book of Genesis, and is in line with the Thomist understanding of the Creator and of the creative act. Indeed, Thomas Aquinas, the Doctor Angelicus, stresses the inescapable fact that there is nothing that *is*, or *could be*, that is not itself under the Creator-God's sovereignty.

7 As Thomist scholars have particularly affirmed: "Analogy is axiomatic in metaphysics" (Phelan 2).

closer to the Platonists' One than to the biblical God.[8] Following her investigation of the Neoplatonic nature of Eru, Flieger described the creation-act along the lines of an emanationist theory that has profound implications for the rest of Arda's unfolding history. According to this emanationist belief, emanation implies diminution, falling away from Eru's perfection and light. In fact, the whole concept of emanation as diminution, as splintered light, lies at the heart of Flieger's impressive work, in which she makes use of this emanationist motif through the examples of the Lamp and the Trees.[9] According to this account of Tolkienian creation, Catholicism would serve only as a source for inspiration, providing the *image* of light (Flieger, *Splintered Light* 49).[10] Nothing more.

In turn this "splintered light" led to a diminution of being, "splintered being" (Flieger, *Splintered Light* 49-56). The crucial implication is this: with every stage of created reality, we observe a move away from the perfect One. In a typical Neoplatonic fashion, this would imply a "corruption or dilution" of being (McIntosh 194). Hence:

> Approaching Tolkien in light of the Plotinian and Dionysian tradition of Neoplatonism, Flieger both here and in her recently revised study, *Splintered Light*, stresses the apophatic or negative dimension of Tolkien's fictional theology at the expense of its more cataphatic or positive aspects, going so far

---

8 There is often a good deal of theological misunderstanding, as with Tolkien's "natural theology" (*L* 220). Madsen for example concludes: "Middle-earth is a monotheistic world – remotely; it has no theology, no covenant, and no religious instruction; it is full of beauty and wonder and even holiness, but no divinity. Even the reader need not worship anything to comprehend it. It is more important for the reader to love trees" (Madsen 39). It is obvious from Madsen's (39) following statement that she does not comprehend the meaning of "natural theology": "'Natural theology,' in the *Oxford English Dictionary*'s definition, is 'theology based upon reasoning from natural facts apart from revelation.' Unless one is willing to call God a natural fact it is difficult to see how this can be theology at all."

9 Cox (58-59) argues along much similar lines, but from a more direct philosophical perspective: "while Tolkien follows the Timaeus [...] in creating the Ainur, he follows neo-platonic tradition, beginning with Plotinus, in depicting innumerable series of imitations that radiate outward from a point close to the greatest creative power through stages of gradual diminution."

10 The image of "light" is prevalent in several letters, including the following: "Your reference to the care of your guardian angel [...] reminded me of a sudden vision (or perhaps apperception which at once turned itself into pictorial form in my mind) I had not long ago when spending half an hour in St Gregory's before the Blessed Sacrament when the Quarant' Ore was being held there. I perceived or thought of the Light of God and in it suspended one small mote (or millions of motes to only one of which was my small mind directed), glittering white because of the individual ray from the Light which both held and lit it. (Not that there were individual rays issuing from the Light, but the mere existence of the mote and its position in relation to the Light was in itself a line, and the line was Light). And the ray was the Guardian Angel of the mote: not a thing interposed between God and the creature, but God's very attention itself, *personalised*" (*L* 99).

as to represent Tolkien's Eru as an almost deistic entity who has abdicated the real work of creation to the intermediate agency of the angelic Ainur. (McIntosh 19)

After reminding us that Eru is a "disengaged figure" (Flieger, *Splintered Light* 43), the Neoplatonic account of creation by the Ainur is presented as a mediatory act between Iluvatar's creative act and the actualised creation. This leads Flieger to conclude that "the concept of the Valar is especially important to the cosmology. While their position in the hierarchy suggests angelic beings, their role in the scheme of things is, from a strictly Christian point of view, eccentric" (Flieger, *Splintered Light* 54). This conclusion is shared by other scholars noting that creation by the Ainur represents a "divine distance" clearly not characteristic of the biblical God. In a way then, it is the Ainur that serve as the *agent* of creation, resulting in a created order that would not completely be according to Iluvatar's will but reflect the free-will creative act of the Ainur.[11] For many, this would imply that the true creators of Arda are indeed the Ainur, relegating Eru to this distant figure already alluded to: "together they [the Ainur] sang the universe into existence" (Birzer 53).

This would, supposedly, be further supported by Eru's approbative declaration: "Behold your Music!" This confirmation addressed to the Ainur might well validate the interpretation of creation as primarily an act of the Ainur. Flieger puts it this way: "the Music is not the physical act of creation, but only its blueprint. It is the pattern for the world *in potentia*" (Flieger, *Splintered Light* 58). From this, it would be easy to conclude with Davis that "Tolkien's music of creation actually *creates* the *entire* cosmos" (emphasis original), and that the Ainur's Music represents the vibratory force in creation, and it is that force which has the power to create and sustain worlds" (Davis 6, 8).[12] Accordingly,

---

11 "If creation is a free act of God, then not only is God free to create or not to create in the first place, but he must also be free to create more than simply one single effect, meaning that God could be the direct and unmediated cause of the being of all things, contrary to the fundamental premise of much Neoplatonic philosophy" (Collins 262). See Plotinus, *Enneads* 5.4.1.
12 See also Eden (185-188), who clearly identifies the Ainur (and *their* Music) as "the creative and omnipotent force," or as "the creational and binding force that sets in motion the entire drama of Middle-earth," further as "the generational force out of which much of the drama of Middle-earth develops," the "creational and cosmological power," and again as "the ultimate power in the cosmological history of Middle-earth."

many conclude that the real creators are the Ainur. They are the true cause of Arda's creation.[13]

However, I believe this contention is a tragic mistake for it fails to see that causality is not univocal or uniform. To believe so would be to fundamentally misinterpret Tolkien on causality, especially seen from a Thomist perspective. For Thomas, what we call secondary causes never erase or replace primary causes. In other words, "Ainur-causality" will never replace or affect "Iluvatar-causality."[14] It is true that Thomas rejected creation by angels, as a form of emanationism, especially since he made a clear distinction between making and creating, the latter being a specific "out of nothing" act.[15] But if Thomas did so, it is because "the act of creation belongs to God alone, and bodies cannot, strictly speaking, 'create', because their making always acts on already-existing matter, to which it gives accidental form" (Candler 10).

By contrast, the emanationist account of the Ainulindalë strongly maintains that Arda is the result of limited and imperfect beings. This perspective is important because the implications are far-reaching. Indeed, it can serve as the interpretative framework for Tolkien's qualification of history as a "long defeat." If Eru really is absent from his creation and if Arda is merely the creation of limited angelic beings, then Arda's history can only be seen as a history of decay, of diminution: it is imperfect, representing only a partial and, at best, an imperfect echo of Eru's original Music. If "Tolkien carefully restricts Eru's

---

13 So Flieger ("Naming the Unnameable" 132): "It is the Ainur, not Eru, who actually create Tolkien's world. They sing its plan in the Great Music which they make from the themes Eru propounds to them, and from that plan fabricate the material world. The rest of Tolkien's vast mythology is enacted without Eru, involving chiefly the Ainur and the Children of Iluvatar. Father of All he may be, but he has no further role in the action [… However, he] remains throughout the Unknown God, unknowable and unreachable in his oneness, perceivable and approachable only to the extent by which the part can represent the whole." Even though she also rightly maintains that "[t]here is only one Prime Mover–Eru, the One. The Ainur, and more particularly the Valar, are sub-creators. They participate in the physical making of the world but could not have done so had not Eru first given them the theme" (Flieger, *Splintered Light* 55).
14 For example, I do not think we can talk about the Music as the "creative and omnipotent force" (*contra* Eden 185). To take this direction implies, I believe, a confusion in scholastic causality; a confusion between "source" and "instrumentality"; between "final cause" and "efficient cause."
15 Strictly speaking, when we deny that angels could create, that means "out of nothing" (Garrigou-Lagrange 366, from Augustine IX, 15). The notion put forth by Tolkien might not, then, seem so eccentric, even though it might be seen as innovative. As McIntosh points out: "Tolkien's conception of the Valar's sub-creative power, therefore, is more complex and dynamic than simple and static: the more they invest themselves into the material shaping and making of the world, the more power or influence they wield over it, and yet the less power they retain in and for themselves, and thus the more like the conventional, governing angels theorized about by St. Thomas they become" (295-296).

role to an implicit guardianship, a mysterious providence throughout the long ages of the Valar's protection of Arda" (Egan 81), we could ask whether this providence is not so distant as to render the future of Arda utterly unknowable. The only thing that could be predicated would be that (1) Arda was created and (2) Arda still exists. Its future is open to question.

If this account of Arda's origin were true, this would leave us with very little to say about the becoming of Arda, nature, and all that Tolkien cherished most. This would leave us with very little to hope for. But we will come back to this point later. In any case, the implications here are serious: history can only be a history of diminution. What of nature then? It must be subject to the same history. Arda's history should necessarily be a history of the decaying of nature.

Thomist Reinterpretation

What can be said of the previous emanationist option? At first, it seems to present a very comprehensive, coherent, and cogent account of natural creation in Tolkien's mythology. However, most of the arguments are grounded in a Neoplatonist metaphysics. By contrast a second option has been presented, interpreting creation and nature though the lens of Thomist metaphysics. Prominent among those promoting a Thomist interpretation of Tolkien are Jonathan McIntosh and Alison Milbank. The former has strongly argued for such a Thomist reinterpretation in his dissertation *The Flame Imperishable*, in which he particularly argues against the notion of a Tolkienian emanationist account of creation. According to McIntosh, "there has been a marked tendency in the Tolkien literature [...] to read his creation-drama and the Music of the Ainur in particular in terms of the emanationist logic of Neoplatonic philosophy." (180). Of course, one could see Thomas as presenting a profoundly different account of emanationism. Naturally, he would agree that everything comes from the creator-God, the source of all that exists. However, such an emanation would not function as a diminution from being but is defined by the analogical relationship beings entertain with the Being from whom all emanate. Certainly, the emanationist account is a powerful one. Thomas himself was in fact well aware that emanationism was a creational option. In his *De potentia dei*, dealing with the question of whether a creation "out of nothing" is even philosophically possible, Thomas considers the objection that "the same thing cannot be the principle of both perfection and imperfection" (Thomas, *On Creation* 6). Even if Thomas does not here explicitly debate Neoplatonic emanationism, it is quite obvious that he sees it as a possible, but mistaken, philosophical outcome. This would seem to argue for a dual principle in creation: one of perfection and another one of imperfection (or limitation), as the previous picture of creation would present the dual role of Eru and the Ainur – the latter being, of course, a "principle" of imperfection. In fact, if Eru is not the principle of perfection and imperfection, he must be, even though perfect himself, the origin of an imperfect and mediated world. Aquinas himself takes another road and implies that this objection would require the identification of another source or origin, which cannot be the case.

Further, Thomas is aware that creation means change and that "the greater the distance between the terms, the greater the change" (Thomas, *On Creation* 14). The implications could be dramatic: falling away from the source of creation could of course imply falling away from being, going through a diminution of being.[16] Opposing such a notion we can see Thomas presenting a notion of creation as participation.[17] The first observation of a Thomistic account of creation is very similar to that of emanationism:

> Now since God is being itself by His own essence, created being must be His proper effect; just as to ignite is the proper effect of fire. Now God causes this effect in things not only when they first begin to be, but as long as they are preserved in being; as for instance light is caused in the air by the sun as long as the air remains illuminated. (Thomas, *ST* 1.8.1)

However, one should not believe that the two accounts are identical. Here lies the crucial part, the main and radical difference. Says Thomas (*ST* 1.8.1): "Therefore as long as a thing has being, God must be present to it, according to its mode of being. But being is innermost in each thing and most deeply

---

16 In his *Summa Theologiae* (Ia.45, henceforth *ST*), Thomas deals with the question of emanation, concluding with an "emanation of all being from the universal cause." But again, this demonstrates that there are different possible explanations of what "emanationism" might look like.

17 Regarding participation, notice that the Thomist construction is complex. For further explanations, see for example Wippel 121ff. Velde stresses the crucial importance of participation in Thomism: "The concept of participation stands at the very heart of Thomas's account of creation" (118). See also Thomas's arguments in *ST* Ia.44.i.

inherent in all things [...] Hence it must be that God is in all things, and most intimately."

Hence, for Thomas, the fact that creation "emanates" from God as from its source does not necessarily imply that creation is a diminution of being. If participation implies different degrees of perfection, it does not imply that a thing that has "less perfection" tends towards nothingness.[18] It would be the case if "being" was predicated univocally. In this case, it would indeed be correct that emanation from a perfect being would entail either identity of being (creation would be the same being as its creator) or a diminution of being. Thomas famously resolves the dilemma in arguing for an *analogical* relationship of being. As such, as in our previous quote, "God must be present to it, *according to its mode* of being." *According to its mode*, or according to its analogical relation to God. Hence, we can easily see that

> Tolkien's Eru is more than merely the distant, creative or 'emanative' source of the world's existence, but is the one who has self-consciously 'designed' the world in such a way as to permit his creatures to learn something of his own mind through the study of his effects. This point is made clear enough, moreover, in the Ainulindalë when it is reported how the Ainur, through the glimpse they catch of the Children of Iluvatar in their Vision, were able to see 'the mind of Iluvatar reflected anew, and learned yet a little more of his wisdom, which otherwise had been hidden even from the Ainur' (*S* 18). (McIntosh 75)

The conclusion here is that Eru first creates the Ainur and then, and *only then*, he reveals to them the further elements of creation.[19] Hence, the Ainur's knowledge will, *partially, analogously*, reflect ideas of the divine mind. This leads us to further conclude that it is Eru who gives *real*, actualised, existence to what the Ainur have perceived through the Music or in the Vision. This is fundamental to a balanced understanding of the Ainulindalë.[20] As McIntosh concludes: "In the Ainulindalë, then, the sub-creative activity of the Ainur presupposes a recognizably Thomistic understanding of sub-creative possibility in terms of imitability of the divine mind or essence" (173). Indeed, this is

---

[18] See Thomas, *ST* Ia. 44.I and *Summa Contra Gentiles*, II.15.
[19] McIntosh presents a fascinating exploration of the implications of the Music and the Vision, here also interpreted through Thomist metaphysics, see McIntosh, chapter three, "The Metaphysics of the Music and Vision" (179-241).
[20] See also Houghton (175-178).

strangely similar to Tolkien's statement that "they [the Valar] shared in [the World's] 'making' – but only on the same terms as we 'make' a work of art or story. The realization of it, the gift to it of a created reality of the same grade as their own, was the act of the One God" (*L* 235n).[21]

If this is so, then creation takes its value, its integrity, from the Thomistic metaphysics of creation according to which everything that is created, by Eru through the instrumentality of the Ainur, including the fields of the Shire, the woods of Fangorn of the trees of Lothlórien, participate in being. As one Thomist scholar puts it: "Being (*ens*) is predicated of God alone essentially, and of every creature only by participation; for no creature is its *esse*, but merely has *esse*" (Wippel 105). Their being can be loved because of the being through which they have existence.

The conclusion is very different from the emanationist account. Arda, its being, with the beings of all its creatures, takes its existence from the ground, the origin of being, Eru, through Ainur-agency.[22] This further establishes a relation of analogy and dependance between Eru and its creation – whether Arda or the Ainur. In fact, "creation in the creature is nothing more than a certain relation to the Creator, namely, a relation of dependence" (Thomas, *ST* Ia.45.x).[23] Regarding the participation of the Ainur in the act of creation, here again Thomas illuminates Tolkien's position: the Ainur participate in "the proper action of another, not by [their] own power, but instrumentally, inasmuch as [they] act by the power of another [Eru]" (Thomas, *ST* Ia.45.v). McIntosh aptly sums up the point:

> Where the doctrine of creation proper is concerned, in summary, careful scrutiny reveals Tolkien's mythology to be in remarkable agreement with St. Thomas's teaching that God and God alone creates, an activity both men understand in the precise, metaphysical sense of a 'giving,' 'sending,' 'sustaining,' or 'emanation' of the very being, existence, or reality of a thing. (259)

---

21 As we hear Eru say to Manwë in the "Converse of Manwë and Eru": "Have I not given to the Valar the rule of Arda, and power over all the substance thereof, to shape it at their will under My will?" (*MR* 362).
22 "However, once it has been actualised by Ilúvatar, he shows it to the Ainur as containing their own minstrelsy: he shows them themselves" (Milbank 192).
23 See also Thomas, *ST* Ia.8.i; *ST* Ia.44.i-ii.

The importance of this Thomist Tolkienian account of creation is that it provides the only possible ground for the care and love of the created order. Nature exists *and* it has an origin. This dual affirmation is both at the heart of Tolkien's metaphysics of creation and at the heart of Thomism. Indeed, it might well be the only viable metaphysical explanation for his environmental vision, especially since Thomism, starkly contrasted with Neoplatonism, stresses the importance and value of creation. As Chesterton had already noticed, the Platonists "thought of God too exclusively as a Spirit who purifies or a Saviour who redeems; and too little as a Creator who creates" (Chesterton 96).

Creational Hope

After this discussion, although more brief than would be necessary, of Eru's creation and its implications for Arda's history, we can move to the implications for the integrity and future of creation. We come now to the crucial issue of "creational hope", hope for creation. Throughout Tolkien's mythological corpus, hope seems ever present, but always in the background. Always in reach, but never attained. This has led Flieger to say that hope is only that: hope. It is never incarnated in reality. And further: "the doubt must be genuine, it must come from the knowledge that there may be no happy ending, that the thing which we greatly fear will indeed come upon us" (Flieger, *Splintered Light* 30). In her introduction to *Splintered Light*, Flieger indicates that Tolkien's faith was less hopeful than either Williams's or Lewis's.

Whether Flieger is right in her assessment of Tolkien's personality or not – she probably is – what is certain is that in an emanationist account of creation, there can be no hope beyond mere wishful thinking. In fact, if imperfection is of the created order, of the nature of the world, then the diminution of "light" and so, of nature, is a creational fact: there is nothing to be done against this state of affairs. There would be no "happy ending," no matter how you define "happy." Here, one can wonder whether hope defined as an outcome "always in doubt" (Flieger, *Splintered Light* 30) can properly be called hope. By contrast, says Tolkien, hope is *Amdir*, which is "looking up" (*MR* 320), and there must be an "up" to look up to. Hope must be directed at something, or someone. But hope is not merely a direction to look for, it is something to long for. In

Thomistic terms, hope is an "appetite of the soul" directed towards a future good. This does not mean that this good is in the present, seen and lived out. It simply means that this hope is constitutive of reality itself, and as such, hope as an attitude becomes, properly speaking, a virtue.[24] It is the virtue of Éomer's refusal to give in to despair in battle; the virtue of Sam going on despite loss of hope; the virtue of Théoden as one who rekindles hope![25]

It has not been noted enough that hope, uncertain but present, is one of the driving elements of the drama of Arda. As Tolkien (*MR* 349) indicates, Arda (the "kingdom of Manwë" or the "Solar System", or Earth) is, properly speaking, the *dramatic* center of the scene on which unfolds the war of the "Children of Eru" against Melkor. It is clear, then, that Tolkien is using "dramatic" not because Arda is liable to be destroyed but in the sense of a historical-theatrical unveiling of the Story. But it is also clear that within this dramatic turn of the story, imbedded in its very heart, lies hope. This is quite visible in the sense of loss and history that is felt by every person in Middle-earth:

> Within every community – the Shire, Rohan, Gondor, and even Rivendell, – there is a certain security that allows ordinary routine to take place, but each community is also marked by a sense of loss or falling off, a dim awareness, either strongly or weakly felt, of the fragility of this borrowed time, and a sense of fatigue to face or change its fate." (Tomko 215)

However, it is absolutely crucial here to realize that a sense of loss does not necessarily mean despair.[26] On the contrary. When Tolkien says that "actually I am a Christian, and indeed a Roman Catholic, so that I do not expect 'history' to be anything but a 'long defeat'" (*L* 195), he does not imply that we should despair. A "long defeat" is not ultimate defeat; as one might forget, and as Hart reminds us, "ultimate triumph is entirely compatible with many penultimate

---

24 Thus, Thomas says: "first, because their object is God, inasmuch as they direct us aright to God: secondly because they are infused in us by God alone" (*ST* IIa.62.i).
25 Or again Merry's "overcoming of despair and the raising of hope – signified by the ancient Horn of the Mark which is given to him by Éomer at their parting" (Caldecott 41). Such an attitude in the face of almost total despair is in Tolkien, I believe, a complex mingling of Thomist virtues and "Northern courage." Here, we must acknowledge the complexity with which Tolkien has tried to integrate the value of Northern epics and virtues in a broader Christian ethical framework. On that matter, see for example Martin Simonson, "Tolkien's Triple Balance: A Redemptive Model of Heroism for the Twentieth Century", esp. 21-25. However, the ground for Tolkien's balanced heroism is a metaphysical, Thomist one.
26 It is true that Tolkien's world is dark, "darker than his critics realize" (Caldecott 112), even leading main characters to express a deep sense of futility. And yet true hope beyond despair, is what defines the Free people.

defeats and struggles, as Christian eschatology is all too aware" (46). Indeed often the end of Tolkien's sentence is forgotten: "though it [the long defeat] contains (and in a legend may contain more clearly and movingly) some samples or glimpses of *final victory*" (*L* 195, italics mine). Hence, Arda's history is not one of long decay or diminution but a long dramatic history moving towards an unseen but hopeful fulfillment.

Hope for Creation is Hope for Eru's Children

This unseen hope is translated into Arda's history in two different ways. The first is hope for creation, hope for Arda. However, there is actually not much material in Tolkien that directly and explicitly deals with the hope for the restoration of creation. Hope for creation is implicit rather than explicit, consciously and intricately woven into the patterns of Eruhini history so as to render it almost imperceptible. In fact the most obvious way to see hope for creation in Tolkien's mythological corpus is to realize that this hope is closely linked to hope for Eru's Children. As Tolkien himself indicates: "According to the fable Elves and Men were the first of these [divine] intrusions, made indeed while the 'story' was still only a story and not 'realized'; they were not therefore in any sense conceived or made by the gods, the Valar, and were called the Eruhini or 'Children of God'" (*L* 235-236).

In fact, "natural eschatology" is deeply woven into "human" (human, so to speak!) eschatology. The hope "beyond the circles of the world" is not merely the hope of Elves and Men but of Arda itself, which groans and suffers the consequences of Melkor's rebellion and the Eruhini's long war against Melkor.[27] This is so because the history of the Elves – particularly the Elves – is engraved into Arda. This has already been noted by Tolkien scholars such as Alison Milbank: "To a degree greater than humanity they [the Elves] are wedded to the material cosmos [...]" (192). Thus, there is solidarity between nature and "free races" in Middle-earth as there is a solidarity between humanity and nature in Paul's epistle to the Romans (Rm 8.19-22). The Elves will have part in the restoration of Arda, because of their love for it (*MR* 343).

---

27 "To answer mortals' suffering on earth with the hope of a compensation from beyond the earth is in fact unconvincing" (Madsen 43).

But what exactly will the restoration of Arda consist of? In one of the most fascinating parts of Tolkien's unpublished papers, the "Athrabeth Finrod ah Andreth" (The Debate of Finrod and Andreth), Tolkien goes, in the text and in his commentary, further than ever before in explaining what lies in the future of Arda. In this clearly eschatological essay, an Elf (Finrod) and a woman (Andreth) debate the fate of Elves as well as the mortal nature of Men. But beyond the debate over human mortality, Finrod has "a Vision of Men as the agents of the 'unmarring' of Arda, not merely undoing the marring or evil wrought by Melkor, but by producing a third thing, 'Arda Re-Made' – for Eru never merely undoes the past, but brings into being something new, richer than the 'first design'" (*MR* 333). Clearly then, whatever the future will be, it does involve three things: the role of the Elves in the war against Melkor, the agency of Men in a manner still unseen, followed by the unmarring of Arda.

Thus, what I suggest we should call "creational hope" is the future of Elves at the end of Arda, and the future of Arda at the end of the Elves' war. This is "naked *estel*," the pure hope that Eru would "do right" by his creation, and more than just "right," that he would bring about "joys unforeseeable" (*MR* 332). This hope beyond the walls of the visible world is shared by Aragorn in his last moments: "In sorrow we must go, but not in despair. Behold! We are not bound for ever to the circles of the world, and beyond them there is more than memory" (*RK* Appendix A.v). This could seem to validate Andreth's point: "We were not made for death, nor born ever to die. Death was imposed upon us" (*MR* 309). Is that hope sufficient? Of course not. Hope reaches beyond death, beyond the known world. This, the Elves are aware of, even though it is more difficult for Men to see. Andreth, from the standpoint of human knowledge, can only state "still many Men perceive the world only as a war between Light and Dark equipotent" (*MR* 321). Even then, she implies that this belief might be mistaken, as Finrod himself seems to believe, and there is an element which is even more crucial. If the Elves assumed that the brevity of Men's lives was due to the character of their *fëa* (soul), it also followed from this that Men's bodies (*hröar*) were frail and brief in their longevity precisely because of the design of Men's *fëar* – the approximate equivalent of "souls" (*MR* 331). How is that relevant? Simply because the hope of both Men and Elves is that when Eru heals Arda, even Eä itself, he will also heal both *hröar* and *fëar* (*MR* 342).[28] Everything, absolutely everything, will be made anew! This is the hope for creation to which we now turn.

Hope for Creation

"It would be a poor life in a land where no mallorn grew" (*FR* 339), complains Haldir as he leads the company into Lothlórien. But this could as well be a statement of hope: hope that the natural world will share in the future destiny and restoration of the Elves. Here, the important question is this: will the un-marring of Arda be merely the un-making of evil? In other words, will Arda be only what it was before Melkor's rebellion? We could be tempted to answer affirmatively. Of course, the un-marring of Arda will be the un-making of what Melkor brought to the world; however, this is too limited. Even Dickerson and Evans's work, with all the great insights they offer into Tolkien's Catholic environmental ethic, miss one important dimension: eschatology, the future of Arda and of Eä. In their summary of Tolkien's environmental vision they mention the following main elements:

1. The universe is the work of a divine creator.
2. The created world is good.
3. Creation has a purpose.
4. The created order and its inhabitants are vulnerable to evil embodied in a cosmic enemy.
5. The mission of people dwelling in the world is to acknowledge the goodness of the earth, fulfill its purpose, and assist in its restoration from evil. (Dickerson and Evans 24)

However, I believe we should move one step further:

6. The hope that the creator himself will bring about Arda-Remade.

This hope is truly characteristic of the "Athrabeth Finrod ah Andreth." For Finrod implies, of course with a partial Elvish knowledge, that hope for the

---

28 This can probably be so because "fëar were held to be directly created by Eru, and 'sent into' Eä; whereas Eä was achieved mediately by the Valar" (*MR* 336). Hence healing of *fëa* is an act of Eru. In the same manner, healing of *hröa* must be an act of Eru even though *hröa* were mediately created by the Ainur. Eru must still remain the "healer" since healing *hröa* means re-establishing its proper relation to *fëa*.

Eruhini and hope for Arda can only be accomplished together. And in that, Tolkien confirms this Elvish insight:

> But Eru could not enter *wholly* into the world and its history, which is, however great, only a finite Drama. He must, as Author, always remain 'outside' the Drama, even though the Drama depends on His design and His will for its beginning and continuance, in every detail and moment. Finrod therefore thinks that He will, when He comes, have to be both 'outside' and inside [...] (*MR* 335, see also 322)

Being *then* (and not before) both inside and outside the world, Eru will be able to bring about such a complete and radical restoration that what will be then will not be Arda anymore. Or rather, Arda remade will be greater even that unmarred Arda. Finrod again: "For that Arda Healed shall not be Arda Unmarred, but a third thing and a greater, and yet the same" (*MR* 318). And here lies the greatest hope of Elves and Men, but not merely the hope of Elves and Men. It is the hope of everything alive; trees, Ents, Hobbits, and still more; it is the hope of everything created, including the Ainur's hope.

In fact, one of the distinctive features of Christian eschatology is that nature that has been "marred" will one day be "healed", be made new through God's grace.[29] Indeed, as the "Athrabeth" and Tolkien's commentary both make clear, Estel is dependent upon Eru bringing about a restoration of Arda (*MR* 322). Estel is thus dependent upon Oienkarmë Eruo (The One's perpetual Production) "which might be rendered by 'God's Management of the Drama'" (*MR* 329). Hope lies in Eru's Music and Vision to which he, and only he, gives existence.[30] If Elves, Men, and even the Ainur cannot produce hope, it is because they live in the perspective of limited knowledge and being, at the difference of Eru: "'Or again, since Eru is for ever free, maybe he made no Music and showed no Vision beyond a certain point. Beyond that point we cannot see or know, until by our own roads we come there, Valar or Eldar or Men'" (*MR* 319).[31]

---

29 As the great neo-Thomist scholar Etienne Gilson (21) remarked: "The true Catholic position consists in maintaining that nature was created good, that it has been wounded, but that it can be at least partially healed by grace if God so wishes."

30 "In the Ainulindalë creation takes place through a process of Iluvatar giving 'Being' or 'Reality' to the sub-creative designs previously thought or imagined by the Ainur" (McIntosh 273).

31 "Now none of us know, though the Valar may know, the future of Arda, or how long it is ordained to endure. But it will not endure for ever. It was made by Eru, but He is not in it. The One only has no limits. Arda, and Ëa itself, must therefore be bounded" (*MR* 311-312). If Finrod can only conjecture about the Valar's knowledge, we know that if their knowledge extends beyond that of the Elves, it does not extend beyond the "circles of the world."

In "Laws and customs among the Eldar", Manwë makes a similar declaration: "For Arda unmarred hath two aspects or senses. The first is the Unmarred that they [the Eldar] discern in the Marred [...]: this is the ground upon which Hope is built. The second is the Unmarred that shall be: that is, to speak according to Time in which they have their being, the Arda Healed, which shall be greater and more fair than the first, because of the Marring: this is the Hope that sustaineth" (*MR* 245). This is the Elvish hope. As Tolkien makes clear: "The Elvish conception of the End was in *fact catastrophic*. They did not think that Arda (or at any rate Imbar) would just run down into lifeless inanition" (*MR* 339). And even more precisely:

> The Elves expected the End of Arda to be catastrophic. They thought that it would be brought about by the dissolution of the structure of Imbar at least, if not the whole system. The End of Arda is not, of course, the same thing as the end of Ëa. About this they held that nothing could be known, except that Ëa was ultimately finite. It is noteworthy that the Elves had no myths or legends dealing with the end of the world. (*MR* 342)

This end of the Drama, that will be the end of the War, is by no means despair and destruction. It is also by no means the hope of the Free Peoples alone – even less the hope of the Children of Eru alone. It is the hope of all of Ëa.

In their book, Dickerson and Evans concluded that "Tolkien's environmental ethic is presented as a transcendent one" (24). We have tried to explain further the metaphysical foundation of Tolkien's transcendental vision of nature which took root in his "imbibed" Thomism (Milbank 188). Indeed, the Bent World will be made right, straight again, and the *whole* of Arda will be remade. That is Tolkien's eschatological hope, the foundation of his environmental vision.

About the Author

Yannick Imbert is professor of Apologetics and Church History at the Faculté Jean Calvin in Aix-en-Provence, France. He holds a Ph.D. from Westminster Theological Seminary (Philadelphia) for which he has written a dissertation titled 'Who Wrote the Stories Anyway: A Reformed Evaluation of Tolkien's Theory of Imagination'. He has written on Tolkien's works in several journals, including for recent issues of the *Journal of Inklings Studies*.

Bibliography

AUGUSTINE. *The Literal Meaning of Genesis*. Translated by John Hammond Taylor. Vol. 2. New York: Newman Press, 1982.

BIRZER, Bradley. *J.R.R. Tolkien's Sanctifying Myth: Understanding Middle-earth*. Wilmington: ISI Books, 2003.

CALDECOTT, Stratford. *The Power of the Ring: The Spiritual Vision Behind the Lord of the Rings*. New York: Crossroad, 2005.

CANDLER, Peter M. "Tolkien or Nietzsche, Philology and Nihilism." University of Nottingham Centre of Theology and Philosophy. http://meologyphilosophy-centre.co.uk/papers /~Candler TolkeinNietzsche.doc (accessed 06/15/2014).

CHESTERTON, Gilbert K. *St. Thomas Aquinas*. London: Hodder & Stoughton, 1933.

COLLINS, James. *The Thomistic Philosophy of the Angels*. Washington, D.C.: Catholic University of America Press, 1947.

Cox, John. "Tolkien's Platonic Fantasy." *Seven* 5 (1984): 53-69.

DAVIS, Howard. "*Ainulindale*: The Music of Creation." *Mythlore* 9.2 (1982): 6-10.

DICKERSON, Matthew and Jonathan Evans. *Ents, Elves, and Eriador: The Environmental Vision of J.R.R. Tolkien*. Lexington KY: University Press of Kentucky, 2011.

DROUT, Michael (ed.). *The J.R.R. Tolkien Encyclopedia*. New York: Routledge, 2006.

DUBS, Kathleen E. "Providence, Fate, and Chance: Boethian Philosophy in *The Lord of the Rings*." *Twentieth Century Literature* 27.1 (Spring 1981): 34-42.

EDEN, Bradford Lee. "The 'Music of the Spheres': Relationships between Tolkien's *The Silmarillion* and medieval cosmological and religious theory." *Tolkien the Medievalist*. Ed. Jane Chance. New York and London: Routledge, 2003. 193-193.

EGAN, Thomas M. "*The Silmarillion* and the Rise of Evil: The Birth Pains of Middle-earth." *Seven: An Anglo-American Literary Review* 6 (1985): 79-84.

FISHER, Matt. "Working at the Crossroads: Tolkien, St. Augustine, and the Beowulf-poet." *The Lord of the Rings, 1954-2004: Scholarship in Honor of Richard E. Blackwelder*. Ed. Wayne G. Hammond and Christina Scull. Milwaukee WI: Marquette University Press, 2006. 217-230.

FLIEGER, Verlyn. "Naming the Unnameable: The NeoPlatonic 'One' in Tolkien's *Silmarillion.*" *Diakonia: Studies in Honor of Robert T. Meyer.* Ed. Thomas Halton and Joseph P. Williman. Washington, D.C.: Catholic University of America Press, 1986. 127-132.

Splintered Light: Logos and Language in Tolkien's World. Kent OH: Kent State University Press, 2002.

GARRIGOU-LAGRANGE, Réginald. *The Trinity and God the Creator.* n.p.: Ex Fontibus, 2012.

GILSON, Etienne. *Christianity and Philosophy.* Translated by Ralph MacDonald. New York: Published for the Institute of Mediaeval Studies by Sheed & Ward, 1939.

HART, Trevor. "Tolkien, Creation, and Creativity." *Tree of Tales: Tolkien, Literature, and Theology.* Eds. Trevor Hart and Ivan Khovacs. Waco TX: Baylor University Press, 2007. 39-54.

HOUGHTON, John. "Augustine in the Cottage of Lost Play: The Ainulindalë as Asterisk Cosmology." *Tolkien the Medievalist.* Ed. Jane Chance. New York and London: Routledge, 2003. 171-182

HUTTON, Ronald. "The Pagan Tolkien." *The Ring and the Cross. Christianity in the Writings of J.R.R. Tolkien.* Ed. Paul E. Kerry. Madison NJ: Fairleigh Dickinson University Press, 2011. 57-70.

KOCHER, Paul. *Master of Middle-earth: The Fiction of J.R.R. Tolkien.* Boston MA: Houghton Mifflin, 1972.

MADSEN, Catherine. "'Light From an Invisible Lamp': Natural Religion in *The Lord of the Rings.*" *Tolkien and the Invention of Myth: A Reader.* Ed. Jane Chance. Lexington KY: University Press of Kentucky, 2004. 35-47.

MILBANK, Alison. "Tolkien, Chesterton, and Thomism." *Tolkien's The Lord of the Rings: Sources of Inspiration.* Ed. Stratford Caldecott and Thomas Honegger. Zurich and Jena: Walking Tree Publishers, 2008. 187-199.

MCINTOSH, Jonathan S. *The Flame Imperishable: Tolkien, St. Thomas, and the Metaphysics of Faërie.* PhD dissertation, University of Dallas TX, 2009.

MORSE, Robert E. "Rings of Power in Plato and Tolkien." *Mythlore* 7.25 (1980): 38.

PHELAN, Greald B. *Saint Thomas and Analogy.* Milwaukee WI: Marquette University Press, 1941.

PLOTINUS. *Enneads.* Translated by A. H. Armstrong. Loeb Classical Library. 7 vols. Cambridge MA: Harvard University Press, 1966.

Rose, Mary Carman. "The Christian Platonism of C.S. Lewis, J.R.R. Tolkien, and Charles Williams." *Neoplatonism and Christian Thought*. Ed. Dominic J. O'Meara. Norfolk: International Society for Neoplatonic Studies, 1981. 203-212.

Simonson, Martin. "Tolkien's Triple Balance: a Redemptive Model of Heroism for the Twentieth Century." *Sub-creating Middle-earth: Constructions of Authorship and the Works of J. R. R. Tolkien*. Ed. Judith Klinger. Zurich and Jena: Walking Tree Publishers, 2012. 21-42.

Thomas Aquinas. *On Creation*. Translated with introduction by S.C. Selner-Wright. Washington, D.C.: The Catholic University of America Press, 2011.

Summa Theologiae: Latin Text and English Translation, Introductions, Notes, Appendices, and Glossaries. 61 vols. Andover: Blackfriars in conjunction with Eyre & Spottiswoode, 1964.

Summa Contra Gentiles. 4 vols. Translated by C. J. O'Neil. Notre Dame: University of Notre Dame Press, 1975.

Tolkien, John Ronald Reuel. *The Fellowship of the Ring*. First published 1954. London: HarperCollins, 1997.

The Letters of J.R.R. Tolkien. Edited by Humphrey Carpenter, with the assistance of Christopher Tolkien. First published 1981. London: George Allen & Unwin; Boston MA: Houghton Mifflin, 2000.

The Silmarillion. Edited by Christopher Tolkien. London: George Allen & Unwin; Boston MA: Houghton Mifflin, 1977.

Morgoth's Ring. (*The History of Middle-earth*, vol. 10). Edited by Christopher Tolkien. London: HarperCollins; Boston MA: Houghton Mifflin, 1993.

Tomko, Michael. "'An Age Comes On': J.R.R. Tolkien and the English Catholic Sense of History." *The Ring and the Cross. Christianity in the Writings of J.R.R. Tolkien*. Ed. Paul E. Kerry. Madison NJ: Fairleigh Dickinson University Press, 2011. 205-223.

Velde, Rudi A. *Participation and Substantiality in Thomas Aquinas*. Leiden and New York: E.J. Brill, 1995.

Wippel, John F. *The Metaphysical Thought of Thomas Aquinas: From Finite Being to Uncreated Being*. Washington, D.C.: Catholic University of America Press, 2000.

Christopher Roman

Thinking with the Elements: J.R.R. Tolkien's Ecology and Object-Oriented Ontology

Abstract

What I want to accomplish in this paper is thinking about an environmental ethic that Tolkien builds throughout his work as it encounters object-oriented ontology. The "natural" world is complicated in his mythology as he presents objects that resist an easy romanticizing of nature as some sort of pastoral ideal. In Tolkien's text the changing environment is best described as an actant: a very real landscape that can manipulate and be manipulated, and ultimately transforms and changes non-teleologically. The various agents at work in Middle-earth – Elves, Hobbits, Humans, Ents, horses, rings – all work within and are affected by the landscape. They affect this landscape, as well. Tolkien's work puts forth the problem of thinking with the object: What would a fox say if it saw a hobbit? How would a ring feel if it was taken up by an unintended force? What does a horse think of its rider? The environmental ethic in Tolkien's universe resists complete revelation and challenges mastery to reveal a dark ecology that underscores the problems of war, greed, and evil in Middle-earth.

> Might not the challenge for philosophical thought today be to proceed altogether without the guardrails of the human-animal distinction and to invent new concepts and new practices along different paths?
> Matthew Calarco, *Zoographies*
>
> For it is said that, though the fruit of the Tree comes seldom to ripeness, yet the life within may then lie sleeping through many long years, and none can foretell the time in which it will awake.
> Gandalf, *The Return of the King*

J.R.R. Tolkien created a vast mythology that is noted for its attention to linguistic, geographical, and spatial detail. It is a deep world.[1] A remarkable aspect of Tolkien's universe is the underlying enmeshed environments he represents. Dark clouds off in the distance affect the biological and spiritual

---

1 For a geographical reading of Tolkien's world that thinks about sustainability through a scientific lens see Ina Habermann and Nikolaus Kuhn's "Sustainable Fictions: Geographical, Literary and Cultural Intersections in J.R.R. Tolkien's *The Lord of the Rings*." For a reading of Tolkien in terms of environmental education, see Alun Morgan, "*The Lord of the Rings – A Mythos in Unsustainable Times.*"

forces miles away. A river flowing through Mirkwood disturbs the psychology of those who touch it even though it may be drinkable for others. The dam of a river clears the water for industrialized processes that need timber to stoke the engine fires which in turn inspires the Ents to rise up against those same industrial processes. These interlocking events reveal the way Tolkien invoked an ontology of objects at work in his world. As Tolkien writes in "On Fairy-Stories" (107): "the realm of fairy-story is wide and deep and high and filled with many things: all manner of beasts and birds are found there; shoreless sea and stars uncounted; beauty that is an enchantment, and an ever-present peril; both joy and sorrow as sharp as swords." Fairy-stories create and reflect worlds using the problem of aesthetic concerns as they are imbricated with the ecological. If all manner of beasts can exist, how do they communicate? Who are they in commune with? What does the crossroads of aesthetics and ethics of *Faërie* look like? Much attention has been paid to Tolkien's environmentalism, but I want to extend that focus to the way Tolkien's texts expand and allow for perspectival shifts that explore the enmeshments of objects and their ability to express surprising agential power (especially surprising for the characters that readers identify with).[2] The effect of objects is felt strongly throughout Tolkien's work and in order to account for them, this essay examines those elements that work in surprising ways to challenge an anthropocentric reading of Tolkien's work.

What I want to accomplish in this paper is to explore an environmental ontology that Tolkien presents in his work in terms of an object-oriented ontology. Middle-earth is complicated by the various commitments to "nature" and the ethical response to it, and Tolkien works against an easy romanticizing of the natural world as some sort of pastoral ideal by presenting us with the

---

2 Important trail-blazing texts in regards to Tolkien's environmentalism are Matthew Dickerson and Jonathan Evans, *Ents, Elves, and Eriador: The Environmental Vision of J.R.R. Tolkien*, the publications by Patrick Curry, most notably his *Defending Middle-earth* and *Deep Roots in a Time of Frost*, and Liam Campbell's *The Ecological Augury in the Works of JRR Tolkien*.

problem of the object and its interactions in the world.³ In Tolkien's work the environment is best described as an acting agent: very real landscapes that can manipulate and be manipulated; something that transforms and changes. As Alfred Siewers describes, Tolkien borrows from the medieval Celtic literary tradition of the Otherworld which presents landscapes as "integrative [...] more a horizontal experiential engagement [...], as are Tolkien's fantasy landscapes: a polycentered reality, not merely an objectification of earthly reality as human desire" (Siewers 141). The various agents at work in Middle-earth – metal, plants, Elves, Hobbits, Humans, Ents, rings, swords, water, light, rocks, horses – are all enmeshed in the world. This enmeshment reveals that objects in Middle-earth act in unexpected ways. Reading Tolkien's work with an eye toward an object-oriented ontology shows the ethical problem of mastery or attempted mastery of environments while Tolkien explores and acknowledges the enmeshment of the world. As Matthew Calarco argues in his *Zoographies* (90): "the shared intuition and hope of most posthumanist philosophers seems to be that a less destructive and more sustainable form of politics can be developed by beginning from a kind of relational ontology."⁴ To push Calarco's description of sustainable and relational politics further, it is worth thinking about relations beyond just the races of Men, Elves, Hobbits and Dwarves and notice how objects circulate as agents.

Before I delve into an analysis of Tolkien's ecological ontology, let me discuss some basic tenets of object-oriented ontology or, as I will refer to it during the duration of this essay, OOO. OOO advocates for what we might call a flat ontology, one that proposes a non-hierarchical world between objects. Part of

---

3   For a reading of Tolkien's ending of *The Lord of the Rings* as romantic pastoralism see Meredith Veldman, *Fantasy, the Bomb, and the Greening of Britain: Romantic Protest*, 1945-1980. Veldman (90) writes: "decades aheads of the Greens, he denounced the exaltation of mechanization and the narrow definition of economic progress that resulted in the degradation of the natural environment and he did so in romantic terms: in Tolkien's Middle-earth, nature expressed a reality beyond human comprehension and worthy of human respect." Although I agree with Veldman's conclusion that Tolkien is critiquing mechanization, her assertion that nature is beyond human comprehension as a kind of romanticism returns us to an easy environmentalism which claims a primal origin, rather than a realism that Tolkien is working within his world, in which the environment has its own agency that may or may not work with the human.
4   For an eco-theological reading of Tolkien's world see Matthew Dickerson, "Water, Ecology, and Spirituality in Tolkien's Middle-earth." Dickerson's essay includes a meditation on pollution of waters in Middle-earth as a reflection of Tolkien's theological concerns with a fallen world. See especially 21-24. Dickerson ends with a plea to "listen to water" (30), an ethical concern towards the object that is mirrored in this essay.

the philosophic question for centuries is how we know objects, and usually the answer has been that the relation between objects and humans is only relevant in terms of our access to them. As philosopher Levi Bryant (*Democracy* 40) writes: "a post-humanist, realist ontology is not an anti-human ontology, but it is rather [...] an ontology where humans are no longer monarchs of being, but are instead among beings, entangled in beings, and implicated in other beings." For Bryant (*Democracy* 53), ontology "does not tell us what objects exist but that objects exist, that they are generative mechanisms." Further, Bryant ("Ontic Principle" 269) points out that objects exist if they make a difference: "if it is the case that there is no difference that does not make a difference then it follows that the minimal criterion for being consists in making a difference [...] if a difference is made then the being is." Objects, then – a pen, a poem, the moon, a unicorn, a volcano – all exist. They exist because they make a difference.

Object-oriented ontology has affected the way philosophers and theorists consider the relationship between nature and culture. For example, Timothy Morton writes that ecology is a way to think about coexistence. As Morton writes in *The Ecological Thought* (4): "ecology includes all the ways we imagine how we live together. Ecology is profoundly about coexistence. Existence is always coexistence. No man is an island. Human beings need each other as much as they need an environment." The environment is a thinking-through of the ways we live together, or a praxis. This is essential for thinking about Tolkien's work, since, as is clear for a great majority in *The Fellowship of the Ring*, as well as *The Two Towers*, the problem faced by the hobbits, Gandalf, and Aragorn is just how divisive Middle-earth has become. This divisiveness is not only to be found among the so-called major races, but can be linked, as well, to the lack of an ethical thinking-through with the non-human agents that act and work throughout the mythology.

Ethics is often defined in terms of what we may owe other *people*. Further, if we think about an ethics of responsibility, there is an emphasis on outcome-oriented ethics – so, one can think about such things as medical ethics and the principle of 'do no harm' that coincides with the idea of an outcome-oriented approach to medicine. OOO proposes that an answer to an ethics-without-subject is that ethics must be defined locally without preconceived reactions or outcomes. As Bryant (*Democracy* 269) points out OOO "recognize[s] the locality of local manifestations and the openness and excess of virtual proper being, refusing any reduction of the being of beings to their local manifestations." If we take care of trees, for example, we might invite in unintentional wildlife, like foxes, who then invade our garbage. That fox becomes part of this ecology and reveals the "openness and excess" of tree culture: their mysterious (to us) responses and our inability to reduce the fox or the tree to its local being (in our yards, or under our control, for example). The fox, too, enacts agential power beyond that of its relation with the human. Or, as Ian Bogost (11) frames the problem: "in a world of panexperiential meshes, how do things have experiences?" If we think of nature as object, then we think of nature through panexperiential meshes with those who may not speak our language or have identifiable human traits – in other words, an ethic with things that are not human. The ethic is open-ended, unpredictable, and in flux.

In thinking in terms of OOO, we can see how Tolkien rethinks relations. As a writer intrigued and heavily influenced by language and linguistics, Tolkien was aware of how language could open or close doors. When Frodo speaks Elvish, he is immediately welcomed where before he was looked at suspiciously, for example. As anthropologist Eduard Kohn (21) writes:

> we are colonized by certain ways of thinking about relationality. We can only imagine the ways in which selves and thoughts might form associations through our assumptions about the forms of associations that structure human language. And then, in ways that often go unnoticed, we project these assumptions onto nonhumans.

As part of Kohn's project, he, like Tolkien, wants to take seriously the concept that "forests think." An ethical route in thinking through relations is to dislodge a purely anthropocentric thinking based on human-language relationality and consider how relations in the world may be refigured, changed, and reconsidered in a more capacious understanding of language itself.

Mineral: Natureculture and the Stone Giants

Perhaps the way into thinking with OOO is through exploring one of the minor events in *The Hobbit*: the encounter with the Stone Giants. As OOO rejects the ideas that objects are only relevant in terms of our access to them, objects in themselves do not give up all of their properties. In other words, humans are unable to truly know all aspects of an object. When we look at or use an object – such as a chair – we may have access to sitting on it, but we do not have access to its relations, to its relationship with the floor, its connection to its joints, or its sense of stitching. This is all to say: how may mountains relate?

If the relationship between human and the world is not *the* relationship – this changes our sense of the "natural" world. In other words, nature is an object, too, and we are enmeshed in it – there is no such thing as a culture/nature divide; rather, following Donna Haraway, we can think of Tolkien's naturecultures. Haraway's purposeful running together of the words nature and culture speak to the entanglement of nature and culture and our inability to truly separate the two.[5] How are objects, then, entangled and implicated with concepts of natureculture? Tolkien addresses this by thinking in terms of landscapes. It is sometimes difficult to avoid anthropomorphizing the natural world;[6] OOO asks us to realize our enmeshment in the world and challenges our notion of ethical responses to that world.

The Stone Giants underscore this OOO-reading. As Jeffrey Jerome Cohen writes (55): "The slowest and the swiftest, rock and flame, are the most challenging to contain within customary frames." And it is in *The Hobbit* that we get the sense that Gandalf cannot fully "contain" the company's adventure: "even the good plans of wise wizards like Gandalf [...] go astray sometimes when you are off on dangerous adventures over the Edge of the Wild; and Gandalf was a wise enough wizard to know it" (*H* 53). The emphasis on the unknown here and Gandalf's inability to master it speaks to the unknowability of the thunder-battle itself. Environments are not always "friendly" to those traveling within them. Time scales and geological scales may increase in magnitude leaving the human

---

5 See Donna Haraway, *The Companion Species Manifesto: Dogs, People, and Significant Otherness.*
6 Jane Bennett (xvi) writes: "we need to cultivate a bit of anthropomorphizing – the idea that human agency has some echoes in nonhuman nature – to counter the narcissism of humans in charge of the world."

behind; the inability to grasp the sheer greatness of the mountain landscape, the time scale of its rising and creation, erosion and shifting, is set in relief to the Company as they witness the power around them. As the group travels up the mountain, Tolkien describes the environment's agential strength: "the lightning splinters on the peaks, and rocks shiver, and great crashes split the air and go rolling and tumbling into every cave and hollow; and the darkness is filled with overwhelming noise and sudden light" (*H* 53).

Bilbo has "never seen or imagined" what he is seeing (*H* 53). The Stone Giants "were hurling rocks at one another for a game, and catching them, and tossing them down into the darkness where they smashed among the trees far below or splintered into little bits with a bang" (*H* 53-54). Bilbo's inability to imagine such activity coupled with the company's inability to control their route across the mountain so that they must seek shelter in another unknowable aspect of the rock, a cave, suggests the ways that Tolkien rejects an easy relationality with the environment. The Stone Giants are blissfully unaware of the company as they play their "game." Despite its criticisms, this is a scene where Peter Jackson's first *Hobbit* film truly captures the spirit of the book. By punching up the action and splitting the group so that they are riding the Stone Giants as they play, Jackson is pointing out the excess of the Stone Giants (what are they? what are they doing? why are they doing it?) and the helplessness that the company feels against the mountain and these strange creatures. Neither book nor movie offer narrative framing here; the Company is simply caught up in the landscape. These various forms of rock prove themselves to be hyperobjects, objects that escape the human scale and proves our inability to master it.[7] The company is not going to master the Stone Giants – at best, they will be carried along; at the worst, the Giants may kill them.

The use of rock in this example reveals an uneasy relationality with geological scales that resist easy human-scale narrative framing. Gandalf's inability to impose a full narrative frame as they trek into the mountains, reveals how the Stone Giants escape anthropomorphic timescales. The company can neither control what happens on the mountain nor control the curious behavior of the Stone Giants. They are mere spectators to an unknowable and powerful force.

---

7 See Timothy Morton, *Hyperobjects: Philosophy and Ecology after the End of the World.*

Animal: Foxes, Beorn, and Shadowfax

Powerful forces are key, as well, in meditating on the animal in Tolkien's work. In order to frame this aspect of the discussion, I want to employ Morton's example of the dinosaur footprint:

> When one object has an effect on another, this must only be through some kind of aesthetic dimension. Thus when the dinosaur [...] steps into some mud, she leaves a footprint. She translates the mud into dinosaur-ese. She dinosauromorphizes it, just as I, a human, anthropomorphize it when I put my hand in it or speak about it. (Morton, *Realist Magic* 82)

Morton is highlighting here the perspectival change that I discussed at the beginning of this essay, a shift Morton calls "interobjectivity." The paleontologist working with the fossil "can influence the footprint, and the footprint can influence her, in this shared sensual space. It's as if this level of reality is a vast mesh of crisscrossing lines, marks, symbols, hieroglyphics, riddles, songs, poems and stories" (Morton, *Realist Magic* 82). This "mesh" is explored in various guises throughout Tolkien's texts, and like the mineral discussion above, the animal also reveals Tolkien's interest in object relations and the way they work in Middle-earth.

At the beginning of *The Fellowship of the Ring*, Tolkien writes a curious passage: "a fox passing through the wood on business of his own stopped several minutes and sniffed. 'Hobbits' he thought. 'Well, what next? I have heard of strange doings in this land, but I have seldom heard of a hobbit sleeping out of doors under a tree. Three of them! There's something mighty queer behind this.'" (*LotR* 71). This moment of perspective change is a rubric for thinking about the object's ability to hide itself. The narration gestures toward a fox-conciousness. As well, by suggesting the fox's curiosity and categorization of the "queerness" of the event, Tolkien suggests an ability of those we take for granted to frame themselves in surprising ways. The fox is thinking about the hobbits – they may not realize it, but the curiosity expressed by the fox gestures toward the aliveness of the objects around us. In his *The Animal That Therefore I Am* Jacques Derrida writes (3-4): "I often ask myself, just to see, who I am – and who I am (following) the moment when, caught naked, by the gaze of an animal, for example the eyes of a cat, I have trouble, yes, a bad time overcoming my embarrassment." Derrida alludes to how the human may not take account of being seen by the animal-other. Tolkien's passage reflects a similar relationship: the fox looks out from the page. Tolkien forces us to think about the fox thinking. This brief interlude of inhabiting the animal-body is indicative of Tolkien's efforts to dismiss pure anthropocentrism by shifting away from the traveling hobbits and measuring their "queerness" through the eyes of the animal-other. This passage relates the fox-ness that is alive in the world; both the sleeping hobbits and the readers have been judged: who are you to be going on this adventure? What kinds of beasts are you?

Beorn's role in *The Hobbit* is marked by its chapter heading: "Queer Lodgings." Here, too, we see Tolkien experimenting with an environmental ontology that considers the perspective of the non-human. Because of Beorn's were-bear status, he falls into an in-between category, one that may or may not be friendly and one that may or may not destroy the dwarves and Bilbo. As Derrida (4) meditates, the cat sees "without biting, although that threat remains on its lips or on the tip of the tongue." Beorn is a threat, a danger; one that defies categorization, and one that stares at us in his bear-ness. Beorn is a kind of becoming-animal, one that transcends the split between beast and human. From the perspective of Bilbo and the dwarves, everything about Beorn's life is "queer." Gandalf comments that Beorn's lineage is unknown; he may be from a long line of "great and ancient bears of the mountains" or "descended from the first men who lived before Smaug" (*H* 107). His very genetic material is an unknown, as if to categorize Beorn by his "nature" would make him more recognizable. Of course, it would not. Even genetic material is never fully actualized depending on its material entanglements.

Beorn's land is also marked as queer in that it is bear-ized. In other words, Bilbo finds himself in fields and a house that is designed partially from a bear's perspective. Beorn's land is bounded by his preferred crop: honey. "We are getting near," remarks Gandalf as bees become larger, "we are on the edge of his bee-pastures" (*H* 108). There is a sense of whimsy and fairy, to be sure, but the remarkable thing about this particular chapter is that, like the fox, Tolkien is experimenting with being inside the head of a non-human being. Not only are the pastures particularly bee-focused, but Gandalf also remarks that he has heard Beorn speak in "the tongue of bears" (*H* 107). There is a were-bear natureculture that Bilbo is unaware of; Tolkien presents us with another mode of being. Beorn's aesthetic concerns bend toward the enmeshment of beings. But, there are hidden, withdrawn aspects that surprise the Company. For example, although identifying bear-speech it is never revealed that anyone other than Gandalf understands it and Beorn himself does not speak it to the assembled Company. However, it is Gandalf's gift to learn to speak with Beorn, and it is the telling of the unique interrupting narrative, showing Gandalf's ability to think-through with the becoming-animal, that allows them to be welcomed by Beorn. Here Tolkien is addressing the problem of communicating with the non-human because of the very indeterminancy of outcome, response, and linguistics. One must listen, humble oneself before the mysterious agent, but also attempt to reach out. Although Bilbo admires Gandalf's plan, part of the thrill and joy of this interaction is that there is nothing to indicate that it might not backfire, and the path that the dialogue takes proves riveting.

Beorn's hybridity enmeshes him with his environment. We could call it a sustainable environment, since nothing is wasted and Beorn's bear-apiculture is a form of preservation. But, we can also see that Beorn takes into account his environment. As I will outline here, each aspect of his domestic life reveals an ecology that is enmeshed with the non-human with an emphasis on thriving. Beorn's bear-ethics are performed in the commitment that Beorn shows to various agents in his community. The bees grow bigger, for example, because Beorn has managed fields for them; he may harvest honey, but the actors are cared for (a sentiment we may well heed considering recent international honey-bee hive collapses). Beorn's community is also made up of the non-human; as Gandalf notes upon their arrival into Beorn's courtyard the horses go "to tell him of the arrival of strangers" (*H* 108). When it is time to serve his guests, Beorn speaks to the horses and dogs "in a queer language like animal noises turned into talk" (*H* 115). While Beorn may speak bear, he can also communicate with horses and dogs in a communal language that, again, escapes Bilbo and the other members of the Company. Even animal-behavior is given agential power, as it is remarked, "the dogs could stand on their hind-legs *when they wished*" (*H* 115; emphasis added). Beorn is also considerate of his animal-family as an enmeshed community: all the furniture is made very low so that they can use it (and serve food). Finally, as Gandalf remarks, the company must return the ponies that Beorn lent to them because "he loves his animals as his children"

(*H* 124). This queer family suggests the ways in which Beorn has taken account ethically, biologically and communally of animals and plants in order to live together harmoniously on the edge of the Wild.

As Sarah Ahmed points out in her *Queer Phenomenology* (157), "moments of disorientation are vital. They are bodily experiences that throw the world upside down, or throw the body from the ground." For Ahmed, a queer phenomenology places oneself in the position to see at new angles. I want to end my discussion of the animal with a gesture toward horses and thinking about a horse-phenomenology that "throws the body." Tolkien shows in his writings a great respect for horses. But their domesticity in our modern sense makes them subjected – in other words horses are there for our use without their response. Of course, this is a difficult thing to wrap our minds around if we think anthropocentrically. Tolkien renders horses as agents, especially in the case of Shadowfax. Immediately after the rise of the Ents, the reader rejoins Aragorn, Gimli, and Legolas in their hunt for Merry and Pippin. Aragorn infers that something strange is going on in the landscape because of the horses:

> 'I am thinking of the horses. You said last night, Gimli, that they were scared away. But, I did not think so. Did you hear them, Legolas? Did they sound to you like beasts in terror?' 'No,' said Legolas, 'I heard them clearly. But for the darkness and our own fear I should have guessed that they were beasts wild with some gladness. They spoke as horses will when they meet a friend that they have long missed.' (*LotR* 477)

In this instance, we have to admire the Elves; their need to understand has led to empathy – they learn tree-language, they learn horse-language. Legolas, and Aragorn we suspect, can identify gladness and joy in horse-language. But this mystery will be solved only later.

After Gandalf's new identity as Gandalf the White has been revealed, he sets out for Rohan with Aragorn, Gimli and Legolas. When seeing Shadowfax, Legolas is in disbelief, like Bilbo in the face of Stone Giants, because he has never seen a horse like this. Tolkien changes our perspective on horse-experience by characterizing the horse as being on equal terms with the other members of the Fellowship. Gandalf first introduces the horse; in Tolkien's flat ontology the horse is equal – there is no hierarchy: "that is Shadowfax. He is the chief of Mearas, lords of horses. […] Does he not shine like silver, and run as smoothly as a swift stream? *He has come for me*: the horse of the White Rider. *We* are going to battle *together*" (*LotR* 493; emphasis added). In this introductory speech, we see Gandalf creating a partnership with the animal; he is not the rider of the horse, but they are on equal terms. Gandalf is ethically committed to Shadowfax; he does not attempt to master him. Shadowfax has come for Gandalf and they are riding together.

Tolkien next describes Shadowfax greeting Gandalf: "as soon as Shadowfax saw Gandalf he checked his pace and whinnied loudly; then trotting gently forward he stooped his proud head and nuzzled his great nostrils against the old man's neck" (*LotR* 493). Tolkien draws attention to the horse's movements, horse-culture – the greeting, the gentle movement toward a friend, the nuzzle. Rather than shake hands or hug, a horse nuzzles the neck. When they do set off, Gandalf does not control the movements of Shadowfax. Instead, Shadowfax chooses the route they will take to get to Rohan: "after a little while he turned suddenly and choosing a place where the banks were lower, he waded the river, and then led them away due South into a flat land, treeless and wide" (*LotR* 493). This passage takes us into horse-consciousness, horse-ness. The mystery of the horse-discussion of the night before is solved, as well; as Legolas comments, "our horses met Shadowfax, their chieftain, and greeted him with joy" (*LotR* 493). Even Legolas cannot fully comprehend the complexity of this horse-language. His conjecture suggests this horse-culture mystery. The joy of the horse withdraws as it is enacted before them; they cannot know how horses experience joy with each other.

Shadowfax is interacting with the environment, turning the reader's perceptions of the trail to Rohan towards horse-thought. How would a horse choose the path through the landscape, how would it make a path, especially with a rider? Gandalf is not mastering the horse, and in fact Shadowfax has no saddle or bridle. What happens when we give ourselves over to the animal? What happens when we think with instead of against the animal? In terms of the fox, Beorn, and Shadowfax, our sense of landscape and natureculture is shifted. Our connection with the earth is revealed to be more enmeshed and mysterious, and we can no longer place ourselves as other than the animal or above the animal, but with.[8]

---

8 For a succinct history of the philosophic puzzle between animal and human see Gilbert Simondon's *Two Lessons on Animal and Man*.

Vegetable: The Ethics of Elves and the Problem with Trees

Perhaps the most poignant meditation on enmeshment in Tolkien's works concerns the relationship between Elves and forests. From the beginning, Tolkien highlights the Elves in his cosmography. They grow things, cultivate, teach. Their language is deeply embedded in the ecology of Middle-earth. As Dinah Hazel (83) comments, "almost every plant in *The Lord of the Rings* carries lore, symbolism, and cultural connotations that express belief in nature's power and wisdom. Plants have much to offer man, if he listens." As Ross Smith (8) points out, as well: "the relation between word, sound, and meaning was an essential element in Tolkien's approach to understanding language and his linguistic invention [...] in the context of his notions about linguistic aesthetics." The OOO-reading I have been outlining considers the aesthetics of language itself as having both power in the world and in the Otherworld. Tolkien comments on this point, as well: "*Faërie* cannot be caught in a net of words; for it is one of its qualities to be indescribable though not imperceptible" (OFS 114). Smith (74) points out later in his book that "language is in tune with the landscape." Hazel, Smith, and Tolkien are commenting on the power of language to make and reflect the world in Tolkien's Middle-earth that shows language's agency in terms of time, depth, withdrawal, and ecology. Their commentary underscores the deep ecological question of how to speak and listen to the world. Tolkien's understanding of language reflects a relationality that involves history, object, and response. For example, how one understands *athelas*, kingsfoil, or *asëa aranion* and its history, linguistic roots, and context indicates how one will use it, think about it, or even notice it in the forest.

The Elves' relation to the world is central in thinking through the ethical and ecological world Tolkien presents us with. In his letters, Tolkien critiques the Elves and their power: "they [...] became obsessed with 'fading,' the mode in which the changes of time (the law of the world under the sun) was perceived by them. They became sad, and their art (shall we say) antiquarian, and their efforts all really a kind of embalming" (*L* 151). Tolkien's reflection on the Elves' aesthetic and ecological concerns situates them within the bounds of what we could call an extreme preservation, an embalming, which, of course, is something done to the dead. One cannot embalm without killing what was once alive – in this way we can think of the Elves as already misperceiving the power of ecological change and their role in that change. The ecology of Middle-earth as a changing object has not escaped them, but in terms of our argument they are rather bent on counteracting this process. The Elves, then, present us with a problem when a static aesthetics meets an equally rigid ethics. The Elves are intimately tied to nature – their knowledge of the natural world is deep. However, they use their knowledge to freeze nature in time. As Dickerson and Evans also point out, the Elves' interest in ecology is "aesthetic"; the Elves' "main concern is for the beauty of Arda (the earth) and indeed of all Eä (creation)" (99). Although Evans and Dickerson frame their argument of ecology and Elves in terms of the Elves' interest in aesthetic beauty against that of the dark industrialization of Mordor or the utilitarianism of the Dwarves, an OOO-reading would see that the problem of the Elves is of reducing environments to their local manifestations only. Their aesthetics does not account for the ways objects may interact with other objects without the Elves' intervention. The Elves suffer from an excessive elf-*pomorphis*. Their need to master the ecology, although benevolent, proves also to be unsustainable; the world's change is ultimately forcing them to leave.

Sustainability, preservation, conservation. These are all important ecological buzzwords that contain nuances that ultimately prove unfruitful to finding a way through our ecological crisis, since these words are almost always used as a cover for human concern with utility and capitalist economic progress. For example, aesthetic concerns over wind farms sometimes trump larger concerns of the economic overuse of fossil fuels and its relation, in turn, to global climate change. The argument stalls at this impasse of aesthetics versus money. Despite its great benefits, wind farms are sometimes set up in ignorance of (or a lack of care for) migratory species, resulting in the death of birds. Wind turbines are a great source of alternative energy; they also cannot be reduced to mere local manifestations. Some key questions to ask of the Elves (and of ourselves): What kind of aesthetics is tenable in the face of ecological crisis? Can the wind farm be beautiful? What if we let Mirkwood experience the full ranges of seasons? The Elves are guilty of a kind of pastoral nostalgia (like those who may object to wind farms on the sole basis of aesthetic concerns) that arrests processes and asserts mastery as the premier aesthetic concern; the Elves raise the issue of where the ramifications of their kind of preservation practice take us. Are there different ways to listen and perceive?

The story of Beren and Lúthien echoes throughout Tolkien's mythology. From Aragorn's song in *The Fellowship of the Ring* to the names of Beren and Lúthien being inscribed on Tolkien and his wife's grave, the story held special import to its author. The song of Beren and Lúthien also encapsulates an important ecological commentary. The events of the "Lay of Leithian" occur during the First Age: Beren is human and Lúthien is an elf. She is one of the most beautiful Elves and, she is daughter of the elf Thingol. Lúthien has a sweet voice which transforms the natural world. One evening while Lúthien dances in the woods, and her friend Daeron plays his flute, she is discovered by Beren as he wanders the woods of her father's kingdom. He falls in love with her. Upon seeing Beren, Daeron warns Lúthien, and she hides. Later Beren catches her, and they grow to love one another.

When Lúthien takes Beren to meet her father, he is appalled that his royal daughter should wish to wed a mortal, and, as is recounted in the "Lay," in order to get rid of him, he sets Beren what he thinks is an unachievable quest, to recover a Silmaril from Morgoth's Iron Crown. While in pursuit of the Silmaril, Beren is captured by Sauron, and is held in the dungeons of Tol-in-Gaurhoth. Lúthien sets out to rescue Beren; through Lúthien's magic and Huan the Hound's strength they defeat Sauron and rescue Beren. All three then set out together to fulfill Beren's task.

Naturally, this summary of course does not relate the power of the tragedy, nor the power of the enmeshed world in the tale. For example, in the first encounter between Beren and Lúthien, Tolkien sets up a landscape in which Lúthien is about to be discovered:

> her arms like ivory were gleaming
> her long hair like a cloud was streaming
> her feet atwinkle wandered roaming
> in misty mazes in the gloaming
> and glowworms shimmered round her feet
> and moths in moving garland fleet
> above her head went wavering wan –
> and this the moon now looked upon
> uprisen, slow and round and white
> above the branches of the night.
> Then clearly thrilled her voice and rang;
> with sudden ecstasy she sang
> a song of nightingales she learned
> and with her elvish magic
> turned to such bewildering delight
> the moon hung moveless in the night
> (*LB* 526-542).

First, note the ways in which Lúthien is enmeshed, literally, in her natural environment. The glowworms dance around her feet, the moths form a garland around her. Even her feet are "atwinkle" – this metaphor has much more to do with stars, the landscape, than toes. This connection roots her to landscapes. But note also the moon. Here the moon is anthropomorphized in terms of "looking" but Tolkien also thinks moon-ese. The moon is uprisen, slow, round, and white – a blazon for the lunar. Lúthien's dancing matches the moon's observation; both are connected. He is a witness to her singing, but her magical power stills the moon. Tolkien writes "moveless." We can imagine the moon rapt – her singing is just that enchanting. Note, as well, that Lúthien learns a nightingale's song that speaks to the ways that Elves learn the world's speech (and teach speech to the world) around them. My reading of the "Lay of Leithian" indicates the ways in which the Elves can cause a sense of stasis, for example, here Lúthien suspends nature. It is a moment of aesthetic beauty, but speaks to the greater problem of the Elves' interest in preservation. However, the moon's stillness also addresses a certain ambivalence of nature – the moon does not warn her of Beren's presence and this encounter is the beginning of a long tragedy (both Beren and Lúthien will die – she gives up her immortality in order to be with Beren).

Another passage later in the poem also relates this enmeshed voice. When Beren and Lúthien are separated after Beren first sets off for the Silmaril, Tolkien describes the river of Esgalduin while Lúthien mourns:

> so days drew on from the mournful day;
> the curse of silence no more lay
> on Doriath, though Dairon's flute
> and Lúthien's singing both were mute.
> The murmurs soft awake once more
> about the words, the waters roar
> past the great gates of Thingol's halls;
> [...]
> she sat and mourned in a low song:
> "Endless roll the waters past!
> To this my love hath come at last,
> enchanted waters pitiless
> a heartache and a loneliness."
> (*LB* 1206-1212; 1219-1223)

Lúthien's previous song has been supplanted by the water's voice, a roar. This is a reverse of the first meeting where nature was stilled by her voice; she is stilled by the voice of the river. How do we read the river's voice? Lúthien hears pitilessness, it roars on. But here is a moment in which Tolkien is invoking the power of the river-voice. It is pitiless for her mourning, but it is also "shrouded" and "dark and strong" (*LB* 1217; 1218). These elements reveal the unknowability of the natural world, especially when it is not being arrested by the Elves' work. She laments its "endlessness" but its endlessness is its very power. Despite the tragedy that will ensue, Esgalduin will continue to roar – or, as it meets the sea, become something even greater. While the emphasis is on the intimacy of the Elves with nature, Tolkien is commenting here on the scale of nature; the roar of the water speaks to its timescale above and beyond even that of the Elves. In fact with the Great Flood that comes at the end of the Second Age, Esgalduin will be swallowed by greater waters. The point here is to see not an easy relationship between the Elves and Nature, but one in which, while they are aware of its power, and are enmeshed in the world, the Elves can still be corrupting in their actions because of their emphasis on preservation. As Tim Ingold (12) comments, "to be sentient [...] is to open up to the world, to yield to its embrace, and to resonate in one's inner being to its illuminations and reverberations." The Elves with all of their ecological efforts spent on "embalming" are not as willing to "yield" to the embrace of the world.[9]

How to listen to the trees, then? To return to the work of Eduardo Kohn in his *How Forests Think*, Kohn outlines the concept of selves that he works with in his study of the ecology of the people, plants, and animals in the Amazon of upper Ecuador (92): "selves are the product of a specific relational dynamic that involves absence, future, and growth as well as the ability for confusion, and this emerges with and is unique to living thoughts." Kohn's rubric opens up the relational-being that describes Ent-being in terms of timescales, language, and causality. The Ents are an example of being within, united with the landscape; allowing oneself over to the object without fully mastering the object's whole being.[10]

For a visualization of this enmeshment that is different compared to that of Tolkien's written text, one can again think about the Peter Jackson films: Merry and Pippin climb a tree in Fangorn Forest to escape an orc, only to suddenly see the tree's eyes open. They are enmeshed in the landscape as it reveals itself, already watching. Tolkien himself comments on the power of the natural in the word "supernatural" that reflects an understanding of the Ents, as well:

> *Supernatural* is a dangerous and difficult word in any of its senses, looser or stricter. But to fairies it can hardly be applied, unless *super* is taken merely as a superlative prefix. For it is man who is, in contrast to fairies, supernatural (and often of diminutive stature); whereas they are natural, far more natural than he. (OFS 110)

This excess bound up with the prefix super- is observed early on in terms of the power of trees in *The Fellowship of the Ring* when the four hobbits enter into the Old Forest. Merry says, "but the forest *is* queer. Everything in it is very

---

9 As well, the Elves have lost hope. As Guglielmo Spirito comments, "we need to consider hope (theological hope), or surrender […]: we are saying, with Tolkien, that tales of communion with animals are not lies" (30).
10 For a psychoanalytical reading of the trees in Tolkien see Elizabeth Harrod's "Trees in Tolkien and What Happened Under Them." For a discussion of the "environmental politic of power" (113) that the Ents enact see Ike Reeder, "The Silence of Trees: Environmental Agency and the Politics of Powers in J.R.R. Tolkien's *The Lord of the Rings*." For a categorization of the representation of trees in Tolkien's Middle-earth see Cynthia M. Cohen, "The Unique Representation of Trees in *The Lord of the Rings*."

much more alive, more aware of what is going on, so to speak" (*LotR* 108). We can draw out of this commentary the idea of the "very much more alive"; the power of the trees is super-life; beyond life. This may have something to do with its queerness; its "positive" excess. Merry further recounts a time when he was in the forest in the dark and thought the trees were "whispering to each other, passing news and plots along in an unintelligible language; and the branches swayed and groped without any wind" (*LotR* 108). This reminds me, again, of Derrida and his cat. Derrida (8) muses:

> I am not about to conclude hurriedly, upon wakening, as Alice [in Wonderland] did, that one cannot speak with a cat on the pretext that it doesn't reply or that it always replies the same thing. Everything I am about to entrust to you no doubt comes back to asking you to respond to me, you to me, reply to me concerning what it is to respond. If you can. The said question of the said animal in its entirety comes down to knowing not whether the animal speaks but whether one can know what responds means.

Derrida highlights here the narrow definition we hold when we say something responds – response in an anthropocentric register is verbal, maybe gestural, immediate. But, isn't this too narrow and indicative of our human-centric demands? How does a tree respond? As with the example of Shadowfax, how does a tree greet you? Studies have shown how trees respond to environmental pressures – they may grow deeper roots or more shallow roots in a longer radius.[11] Or, they tap into human-made water sources; they seek out nutrient-rich waste water. Think about trees that seem to be climbing over rocks or have split themselves in the trunk to grow around something. This is tree-response. For Tolkien, a conversation with a tree, though lengthy, is possible. Again, the assumption that an object will respond as we want it to is subverted in Tolkien's work.

Of course, the Ents are not trees, they are tree herders, tree-like. But they are also perfect examples of the enmeshment of being and landscape. Merry and Pippin's first meeting with Treebeard is one of surprise. Tolkien's description of the Ent creates a picture of integration:

> they were looking at a most extraordinary face. It belonged to a large Man-like, almost Troll-like, figure, at least fourteen-foot high, very sturdy, with a

---

11 For a fascinating video presentation on plants and pain, see the Smithsonian's "Do Plants Respond to Pain?" http://www.smithsonianchannel.com/sc/web/video/titles/12151/do-plants-respond-to-pain.

tall head, and hardly any neck. Whether it was clad in stuff like green and grey bark, or whether that was its hide, was difficult to say. At any rate, the arms, at a short distance from the trunk, were not wrinkled, but covered with a brown, smooth skin. The large feet had seven toes each. The lower part of the long face was covered with a sweeping grey beard, bushy, almost twiggy at the roots, thin and mossy at the ends. (*LotR* 452)

This description reflects the nature of the Ent, not quite tree, not quite humanoid. He is a non-human vegetable. There is skin, but it is like bark; our words for the human body, trunk, arms are the same as the ones we use to describe a tree. Tolkien presses that doubleness. The beard is like a giant upside-down bush: twiggy, mossy. And then the feet have seven toes each: very much more toes, super-toes. Later, Treebeard explains the enmeshed growing-with of Ents and Trees:

We are tree-herds, we old Ents. Few enough of us are left now. Sheep get like shepherds and shepherds like sheep, it is said, but slowly, and neither have long in the world. It is quicker and closer with Trees and Ents, and they walk down the ages together. For Ents are more like Elves: less interested in themselves than Men are, and better at getting inside other things. And yet again, Ents are more like Men, more changeable than Elves are, and quicker at taking the colour of the outside, you might say. Or better than both: for they are steadier and keep their minds on things longer. (*LotR* 457)

Treebeard is underscoring that rather than resist the trees and maintain category differences the trees and Ents have grown like each other. Their natureculture has slowy erased boundaries between their beings, so that, in some cases, some Ents have rooted themselves and become trees. Even in language, Ents have learned to reflect timescales through language which causes an impatience in Merry and Pippin.

Treebeard also indicates that the Elves started it all: "waking trees up and teaching them to speak and learning their tree-talk. They always wished to talk to everything, the old Elves did. But then the Great Darkness came, and they passed away over the sea, or fled into far valleys, and hid themselves, and made songs about days that would never come again" (*LotR*, 457). The Elves turn away, lament the passing, and become too involved in regaining the past. Tolkien's commentary on the Elves' embalming is evident in the appraisal of the Ents, as well. As with the example of Lúthien, the Elves are too preoccupied with stasis. Ents, however, move with their environment, become something more in it.

Conclusion: Parables

In *The Lord of the Rings*, it is the rousing of the Ents that leads to a shift in fortunes for the Fellowship. Their rousing coincides with the victory at Helm's Deep, so that when Gandalf and Théoden arrive at Isengard, Saruman has already been defeated. The Ents' participation in the world, like Beorn's presence in the Battle of the Five Armies, proves to be integral to Tolkien's comment on the need for communities to come together and reflect enmeshment, and, perhaps, avoid ecological catastrophe.

In his "Beowulf: The Monsters and the Critics," Tolkien discusses the significance of the presentation of mythology, and his comments can be applied to his own work as well: "the significance of a myth is not easily to be pinned on paper by analytical reasoning. [...] Its defender is thus at a disadvantage: unless he is careful, and speaks in parables, he will kill what he is studying by vivisection, and he will be left with a formal or mechanical allegory, and, what is more, probably with one that will not work" (BMC 15). Tolkien's world presents us with an ecological problem that resists this kind of "vivisection," for to see objects at work in Middle-earth is to see the way they defy traditional categories of reason and work against a community building that is purely anthropocentric in its concerns. Objects, then, work like parables; and, like parables, there are hidden meanings, meanings that withdraw, meanings that only work if interacting with a certain surface, context, or listener. There are meanings that never appear, as well. The object's parables may only work if we think like an object would think. Even this may not be enough. To set the parable loose in the world often has unintended consequences, even to itself.

About the Author

Dr. Christopher Roman is Associate Professor of English at Kent State University Tuscarawas. He teaches medieval literature, the works of J.R.R. Tolkien, literary theory, creative writing, and composition. His research work is focused on the intersection of theology and ecology and he is currently working on a book-length study of the hermit Richard Rolle's metaphysics. His book *Domestic Mysticism* (2005) examined the works of Margery Kempe and Julian of Norwich for the spiritual families they built through language and his work has appeared in *Mystics Quarterly*, *Speculum*, *Glossator*, and *Florilegium*, as well as various essay-collections.

Bibliography

AHMED, Sarah. *Queer Phenomenology: Orientations, Objects, Others*. Durham NC: Duke University Press, 2007.

BENNETT, Jane. *Vibrant Matter: A Political Ecology of Things*. Durham NC: Duke University Press, 2010.

BOGOST, Ian. *Alien Phenomenology*. Minneapolis MI: University of Minnesota Press, 2012.

BRYANT, Levi R. *The Democracy of Objects*. Ann Harbor: Open Humanities Press, 2011.

"The Ontic Principle: Outline of an Object-Orientated Otology." *The Speculative Turn: Continental Materialism and Realism*. Eds. Levi Bryant, Nick Srnieck, and Graham Harmon. Melbourne: re:press: 2011. 261-278.

CALARCO, Matthew. *Zoographies*. New York: Columbia University Press, 2008.

CAMPBELL, Liam. *The Ecological Augury in the Works of JRR Tolkien*. Zurich and Jena: Walking Tree Publishers, 2011.

COHEN, Cynthia M. "The Unique Representation of Trees in *The Lord of the Rings*." *Tolkien Studies* 6 (2009): 91-125.

COHEN, Jeffrey Jerome. "Elemental Relations." *O-zone: A Journal of Object-Oriented Studies* 1 (2014): 53-61.

CURRY, Patrick. *Defending Middle-earth. Tolkien: Myth and Modernity*. First published 1997. New York: Houghton Mifflin, 2004.

Deep Roots in Times of Frost: Essays on Tolkien. Zurich and Jena: Walking Tree Publishers, 2014.

DERRIDA, Jacques. *The Animal That Therefore I Am*. Ed. Marie-Louise Mallet. Trans. David Wills. New York: Fordham, 2008.

DICKERSON, Matthew. "Water, Ecology, and Spirituality in Tolkien's Middle-earth." *Light Beyond All Shadow: Religious Experience in Tolkien's Work*. Eds. Paul E. Kerry and Sandra Miesel. Madison NJ: Farleigh Dickerson University Press, 2011. 15-32.

and Jonathan Evans. *Ents, Elves, and Eriador: The Environmental Vision of J.R.R. Tolkien*. Lexington KY: University Press of Kentucky, 2006.

HABERMANN, Ina and Nikolaus Kuhn. "Sustainable Fictions: Geographical, Literary and Cultural Intersections in J.R.R. Tolkien's *The Lord of the Rings*." *The Cartographic Journal* 48.4 (2011): 263-273.

HARROD, Elizabeth. "Trees in Tolkien and What Happened Under Them." *Mythlore* 11.1 (1984): 47-52.

HARAWAY, Donna. *The Companion Species Manifesto: Dogs, People, and Significant Otherness*. Chicago IL: Prickly Paradigm Press, 2003.

HAZELL, Dinah. *The Plants of Middle-Earth: Botany and Subcreation*. Kent OH: Kent State University Press, 2006.

INGOLD, Tim. *Being Alive: Essays on Movement, Knowledge, and Description*. London: Routledge, 2011.

KOHN, Eduardo. *How Forests Think: Toward an Anthropology Beyond the Human*. Berkeley: University of California Press, 2013.

MORGAN, Alun. "*The Lord of the Rings* – a Mythos in Unsustainable Times." *Environmental Education Research* 16.3-4 (2010): 383-399.

MORTON, Timothy. *The Ecological Thought*. Cambridge MA: Harvard University Press, 2010.

Hyperobjects: Philosophy and Ecology after the End of the World. Minneapolis MI: University of Minnesota Press, 2013.

Realist Magic: Objects, Ontology, Causality. Ann Arbor MI: Open Humanities Press, 2013.

REEDER, Ike. "The Silence of Trees: Environmental Agency and the Politics of Powers in J.R.R. Tolkien's *The Lord of the Rings*." *A Wilderness of Signs: Ethics, Beauty, and Environment after Postmodernism*. Ed. Joe Jordan. Newcastle: Cambridge Scholars, 2006. 107-115.

SIEWERS, Alfred K. "Tolkien's Cosmic Christian Ecology: The Medieval Underpinnings." *Tolkien's Modern Middle Ages*. Eds. Jane Chance and Alfred K. Siewers. New York: Palgrave MacMillan, 2005. 139-153.

SIMONDON, Gilbert. *Two Lessons on Animal and Man*. Trans. Drew S. Burk. Minneapolis MI: Univocal, 2011.

SMITHSONIAN. "Do Plants Respond to Pain?" http://www.smithsonianchannel.com/sc/web/video/titles/12151/do-plants-respond-to-pain.

SPIRITO, Guglielmo. "Speaking with Animals: A Desire that Lies Near the Heart of Faërie." *Tolkien's Shorter Works*. Eds. Margaret Hiley and Frank Weinreich. Zurich and Jena: Walking Tree Publishers, 2008. 17-35.

SMITH, Ross. *Inside Language. Linguistic and Aesthetic Theory in Tolkien*. Zurich and Berne: Walking Tree Publishers, 2007.

Tolkien, J.R.R. *The Hobbit: or There and Back Again*. Boston: Houghton Mifflin, 1996.

"The Lay of Leithian." *The Lays of Beleriand*. (*The History of Middle-earth* vol. 3.) Ed. Christopher Tolkien. New York: Ballantine, 1985. 183-393.

The Lord of the Rings: One-Volume Edition. Boston: Houghton Mifflin, 1994.

"Beowulf: the Monsters and the Critics." *The Monsters and the Critics and Other Essays*. Ed. Christopher Tolkien. New York: HarperCollins, 1983. 5-48.

"On Fairy-Stories." *The Monsters and the Critics and Other Essays*. Ed. Christopher Tolkien. New York: HarperCollins, 1983. 109-161.

"To Milton Waldman." *The Letters of J.R.R. Tolkien*. Ed. Humphrey Carpenter with the assistance of Christopher Tolkien. Boston: Houghton Mifflin, 2000. 143-161.

VELDMAN, Meredith. *Fantasy, the Bomb, and the Greening of Britain: Romantic Protest, 1945-1980*. Cambridge: Cambridge University Press, 1994.

Magdalena Maczynska

On Trees of Middle-earth – J.R.R. Tolkien's Mythical Creations

Abstract

Trees are the central motif of numerous mythologies; they symbolize the whole universe, indicate the axis mundi, or grant life and wisdom. Therefore, one is not surprised that J.R.R. Tolkien reflected his literary inspirations and deep respect for trees in his own mythopoeia. The cosmological myth included in Quenta Silmarillion indicates the important role played by the sacred trees of Valinor. Being the primeval source of light and heavenly bodies, the trees symbolically link all tales in the legendarium. Trees in Middle-earth are equally wondrous for they are alive, literally. They have their own distinct characters and are able to actively influence their surroundings – they may become a threat or provide help; consequently, the forests of Middle-earth are autonomous and unique. In equal measure being entangled in the conflict between light and darkness, the woods are as varied as the protagonists themselves. In order to highlight the majesty of trees Tolkien created beings that do not have their direct counterpart in European mythologies. The Ents are the embodiment of forces lying dormant in woods; they are the eldest beings inhabiting Middle-earth, nevertheless, their vitality is connected with the existence of the primordial forests whose destruction indicates the Ents' extinction. Tolkien voiced his anxiety connected with the mechanization of the contemporary world, as he saw the threat of dehumanization in the devastation of forests caused by the rampant technological development. The article describes the symbolical meaning, significance and role of trees and forests in Tolkien's mythology. It focuses on various connotations of sacred trees either as the guardians of peace and happiness, the symbols of authority, or the indicators of development of a given community. Additionally, the article traces the protagonists' attitude towards trees that indicates their character and moral bearing.

Mythologies around the world indicate trees as the sources of life and knowledge. They may represent the whole universe with their roots reaching the underworld and their boughs ascending to the domain of gods. Trees indicate the *axis mundi* or provide enlightenment, since their magical properties are widely acknowledged. One ought to point out that the symbolical meaning of trees differs among various peoples, the image of the tree being regarded as the token of life, youth, immortality, or wisdom (Eliade, *Sacrum* 151). The variety of tropes pertaining to trees is elaborated on by J. R. R. Tolkien whose love and reverence for trees is reflected in his writings, as he admitted in one of his letters: "I am (obviously) much in love with plants and above all trees, and always have been; and I find human maltreatment of them as hard to bear as some find ill-treatment of animals" (*L* 220).

The importance of trees in the mythopoeia is established by the *Quenta Silmarillion* which introduces the motif of the sacred trees; in point of fact, the "account of the Two Trees and their place at the heart of events both in the Undying Lands and Middle-earth reveals the iconic status of trees in both his [Tolkien's] work and his life" (Curry 682). Yavanna sings the two wonderful Trees into life, which may be seen as the symbolical beginning of the First Age of the world. The Two Trees of Valinor, the most beautiful and perfect plants in Eä, are inextricably bound with the lot of Aman and Middle-earth, since "about their fate all the tales of the Elder days are woven" (*S* 31). Telperion, the elder, had leaves as if lined with silver that spread around the silver shimmer filling the whole island, whereas Laurelin was golden, with pale green leaves and gold flowers that glowed with a strong yet warm light. The colours are themselves significant because they allude to the Trees' hallowed provenance. Moreover, their exceptional character is marked by the bright light issuing forth from the plants, which, in turn, may be regarded as a symbol of the sacred and the closeness of the divine (Eliade, *Kowale* 168). Trees are crucial to the tales, yet their significance varies as Tolkien introduced themes and symbols related to them on different levels of the legendarium. It is these various aspects of trees as Tolkien's mythical creations that this paper is going to explore.

Trees and the Ordering of the World

Tolkien's cosmogonic myth establishes the Trees' significance in the very process of shaping the structure of the universe. They function as guardians of the imperturbable bliss of Valinor (that lasts as long as the Trees flourish), and yet they indirectly become the reason for the rebellion of the Elves and the downfall of the house of Fëanor. Telperion and Laurelin resemble, therefore, the trees in the garden of Eden, as with them is connected the story of a major betrayal and the abandonment of paradise. However, one must also pay attention to the fact that there is no special law concerning the Sacred Trees of Valinor; granting neither eternal life nor knowledge (as these are already given to the Eldar), they are revered for their own sake. The destruction of the Trees marks the beginning of a new era, the age of battle with darkness that is fought entirely in Middle-earth. The annihilation of the Trees does not change the situation of the Eldar, yet it triggers Fëanor's rebellion. Fëanor himself is so much under the spell of the marvellous light that he devises three gems, the Silmarils in which he manages to preserve the silver and golden glow. After the destruction of the Trees by Ungoliant, Yavanna could end the sudden darkness that pervades Aman only with the help of the jewels. Yet Fëanor is unwilling to hand over the precious jewels because his heart "was fast bound to these things that he himself had made" (*S* 69). Coveting the light, he, nonetheless, plunges into darkness, as he becomes the initiator of the revolt of the Noldor and the leader of their exodus to Middle-earth. The Elves are not driven forth from Valinor, but those who leave these shores are banned from returning. Their fate, like that of the first men, is bound to be formed in exile within the substitute for the former splendour of the sacred Trees.

Yavanna's creations are the sole source of life-giving light in Eä that had existed even before the firmament was adorned with the Sun and the Moon. When one of the Trees was waxing, the other was waning, though twice a day their gleam mingled and the soft glow of gold and silver spread all around. The light is restricted to the vicinity of the Western Islands. Middle-earth being removed from the direct sight of the shores of Valinor was initially plunged in darkness, yet Elbereth "took silver dews from the vats of Telperion, and therewith she made new stars and brighter among the coming of the Firstborn" (*S* 44). Consequently, the land was granted the refracted light of the Trees. The sacred Trees of Valinor are, therefore, the source of light that endures throughout all ages of Arda. It ought to be emphasised that the Trees introduce the count of time (measured by means of the changing lustre) into an everlasting land, which, however, is not subject to decay and fading. This brings to mind the Celtic *Tír na nÓg* where time is also suspended, since the Blessed Isles (a notable name, used also by Tolkien in reference to Valinor) are the only place where the apple trees are in bloom and bear magical fruit at the same time.

The Sun and the Moon shining over Eä originate from the Two Trees of Valinor, since darkness, the aftermath of Melkor's attack, is finally broken owing to the silver flower of Laurelin and the last golden fruit of Telperion, both containing the radiance of the Trees. Elbereth with the help of the Valar sets them in vessels so that "they might become lamps of heaven, outshining the ancient stars, being nearer to Arda; and she gave them power to traverse the lower regions of Ilmen, and set them to voyage upon appointed courses above the girdle of the Earth from the West unto the East and to return" (*S* 109). Having replaced the mighty primeval light that had once filled the world, the Sun and the Moon are the reminder that the Valar constantly watch over Middle-earth. Their light is a token of hope as well as a link between the legends of the First Age and the story of Frodo and the War of the Ring. The annihilation of the Trees of Valinor is a culminating point in the legends of the very beginning of the world. The focus of the legendarium shifts to Middle-earth, thus leaving the Blessed Realm on the margin of the narrative. Middle-earth's history really starts with the light of the new heavenly bodies, the progenies of the Trees.

The sacred Trees do not perish altogether, since Yavanna makes for the Elves of Eldamar "a tree like to a lesser image of Telperion, save that it did not give light of its own being" (*S* 59), the seedling of which was given to the Númenóreans by the Eldar from Tol Eressëa in token of friendship. It is cherished and cared for by the descendants of the Kings of Númenor and only when they eventually forsake the old ways, does it begin to wither. A fruit of the tree is preserved and thus a sapling "of the line of Nimloth the fair; and that was a seedling of Galathilion, and that a fruit of Telperion of many names, Eldest of Trees" (*RK* 301) is carried to Middle-earth with Elendil and those few still faithful to Ilúvatar who manage to survive the annihilation of Númenor. As a result, the White Tree of Minas Tirith, the symbol of the Kings of the house of Elendil, may be seen as a reminder of the bliss that is irrevocably lost due to human haughtiness and presumptuousness. Adorning the banners of Elendil's heirs and the surcoats of the Guards of the Citadel, it signifies the King's power and the continuity of his line. The fate of the Kings of Gondor and the White Tree seem not only to be intertwined but also to correspond to one another. For this very reason, when the line of the

Kings in the South fails, the Tree dies as well. The return of the King is deemed impossible, the more so that according to Tal-Palantir's prophecy the perishing of the Tree would signify the end of the line of Elros. Yet during the long rule of the Stewards of Gondor, the Withered Tree, a sad remnant of the glory of old, is left to stand in the Court of the Fountain. Aragorn's succession to the throne is marked by the restoration of the Tree, for a sapling is found – "it has lain hidden on the mountain, even as the race of Elendil lay hidden in the wastes of the North" (*RK* 301). Such a close connection between tree and king is understandable, for a tree is a symbol of monarchy in many mythologies worldwide. A tree grows tall and mighty, is crowned with leaves, it seemingly dies in autumn and comes back to life again in spring, the same yet somewhat changed. In like manner one may look at a king – he rules his subjects and when his time comes, he has to pass but is, in a way, reborn in his successor (Roux 43).

It is worth mentioning that in Tolkien's legendarium there is one more symbol of the re-established line of Kings, that is to say a green jewel from which Aragorn takes his new Elven name – Elessar. *The Lord of the Rings* does not provide sufficient answers concerning the maker and the history of the gem, though two separate stories on the subject may be found in *The Unfinished Tales*. The comparison of the two texts shows us considerable inconsistencies. One tale maintains that the jewel was made by Enerdhil of Gondolin and then passed West with Eärendil only to be once more sent back to Middle-earth by the grace of the Valar. The other version, though, asserts that there have been two different Elf-stones, one that remained beyond the Circles of the World and another that was wrought specially for Galadriel, which she finally gave to Aragorn to be the heirloom of his house. What is, however, important is the fact that the gem itself is wonderful because its maker has managed to imprison in it "the sunlight [shining] through the leaves of the trees" (*UT* 322). Therefore, its green light makes one think of woods in spring and, furthermore, it possesses the ability to heal the wounds caused by the Dark Power. Thus the fascination exerted by trees is creatively depicted by artists and craftsmen.

The Cultural Significance of Trees in Middle-earth

Trees in Middle-earth are fundamental to various peoples, for they serve as powerful symbols – defining cultures or heritage that (especially with reference to the Elves and the descendants of the Númenórians) have roots in the far West. The Elves, especially the Sindari and those who joined them, have established a close bond with the trees; as a result, trees have become an integral part of their identity. The most renowned sylvan realm is Lothlórien, whose physical appearance reflects the fundamental role the trees play in the Galadhrim culture. The construction of *telain* or *flets* – wooden platforms situated high in the trees – is undoubtedly dictated by the shaping of the land of Lórien, though such closeness with *mallorns* seems to strengthen the bond between the Elves and the trees. The name of the Golden Wood, Laurelindórenan, brings to mind the sacred Tree of Valinor "for which, as is plain, Galadriel's longing increased year by year to, at last, an overwhelming regret" (*UT* 327). The name itself was shortened to Lothlórien and subsequently to Lórien, though the change (being an apt indication of the nearing end of the old ways of the world) is adequate, as the wood no longer flourishes. The subsequent change of names of Galadriel's realm also indicates its gradual decline and eventual abandonment. With the Galadhrim gone, the Golden Wood is to lose its distinction and protection – it will become susceptible to all the physical laws that act upon the whole of Middle-earth. Caras Galadhon (chief dwelling of the Elves of Lothlórien) is built high in the crowns of the tallest and most majestic trees that the hobbits have ever seen – *mallorns* are a living reminder of the Blessed Realm that the rebellious Elves managed to preserve in their abodes; they reflect the longing of the Galadhrim who have tried to recreate their homeland in Middle-earth. *Mallorns* were of exceptional beauty, their leaves "were pale green above and beneath were silver, glistening in the sun; in the autumn they did not fall, but turned to pale gold"; golden blossom adorned the trees in the summer and "as soon as the flowers opened the leaves fell, so that through spring and summer a grove of *malinorni* was carpeted and roofed with gold, but its pillars were of grey silver" (*UT* 216). Their colours correspond to those of the Two Trees of Valinor and allude to their place of origin.

Mircea Eliade (*Patterns* 300) observes that "the tree expresses absolute reality in its aspect of norm, of a fixed point, supporting the cosmos. It is the supreme prop of all things. And, consequently, communication with heaven can only be effected near it, or by means of it." The sacred or special areas described in the legendarium are marked by trees which indicate the centre of a given community – the exceptional trees have been carried to the shores of Middle-earth by those who chose exile or were forced to leave the Blessed Realm. *Mallorns* form the heart of Caras Galadhon, while the White Tree adorns the Citadel in Minas Tirith. Nonetheless, even the Hobbits who have not heard about the Sacred Trees of Valinor have their own Party Tree. Growing in a place of meetings and feasting, the tree may be seen as the symbol of the well-being of the Halflings. Saruman's destruction of it is directed not at the tree itself, but at the Hobbits whose spirit the wizard has tried to break. Therefore, the sign of the revival of the Shire-folk is the restoration of the Party Tree that gains even more significance due to its provenance. Samwise Gamgee plants a *mallorn*, the only one to grow in a corner of Middle-earth whose inhabitants (in general) have not heard of the far West and the Valar. The tree, thus, hallows the Shire by creating a link with Valinor. Seen in this light Galadriel's gift to Samwise is all the more valuable.

Trees in Middle-earth are exceptional not only because they are powerful symbols, but above all because they are alive, literally alive. In Tolkien's legendarium they form another order of creatures. As creations of Yavanna, trees have been granted free will, so they can make their own judgements and choices, and in this respect they are autonomous; while the degree of their independence varies, they resemble animals more than plants. It needs to be emphasised that trees have feelings just like any other sentient beings, though they needed to be taught how to express them. The Elves possess a special kind of sensitivity denied to other creatures, which explains the fact that they are attuned to the emotions of the trees. Having perceived the dormant awareness of woods, the Elves have provided the trees with a means of communication – they have taught them to speak. In a way the Firstborn have woken up the trees and given them their own unique voice. Once roused, the trees do not return to their primeval state, even though the creatures who are able to understand them are diminishing. At the end of the Third Age, Legolas is still able to hear the murmuring trees and understand their emotions and moods. Hence he may ascertain after entering Fangorn Forest that "it is not evil, or what evil is in it is far away. I catch only the faintest echoes of dark places where the hearts of the trees are black. There is no malice near us; but there is watchfulness, and anger" (*TT* 107). Nonetheless, with the passing of the Elves the woods will remain inscrutable, for no other peoples can comprehend the secretive nature of trees. Although the destruction of their physical aspect does not involve the annihilation of their awareness, yet the possibility to interact with trees lessens with time and prevents any communication.

Trees as Sentient Beings

Trees possess knowledge of current events, which they pass to one another whispering after dark as in the Old Forest. The Old Forest is so terrifying to the Hobbits because numerous strange tales concerning the trees are passed around. It is said that they can move their boughs even when there is no wind; they are constantly vigilant, watching those who enter their domain. It needs to be emphasised that the trees can actually move, though they do it time and again – "[o]ccasionally the most unfriendly ones may drop a branch, or stick a root out, or grasp at you with a long trailer" (*FR* 108). The trees do not appear to be defenceless victims, they are said to hem in strangers or even go as far as to attack the hedge that separates the wood from Buckland. Since the Old Forest is the remnant of the primeval woods that – once vast and continuous – occupied large areas of Middle-earth, the trees there still possess the powers that have already dwindled in other woodlands. And yet the hearts of the trees have darkened and are filled with anger due to the years of mistreatment and felling – "there lived yet, ageing no quicker than the hills, fathers of the fathers of trees, remembering times when they were lords. The countless years had filled them with pride and rooted wisdom, and with malice" (*FR* 128). As a matter of fact, many trees pose a direct threat to creatures venturing into their realm. Hostility presides under the eaves of the forest, which is felt by the hobbits the more strongly as they progress deep into the backwoods.

The illustration of the malevolence of the trees that readily comes to mind is Old Man Willow's attack. Old Man Willow is not menaced by the hobbits;

nevertheless, he uses his abilities to put them to sleep and then to crush Merry and Pippin inside his trunk. His enchantment must be immensely powerful, since the hobbits fall asleep immediately at the foot of the willow. Their slumber is deathlike and overwhelming, indicating the extraordinary power of the Willowman. Jane Chance sees in this very tree and its malice the embodiment of the Tree of Death (106).[1] The tree is aware of its advantage in this situation, as Frodo's kick results only in "[a] hardly perceptible shiver [that] ran through the stem and branches; the leaves rustled and whispered, but with a sound now of faint and far-off laughter" (*FR* 115). The hobbits would have never freed themselves from Old Man Willow's mighty spell but for the help of Tom Bombadil, to whom the charms of the tree are merely a trifle. It should be mentioned that Old Man Willow is not in league with Sauron, even though the tree's evil and groundless attack may hint at this. Trees are their own masters, having their own agenda and forming their own alliances. Old Man Willow's malevolence highlights the fact that even "trees may 'go bad'" (*L* 287), like other creatures they are not "unambiguously good. Like sentient beings, they are susceptible to some form of corruption and the Fall" (Dickerson 471).

However, not all enchantments spread by trees are harmful; the willows in Nan-tathren possess such power as to subdue even the longing for the sea. Their leaves blowing in the wind cast a spell of oblivion, which is "a spell of music: day and night would flicker by uncounted" while those captured by the enchantment stood "knee-deep in grass and listened" (*UT* 46). One perceives that trees are presented as extraordinary, they may influence not only their surroundings but also those who venture under their boughs. Furthermore, some of the trees possess great magical powers that they use as they see fit.

Tolkien's love for trees resulted in the creation of a race that is unique to Middle-earth and has no counterparts in European mythologies. It was William Shakespeare who inspired Tolkien to introduce Ents into his own legendarium; the Professor admitted that they appeared due to his "bitter disappointment

---

[1] Chance regards the hobbits' expedition into the Old Forest as a symbolical entry into the underworld and, therefore, Old Man Willow with his malevolent intentions introduces the notion of death. Seen in this light it is the exact opposite of the Tree of Life mentioned in Genesis. However, the tree's connection with the netherworld is stressed by its species – willows are associated with mourning, but more importantly, they have been traditionally regarded as entrances to the netherworld, existing in the liminal sphere between the mundane and the land of the dead (Kowalski).

and disgust from schooldays with the shabby use made in Shakespeare of the coming of 'Great Birnam wood to high Dunsinane hill': I longed to devise a setting in which the trees might really march to war" (*L* 212). In *The Lord of the Rings* Fangorn Forest indeed goes to war – powerful and terrifying Ents get involved in the events that mark the end of the Third Age. It is their first and, at the same time, last such deed. This battle brings to mind Gwydion's achievement of turning trees into warriors. The Welsh *Mabinogion* also tells about *Cad Goddeu* – "The Battle of Trees". Yet here they are not individual living creatures, but a means to win the fight. Tolkien's Ents are utterly independent, for as he liked to stress, the Ents were not invented but simply came along and thus were drawn into his stories (as also happened, according to the author, with many others of his characters); it seems that they joined the War of the Ring of their own accord. The origin of the Onodrim is not stated clearly. A reference in *The Silmarillion* to a special order of spirits – the Shepherds of the Trees – appears to pertain to them; if so, it captures their uniqueness, leaving the question of their beginnings unanswered. It may not be denied that they are the oldest of all the living things, which is subtly emphasised by the fact that for Treebeard the treacherous wizard is still "young Saruman down at Isengard" (*TT* 74). The Ents appear to link the past with the contemporary events, they come out of old stories to prove them true. They are the creatures whose eyes reflect their longevity and wisdom, for "[o]ne felt as if there was an enormous well behind them, filled up with ages of memory and long, slow, steady thinking; but their surface was sparkling with the present" (*TT* 71). Still the Shepherds of the Trees are already forgotten by the end of the Third Age of Middle-earth.

The Ents' major occupation – taking care of and talking to trees – brings attention to their physiognomy which very much resembles that of ordinary, growing trees; so much indeed that the hobbits at first take Treebeard for a tree. The colour and texture of their skin seems to be similar to bark and due to this feature individual Ents remind one of different species of trees that do not closely resemble one another: "some [were] as different as one tree is from another of the same name but quite different growth and history; and some as different as one tree-kind from another, as birch from beech, oak from fir" (*TT* 93). What is more, the Ents learned the Elves' language, in which they communicate with other races, though they still possess a tongue of their own that aptly mirrors their nature: "it is slow, sonorous, agglomerated, repetitive, indeed long-winded" (*RK* 511). It is a tongue that, though not kept absolutely secret, seems to be almost impossible to learn and understand. As any other language, Entish also evolves, yet with time it becomes even more complex and long-winded. There exists a direct link between the Ents and their tongue – Ents grow together with their names which in their own speech reflect the changes their bearers undergo. This tendency is notable, since the reverse process does not take place – the Entish words are everything but short.

Living in the depths of Fangorn Forest, the Ents are not interested in the wars and arguments that break out beyond the borders of their domain. They show no need for contact with creatures from beyond the outer lands, and after Saruman's betrayal they are now even more wary and cautious. They do not want to meddle in matters that (seemingly) do not concern them for the very reason that no one cares for the forests any longer. Therefore, many of their race have fallen asleep, once again becoming very much like trees; they turn into Huorns who live in the remotest parts of the forest – "they are Ents that have become almost like trees, at least to look at. They stand here and there in the wood or under its eaves, silent, watching endlessly over the trees" (*TT* 205). According to Merry, there are very many of them, maybe even thousands half-awake, though vigilant all the same. However, it ought to be noticed that the trees are awakening as well – "[s]ome are quite wide awake, and a few are well, ah, getting *Entish*" (*TT* 77), thus it appears to be a two-way process. Huorns are still able to communicate with the Ents and they do look after the trees in a way – "[t]here is a great power in them, and they seem able to wrap themselves in shadow: it is difficult to see them moving" (*TT* 205), though they move fast and, in addition, they are merciless to the Orcs who fell trees not only for the furnaces of Isengard, but also to satisfy their desire to destroy growing things. Such pointless deeds anger Huorns who go to war together with the Ents; consequently, no Orc is seen leaving the strange and mysterious forest that during one night has appeared near Helm's Deep. Huorns become threatening and wild, since having returned to their "primeval nature" they do not modify their actions according to rational laws (Kocher 121). Their existence may be seen as a state between the wilderness of trees and civilisation which they used to create by themselves.

Their race is dwindling not only because the Ents are becoming treeish, but also due to the fact that no Entings have been born for many a year. The Ents have lost the Entwives, who began to care not only for the trees but for herbs and other plants as well, thus elevating order and plenitude above everything else. The Entwives are not afraid to venture forth into unknown lands and a completely different habitat. For this reason they at first moved to the borders of forests where trees were not growing so densely, later on they established gardens and worked hard in the open spaces so that the sun and the wind made them look ruddy. Still enamoured of the forests, the Ents did not share the passion of the Entwives. Subsequently, they met only on rare occasions and, becoming more and more attached to their own domains, they were not able to live together anymore. After the great wars with Morgoth, the Ents discovered that the old abodes of the Entwives had been destroyed and abandoned and the Entwives were gone to unknown distant places. Long was the search of the Ents for the Entwives, though it proved fruitless. Treebeard is aware that they are irrevocably lost, yet some faint glimmer of hope still echoes in his questions to the hobbits. Nevertheless, he is acutely aware that only in the far West, beyond the Circles of the World, there exists "a land where both our hearts may rest" (*TT* 90). The conflicting desires will not abate in Middle-earth, only the paradisical land of Valinor is believed to bring final repose.

Fangorn understands that the Ents, just like the Elves, will eventually have to fall into oblivion after the war is over. Accordingly, he accepts that having joined in the war, the Ents will eventually meet their doom; it will be "the last march of the Ents" (*TT* 102), one that will be worth remembering, since the Ents – being everything but hasty (which characteristic is regarded by them with contempt) – have been finally roused and angered to such an extent that they appear to be invincible. Nothing save fire or magical spells might have possibly stopped them from breaking the fortified walls of Isengard. They do not fight to overthrow Sauron, they have joined the battle because the forest is endangered. It is worth mentioning that since the first ages, the primeval forests have been disappearing, the areas they used to occupy have been shrinking in an irreversible process. This tendency is alarming, for the well-being of Middle-earth is reflected by the state of the woods. Wherever evil takes root, the trees die. The probable passing of the Ents marks an end of an era of wilderness, a time of transition – the

Fourth Age may either restore the respect for nature or strengthen the reverence for steel and machines. Tolkien leaves this issue open.

The Attitude towards Trees and Alignment

Love for the trees reveals the true nature of Tolkien's characters. Those who respect and care for them are noble and, though not devoid of flaws, good. Tolkien discusses this vital issue whose indicators of worth are either a close connection with nature or utter separation from it. He does not denigrate progress as long as it does not disregard the environment. The Elves have developed a sophisticated culture that blends technological achievement with reverence for nature. No area they inhabit is destroyed, while the Dark Lord and his followers apply their undeniable skills to promote corruption – both physical and moral. Wherever they are situated, their abodes quickly turn to rocky deserts, as if the trees reminded the Dark Lord of the creative powers denied to him. For miles around vegetation is stunted as if mirroring the character of the occupants.

Forests highlight the true nature of protagonists, features that are otherwise hidden are exposed due to their confrontation with the trees. Tom Bombadil with his bright clothes and funny nonsensical songs may seem to be a harmless person. But Tom who possesses profound wisdom and mighty power is utterly fearless in the Old Forest – he is able to command Old Man Willow, for he himself is uncorrupted and untouched by evil. Goldberry supplies some explanation pertaining to Tom himself and the nature of his rule over the wood by stating that "[h]e is the Master of wood, water, and hill" (*FR* 122). One ought to stress the fact that Bombadil is the Master in the sense that he understands and cares for the well-being of the creatures and plants within the borders of his realm. Moreover, being interested in the wood itself, he thoroughly enjoys its vastness and complexity. Tom does not desire supremacy and his rule is not a rule of terror. He makes sure that nothing and no one threatens his domain, but does not directly interfere with the decisions of the trees (as long as these do not threaten others). The forest becomes an integral part of his identity; in fact, Tom's power and protection do not reach far beyond the boundaries of the wood.

By contrast, although powerful, Saruman has no control over Fangorn Forest. He attacks and destroys the trees, as he has the means to do so, but he does not understand them, having learned of the Ents only the things that he found useful for the fulfilment of his plans. His attention is directed towards trees only for as long as he needs them, and as a consequence, his disregard becomes the very reason of his fall. Saruman does not treat trees as living things but as objects because his imagination is mainly preoccupied with artifical contrivances. He destroys the trees surrounding Orthanc in order to create a fortress of metal, reeking with foul fumes and filled with the clangour of machines. Such engrossment in mechanical and artificial devices not only leads him astray, but also hastens the corruption of his character. Trees are connected with the spiritual dimension while metal is heartless, which is emphasised by Tolkien's description of the wizard as having "a mind of metal and wheels" (*TT* 84). Accordingly, Saruman no longer cares for the Entwood and orders a purposeless devastation of the surrounding forests, transforming Isengard into a barren land, a furnace of evil. Saruman commands his minions to cut down trees and leave them to rot; this senseless devastation done only out of spite gains its proper significance when one juxtaposes it with the reverence in which many ancient peoples held trees, the more so that "the tree represents – whether ritually and concretely, or in mythology and cosmology, or simply symbolically – the *living cosmos*, endlessly renewing itself" (Eliade, *Patterns* 267). Therefore, felling a sacred tree was a sacrilege. It may be seen as a bitter irony that the wizard who had so much confidence in metal works and technology should be defeated by the unbound power of nature. He did not treat the Ents as dangerous enemies; in fact, he disregarded them completely, which proved to be one of the reasons for his downfall.

At first Saruman only wanted to gain knowledge, yet soon he became interested in the doings of Sauron, thus he read avidly all the accounts he could find concerning the making of the Ring of Power. The knowledge he came to possess through long years of study convinced him that he was the right person to wield power in Middle-earth. Saruman was assured that he was ready to struggle with the Shadow and finally to reject it. The confidence in his own abilities and wisdom contributed to Saruman's corruption. He succumbed to the Shadow because he wanted to control the wills of others; unlike Tom Bombadil he does not look after his domain and subjects, but tries to subjugate them – thus he transgresses the basic right that Eru has given his children. Saruman the White rejects the true wisdom, goodness and reason, which are usually associated with this colour, only to become Saruman of Many Colours, a slave to Sauron and his own ill-deeds, which he is no longer able to renounce. Patricia Meyer Spacks aptly observes that only by choosing Good can one retain the freedom of will (57). Saruman is unable to admit his own defeat, therefore he plunges deeper and deeper into madness; trying to mar as many things as possible, he devastates the Shire and has the Party Tree cut down. Saruman persists in following the once chosen path, even though it does not give him the knowledge that he had so much desired, because, as Tolkien clearly states, "he that breaks a thing to find out what it is has left the path of wisdom" (*FR* 252).

Trees vs. the Sea

In Tolkien's legendarium one notices two conflicting emotions – the love for trees and the longing for the sea. The sea inspires the spirit of adventure and curiosity, while trees may be regarded as providing support and calm. Sometimes both feelings coexist, as in the case of Galadriel, without annihilating or changing each other; Galadriel still lives in the Golden Wood, cherishing the memory of the Great Sea, whose murmuring reminds her of Valinor. She warns Legolas that when he hears the sound of the waves breaking on the shores of Middle-earth, he will be almost compelled to sail West. The Elves in general, even those born in Middle-earth, harbour both feelings, though it is the sea that triggers the longing for Valinor. Nonetheless, if love for the woods has to be set against love for the sea, the only result is grief and woe that affect the Elves and Men. Tolkien elaborated on this theme in his tale of *The Mariner's Wife*, the story of two lovers who cherish different things. Aldarion is of the royal line of Elros; proud, stubborn and persistent, he would not live on land longer than necessary. He has been haunted in his dreams by the desire to see unknown lands, to travel ever farther beyond the horizon. The valiant captain allows no one to restrain him, as he cannot suffer being ordered around, and thus almost always he takes "the opposite course to any that was counselled" (*UT* 267). Erendis, on the other hand, hates the sea with all her strength because it takes her beloved away for so long. She treats Uinen, the Lady of the Seas, like a potential rival and does not hide her hostility towards the Maia who is known for guiding and preserving the ships of the Númenóreans. Furthermore, Erendis is not interested in what lies beyond Númenor, being only enamoured of her island, its woods and pastures. Such a discrepancy in their desires and preferences is the main reason for the sundering of their union.

The relationship eventually proves tragic, as neither of them wants to lead the life the other favours – Erendis would perish on the high seas, whereas Aldarion grows weak and restless on the mainland. Actually, he feels calm and sleeps well only when he can hear the steady murmur of the waves, while his spouse is at peace in the wide pastures in the centre of the island where she is able to hear the bleating of sheep. Erendis loves trees because of their beauty and majesty, and appreciates them for the simple reason that they exist. By way of comparison, Aldarion cares about forests, yet what he, in truth, needs is only timber for building his strong ships. Therefore, he plants new trees (thus making up for the damage done by the previous generations) with the sole purpose of getting wood for enlarging his fleet. Aldarion sees trees as building material for his ships, he does not consider them to be living beings.

Owing to Aldarion's attitude, Erendis begins to hate even the trees for they remind her of the tall masts of her husband's vessels. She not only despises the sea, but loses the feeling of peace she could find among the woods of her island. Thus, being both proud and unyielding, the spouses grow apart from each other to the point where no reconciliation is possible. The forebodings of the fate that awaits Aldarion and Erendis may be found in the tale itself. It is the custom of the country that the wives or relatives of the mariners bring a bough of *oiolairë* (also known as the Bough of Return), which is set upon the prows of the ships – "[t]he leaves of that tree were evergreen, glossy and fragrant" (*UT* 230). Being a token of the blessing for a long and dangerous voyage, it reminds the sailors of their homes and a safe haven that awaits them. Erendis willingly brings the bough herself when the King denies his blessing, so as to show his dissatisfaction with his son's departure. With this small gesture she draws Aldarion's attention to her feelings. Nevertheless, when he again decides to go to sea and leave her behind, Erendis reluctantly adorns the ship with the bough. Having travelled far and wide, Aldarion on his return voyage looks at the withered bough of *oiolairë* and is dismayed the more so, since "such a thing had never befallen the bough of *oiolairë*, so long as it was washed with the spray" (*UT* 242). During the long cruises the branch is covered by ice just like Erendis's feelings towards Aldarion cool, and it so happens that his wife sets no bough on the prow of his tall ship for the subsequent voyages.

Since Aldarion as well as Erendis have similar characters but love different things, no felicitous conjugal future awaits them. In this legend one perceives the echoes of the Norse myth concerning Njörd and his wife Skadi. She had a house, Trymheim, in the mountains, whereas her spouse preferred to live by the sea. Skadi could not stand the crying of the seagulls, in contrast to Njörd who detested the howling of the wolves. Thus, as neither could live long in peace in the place the other was fond of, they separated for ever to dwell in their beloved places. A similar motif, though with reference to woods and gardens, may be found in the above-mentioned story of the Ents and the Entwives. One cannot choose against one's own nature, hence the spouses are left only with regrets and reproaches that have replaced their love, which at the very beginning must have been true and deep.

Conclusion

The fact that Tolkien devoted so many of his writings to trees should come as no surprise, since he felt a deep love for the woods, and he could neither understand nor explain the mindless felling down of entire groves for the benefit of industrial progress. For the Professor from Oxford machines brought only havoc and destruction; according to him, their widespread use (or rather misuse) portended the emergence of an inhumane world. In the legendarium, trees (regardless of the perspective from which they are presented) are closely connected with the mythological sphere. The Professor's fascination with their nature has rendered intricate depictions of trees as fully-fledged characters. Trees endowed with exceptional features are no longer passive but actively shape the fate of Middle-earth. Tolkien's attitude towards trees may be explained by the fact that he was able to grasp the awe that must have inspired the ancient peoples when they entered the forests – the places they believed to be the abode of magical and inexplicable forces. So strong and unfavourable were Tolkien's opinions of the contemporary mechanized world that he openly stated in one of his letters that "[i]f a ragnarök would burn all the slums and gas-works, and shabby garages, and long arc-lit suburbs, it cd. for me burn all the works of art – and I'd go back to trees" (*L* 96); in point of fact, Middle-earth proves to be a place where trees (still possessing the primeval power) have gained a unique voice and a place of their own in the order of beings.

About the Author

Magdalena Mączyńska graduated from the University of Opole in 2008. Having studied English language and literature, she completed her M.A. thesis on J.R.R. Tolkien's mythopoeia and the writer's creative use of mythical themes present in Norse, Finnish and Celtic mythologies. Simultaneously she studied Russian language and literature and in 2009 completed her B.A. thesis devoted to the motives of evil and death in Leonid Andreev's oeuvre. At present Magdalena Mączyńska is a doctoral student at the University of Opole. Since her main interests remain within the field of fantasy literature, her doctoral thesis focuses on the works of J.R.R. Tolkien, Marion Zimmer Bradley and Philip Pullman.

Bibliography

CHANCE, Jane. *Tolkien's Art: A Mythology for England*. London: Macmillan, 1980.

CURRY, Patrick. "Two Trees." *J.R.R. Tolkien Encyclopedia: Scholarship and Critical Assessment*. Ed. Michael D.C. Drout. New York: Routledge, 2007. 682.

DICKERSON, Matthew. "Old Man Willow." *J.R.R. Tolkien Encyclopedia: Scholarship and Critical Assessment*. Ed. Michael D.C. Drout. New York: Routledge, 2007. 471.

ELIADE, Mircea. *Kowale i alchemicy* [Smiths and Alchemists]. Trans. Andrzej Leder. Warszawa: Fundacja Aletheia, 1993.

Patterns in Comparative Religion. Trans. Rosemary Sheed. Lincoln: University of Nebraska Press, 1996.

Sacrum. Mit. Historia [The Sacred. Myth. History]. Ed. Marcin Czerwiński. Trans. Anna Tatarkiewicz. Warszawa: Państwowy Instytut Wydawniczy, 1993.

KOCHER, Paul H. *Mistrz Śródziemia* [Master of Middle-earth]. Trans. Radosław Kot. Warszawa: Amber, 1998.

KOWALSKI, Piotr. *Kultura magiczna. Omen, przesąd, znaczenie* [Magical culture. Omen, Superstition, Meaning]. Warszawa: Wydawnictwo Naukowe PWN, 2007.

MEYER SPACKS, Patricia. "Power and Meaning in The Lord of the Rings." *Understanding The Lord of the Rings – The Best of Tolkien Criticism*. Eds. Rose A. Zimbardo and Neil D. Isaacs. New York: Houghton Mifflin, 2004. 52-67.

ROUX, Jean-Paul. *Król. Mity i symbole* [King. Myths and Symbols]. Trans. Katarzyna Marczewska. Warszawa: Oficyna Wydawnicza Volumen, Dom Wydawniczy Bellona, 1998.

TOLKIEN, J.R.R. *The Fellowship of the Ring*. First published 1954. New York: Houghton Mifflin, 2002.

The Letters of J.R.R. Tolkien. Ed. Humprey Carpenter, with the assistance of Christopher Tolkien. First published 1981. London: HarperCollins, 1995.

The Return of the King. First published 1955. London: HarperCollins, 1999.

The Silmarillion. First published 1977. London: HarperCollins, 1999.

The Two Towers. First published 1954. London: HarperCollins, 2002.

Unfinished Tales. First published 1980. Ed. Christopher Tolkien. London: HarperCollins, 1999.

Doris McGonagill

In Living Memory: Tolkien's Trees and Sylvan Landscapes as Metaphors of Cultural Memory

Abstract

Trees and wooded environments dominate many of Tolkien's narratives. In woodland realms, beyond the bounds of the familiar world, protagonists get lost, have unexpected encounters, undergo transformations, and confront their destinies. Under trees they find help, protection, and comfort. But the function of trees and forests transcends that of natural protagonists and spaces of initiation. I propose following the trail into the woods as a path to social memory and examining trees and forests in Tolkien's epic as constructions, expressions, and repositories of the cultural imagination.

> "I am (obviously) much in love with plants and above all trees, and always have been; and I find human maltreatment of them as hard to bear as some find ill-treatment of animals." (*L* 220)

Trees and forests loom large in the world of J.R.R. Tolkien's works, literally and metaphorically. As themes and motifs trees dominate Tolkien's plots, imagery, atmosphere, mythology, and narrative structure. Places like the Old Forest, Fangorn, Mirkwood, and Lothlórien, and sylvan characters such as Old Man Willow and Treebeard, together with the Ents, Huorns, Mallorns, and the White Tree of Gondor (with its primordial precursors, Laurelin and Telperion, the Two Trees of Valinor) are well-known to any Tolkien reader. In woodland realms, beyond the bounds of the familiar world, protagonists lose themselves, face the unexpected, and undergo transformations. In forests and under trees they find help, shelter, and comfort – and, occasionally, danger and malevolence. The fate of specific characters (and entire peoples) is symbiotically interwoven with trees – Aragorn and the White Tree of Gondor, for example, or the Huorns' intervention at Helm's Deep, ensuring the survival of Rohan – and in alliance with trees, protagonists acquire great power. By contrast, violations of trees or self-interested manipulations of nature are invariably punished. When the power of Isengard is overthrown by the Ents, Jack Zipes's observation, originally referring to the forests of the Grimms' fairy tales, seems to apply also to Tolkien's texts: "No one ever gains power over the forest, but the forest possesses the power to change lives and alter destinies. In many ways it is the supreme authority on earth and often the great provider" (Zipes 66).

Tree and Leaf, which contains "On Fairy-Stories" and the short story "Leaf by Niggle", expounds the central role arboreal imagery plays in Tolkien's creative imagination, as do multiple references in his letters. The most famous passages refer to the "Tree of Tales" and describe *The Lord of the Rings* as "my own internal Tree " (*TL* 23, *L* 321). Indeed, they reveal the ways in which, for Tolkien, arboreal imagery comes to emblematically represent creative imagination itself.[1] Tolkien criticism has eagerly picked up on these cues. Recent publications, reflecting both the "spatial turn" in Cultural Studies with its shift towards an intense interest in physical, virtual, cultural, and symbolic spaces, and the rise of Environmental Studies, Ecocritism, and the aesthetics of "Environmentality," document a renewed interest in topoanalytical readings of Tolkien's landscapes in general, and in his depiction of forests and trees in particular. Dinah Hazell's 2006 monograph *The Plants of Middle-Earth: Botany and Sub-Creation* dedicates its fourth chapter exclusively to "Forests and Trees" (Hazel 65-87). Patrick Curry's *Defending Middle-earth* (1997/2004) and his volume of collected of essays *Deep Roots in a Time of Frost* (2014) attest to this renewed interest as do Verlyn Flieger's (2012) rebuttal to Curry's "green reading" (Flieger 262-74) or Dickerson and Evans' *Ents, Elves and Eriador* (2006). A 2013 collection of essays edited by Peter Hunt includes two contributions that examine the natural world of Middle-earth, one by Jane Suzanne Carroll, the other by Shelley Saguaro and Deborah Cogan Thacker, both of which pay particular attention to the multi-layered tree trope (Hunt 121-38 and 139-55).[2]

The main aim of the present contribution, however, differs from all these approaches. I propose to interpret Tolkien's representation of trees and sylvan landscapes in light of Hans Blumenberg's theory of metaphor as "memory metaphors," reflective of constructions, expressions, and repositories of the

---

1 See also *TL* 51 and *L* 220, 321, 342, 419-20.
2 See also Brisbois 205.

cultural imagination. In developing my theoretical framework, I also draw on Simon Schama's discourse on collective visual memory (37-242) and Robert Pogue Harrisons's discussion of "Forests of Nostalgia" (155-95). I argue that in Tolkien's epic narrative – from the opening celebration under the "party tree" to the closing of the cycle of renewal with Sam's planting of the Mallorn tree – sylvan spaces and characters reflect cultural memory, fictional and factual, on multiple levels.

A letter written to the editor of the *Daily Telegraph* on June 29, 1972 represents Tolkien's most ardent defence of trees and forests and provides a comprehensive commentary on how Tolkien, in his old age, wanted his depictions of trees and forests to be understood. The commentary bears out the crucial connection between memory and the forest realm:

> In all my works I take the part of trees as against all their enemies. Lothlórien is beautiful because there the trees were loved; elsewhere forests are represented as awakening to consciousness of themselves. The Old Forest was hostile to two legged creatures because of the memory of many injuries. Fangorn Forest was old and beautiful, but at the time of the story tense with hostility because it was threatened by a machine-loving enemy. Mirkwood had fallen under the domination of a Power that hated all living things but was restored to beauty and became Greenwood the Great before the end of the story. (*L* 419f.)

Although the retroactive projection of this protective stance onto the entirety of Tolkien's *oeuvre* can and has been questioned (most directly by Flieger 262-74), forests, more than any other topological setting, preserve the knowledge of the past, good and evil. The internal logic of the narrative is "rooted" in the forests' capacity for memory, which determines appearances, attitudes, and actions. But inscribed in the topological setting are also forms of cultural memory that transcend the text-immanent level and point at broader inter-textual and cultural (historical, mythological, and literary) resonances. In Tolkien's tales, we find echoes of classical, Norse, and Christian religious beliefs. The world tree Yggdrasil of Norse mythology is alluded to along with Barnstock (Barnstokkr) of the *Völsunga Saga* and the Green Man of folklore. In the worship of tree and leaf (in other Germanic languages: *Laub*), Tolkien inscribes his text with the recollection of the dual meaning of *Laub(e)*: foliage *and* holy sanctuary (Schama 585, fn. 61).

But not all woodland realms of Middle-earth resemble a nostalgic paradise. Rather, in accordance with established definitions of the Sublime – most famously among them Edmund Burke's 1756 treatise "A Philosophical Enquiry into the Origin of Our Ideas of the Sublime and the Beautiful" – Tolkien presents the capacity of trees and forests both to compel and to destroy. And parallel to the "historical metaphorics" developed in Ernst Robert Curtius' influential *European Literature and the Latin Middle Ages*, Tolkien's forests bear the signature of both sublime realms, the *locus amoenus* and its inversion, the *locus terribilis*. The former is incarnated, or rather "inarborated," most clearly in Lothlórien, the latter in Mirkwood, the Old Forest, and, with some qualification, Fangorn. Interpreting the hostility of, for example, the Old Forest in context of topoi rooted in collective memory (inspired by the enchanted forests of Grimms' fairy tales) points at a solution to the hermeneutical conundrum Flieger, in her deconstructive reading of the "Eco-Conflict in Middle-earth," considered an irreconcilable contradiction: "Tolkien had written himself into [...] an untenable position. He has espoused two unreconcilable attitudes with regard to nature [...] The paradox may be expressed briefly as follows: civilization and nature are at undeclared war with one another" (Flieger 272).

All woods, trees, Ents, Huorns, Tom Bombadil, even Old Man Willow are associated with memory and act in specific ways as its preservers and guardians. Treebeard is the keeper of "old lists" inventorying all peoples of Middle-earth. The "memory of many injuries" explains the Old Forest's malevolence, the Huorns' march to Helm's Deep, and the transformation of Saruman's industrial wasteland into the Treegarth of Orthanc. Through their ties to memory, sylvan characters act as indicators and agents of change, guaranteeing a balance between civilization and nature, and reversing even the toxic devastations created by Saruman and Sauron. By virtue of their mnemonic capacities, they become antidotes against evil and agents of healing – for societies and individuals (exemplified by the sapling of Nimloth's line or the woodland herb athelas/kingsfoil).

As spaces of transition and initiation, forests bring into focus questions of memory and identity. Characters who enter are in danger of losing their sense of time, purpose, self (The Old Forest, Mirkwood). Or they gain a clearer (re)cognition of where, who, and how they are (Lothlórien). Finally, forests, from the Latin *foris*, abroad or outside (sc. the authority of the state), are uniquely suited as sites of a performative critique of power. The philologist Tolkien, keenly aware of this etymological argument, enacts it in his representations of Fangorn and Lothlórien as discrete realms of memory, largely free of hierarchical power structures.

Following the trail into Tolkien's woods allows us to tread a path that leads to social memory, its multiple layers embedded in the fictional, but retentive and reflective of the historical, mythical, philosophical, and religious. The relationship of fictionality and reality is reminiscent of the sense of "communion" Tolkien invokes in "On Fairy-Stories" (*TL* 18) between Faërie and lived experience: the latter through fantasy is imbued with deeper meaning, while in turn the former, through the "reality effect" of the quasi-historical and quasi-scholarly (what Gray dubs "asterisk-realities," 68), is enriched and bestowed with a sense of historical depth.[3]

Although the landscape settings of the First and Second Ages of Tolkien's world include many forests, among them the vast forests of Beleriand that play an important role in *The Silmarillion*, I focus on Middle-earth during the Third Age, with occasional glances at the preceding ages and the subsequent Fourth Age. Significantly, this Fourth Age is heralded by the discovery of a sapling that is a descendent of the White Tree, Nimloth the fair, whose line can be traced back to Telperion, Eldest of Trees, created early in the First Age. This genealogy alone documents how Tolkien uses trees to imagistically tie together past, present, and future. Tracing representations of trees and forests in Tolkien's "Secondary World," and the memories and sensibilities they retain, also facilitates examination of the basic interconnectedness between the fantasy realm and the real world and provides a productive gateway to the examination of Tolkien's "green" critique of Modernism and technology.

Trees and Metaphors: Blumenberg

Hans Blumenberg interprets myth and metaphors within the larger context of the invention of metaphysical and cultural systems as methods for coping with

---

3 Cf. Saguaro & Thacker 139.

reality that aid us in orienting our thoughts, regardless of the fact that their inherent "truth" is not systematically or logically verifiable. In *Paradigms of a Metaphorology*, Blumenberg examines the role of metaphor and the relationship between figurative and conceptual language. Drawing on Giambattista Vico's notion of a distinct "logic of fantasy," which sets a novel logic of images and imagination against the Cartesian ideal of terminological precision in univocal concepts, Blumenberg argues that figurative speech responds to a logical "perplexity" (*Verlegenheit*) posed by existentially important but theoretically unanswerable questions. Metaphors fill a void that concepts cannot approach, and according to Blumenberg, they can claim a form of legitimacy that is not often acknowledged – a legitimacy based not on their status as "leftover elements" (*Restbestände*) on the irrevocable path toward logicization, but rather on their status as "foundational elements" (*Grundbestände*), translations that intrinsically resist the conversion into logicality and conceptual language (3). For this understanding of metaphors as constituting essential and conceptually irresolvable forms of speech, Blumenberg coins the term "absolute metaphors." The study of these metaphors, his proposed "metaphorology," may provide a tool to assist in examining what could be called the unconscious of the philosophical, "the substructure of thought" (5). Blumenberg turns to metaphors drawn from the physical world in order to demonstrate how metaphors facilitate the discovery of new horizons of meaning and form the indispensable foundation of our history of ideas.[4]

Proposing an interpretation of Tolkien's trees and forests that draws on Blumenberg's theory and reads them as memory metaphors requires methodological circumspection. One needs to ensure not only that one provides a useful tool to deepen the understanding of Tolkien's work, but one needs also to avoid the cardinal sin in Tolkien studies, namely committing to an overly restrictive allegorical or topical reading. The foreword to *The Lord of the Rings* voices Tolkien's distaste for allegorical interpretations and posits over and against allegory the categories of *history* ("true or feigned") and *applicability*. Both, Tolkien explains, reside in the domain of the autonomous reader rather than that of an overly controlling author (*LotR* xxiv).[5] But in its flexibility and

---

4 *Quellen, Ströme, Eisberge: Beobachtungen an Metaphern* (Berlin: Suhrkamp, 2012).
5 Similarly: *L* 262.

its very resistance to restrictive systematization, which understands metaphors as a way of alluding to an otherwise non-representable totality, Blumenberg's attempt at negotiating complementarity between the conceptual and the non-conceptual are highly compatible with Tolkien's notion of "applicability." The methodological validity of the approach is corroborated by a glance at Tolkien's recently published *Beowulf* translation and its notes.[6] Both Tolkien's literary practice – the language of his poetic, evocative translation – and his commentary on translation suggest that he aimed at producing a modern analogue of the Old English text. Rather than rendering *Beowulf*'s prose in formulations of modern concision and fluidity, Tolkien sought to preserve or recreate the character of the original in beautiful images and surprising compounds of his own coinage. His reliance on metaphors to convey the essential characteristics of the material stands out amidst lesser rhetorical devices and subtle rhyme schemes. This reliance is revealing not only with respect to the Old English *middangeard*, but also with respect to the poetic principles underpinning the creation of Middle-earth. In both realms history, fantasy, and mythology intersect, and both employ the poetic beauty and evocative power of metaphor to stage their appeals to the (individual and collective) imagination.

Moreover, this particular interpretation of metaphor is in accordance with the "internal laws" developed in Helms' landmark interpretation *Tolkien's World* (1974) and with Brisbois' 2005 analysis of "Tolkien's Imaginary Nature." Helms identified five internal laws of Middle-earth. These laws, though primarily directed at explaining the morality that informs Tolkien's cosmos, are nevertheless relevant with respect to the analytical approach I suggest, because its implications transcend mere narrative organization and touch on epistemological and – in the discussion of Tolkien's ecological stance – ethical questions. The suggested understanding of metaphor (and the connection of metaphor, memory, and the physical realm of trees/forest) seems a particularly adequate response to the third through fifth laws, which state that "(3) Moral and magical law have the force of physical law. (4) Will and states of mind, both evil and good, can have objective reality and physical energy." And "(5) All experience is the realization of proverbial truth" (Helms 79). This is important because it

---

6 *Beowulf: A Translation and Commentary, with Sellic Spell* (London: HarperCollins, 2014).

confirms the correspondence of Tolkien's representational choices – the favouring of metaphor – with the moral logic governing Middle-earth.

Brisbois' analysis employs a heuristic model that classifies the nature of Middle-earth in a basic binary opposition, Passive and Active nature. "Passive nature" refers to elements of nature that show little involvement in the direct action of *The Lord of the Rings*, while "Active nature" denotes elements that exert a direct effect on the narrative's course of events. On the basis of this binary, Brisbois develops four more "perspectives:" Essential, Ambient, Independent, and Wrathful nature (203-4), and discusses forests in the context of Essential nature – a category that seems to signify nothing more than physical landscape (205). Ambient nature has an indicative function, creates atmosphere or mood, and its method of signification is symbolic (206). Independent and Wrathful nature are both conceived of as forms of Active nature, with Independent nature referring to a part of nature clearly separated from culture and Wrathful nature supplying a heading to the aggressive ("most fantastic") aspects of nature, epitomized in Old Man Willow or the Huorns (211, 214).

Apart from the selective use I will subsequently make of Brisbois' distinctions, I have found this matrix helpful in developing my own analytical approach. Without glossing over the systemic inconsistencies and ambiguities inherent in this categorization,[7] Brisbois' comprehensive view of nature in Tolkien's oeuvre provides a convenient categorical framework for the argument that the connection of memory and trees/forests permeates truly all levels of nature: Passive nature (mere landscapes turned memoryscape), Active nature (Ents, Huorns, Old Man Willow etc.), Essential nature (the lay of the [wood]land), Ambient nature (the atmospheric value and figurative overtones of Lothlórien and its Mallorns), Independent (the sylvan character of Tom Bombadil), and Wrathful (Huorns, Old Man Willow, etc.). Moreover, the connection of woods and memory even permeates the metaphorical speech that various characters and the narrator himself employ. Trees provide important points of reference in the description of physical appearance, moral constitution, and social standing. Thus, Gandalf is described (in his fight with the Balrog) as "a wizened tree

---

7 Problematic seems, for example, Brisbois' assertion that Essential nature is characterized by a marked "pseudo-realism" and must not "contradict the phenomenology of our world too sharply" (205, 208).

before the onset of a storm" (*LotR* 330).[8] Treebeard states about Saruman that his "heart is rotten as black Huorn's" (*LotR* 586). And Legolas, himself a representative of "the folk of the Great Wood," refers to Aragorn as "the Lord of the White Tree" (*LotR* 878). Trees are frequently referred to in order to indicate time: the distant past, the passage of time, an exemplary time of plenty/deprivation, or eternity. As shorthand to denote the ancient days of Valinor, Gandalf uses the expression "while both the White Tree and the Golden were in flower" (*LotR* 598). Tom Bombadil, when explaining to the hobbits "Eldest, that's what I am," illustrates his age by pointing out he "was here before [...] the trees" and remembers "the first acorn" (*LotR* 131). In Treebeard's lament trees serve as indicators for the 'good old times' (before the deforestation that even preceded the Third Age): "Those were the broad days! [...] The woods were like the woods of Lothlórien, only thicker, stronger, younger" (*LotR* 469). Galadriel foresees the coming of "the bare and leafless Day; / The leaves are falling in the stream, the River flows away" (*LotR* 373). And when Treebeard bids farewell to the hobbits, he assures them that their folk have been added to the Long List and that Ents and hobbits "shall remain friends as long as leaves are renewed" (*LotR* 586).

Trees and Memory: Harrison and Schama

The relationship of forests and memory dominates Harrison's analysis in *Forests: The Shadow of Civilization* (1992) and Schama's *Landscape and Memory* (1996). Harrison examines the multiple ways in which the Western imagination has symbolized, represented, and conceived of forests, primarily in literature, religion, and mythology, and offers a selective history that begins in antiquity and ends in our own time. Harrison's argument about the capacity of forests to facilitate modernity's nostalgic gaze into a remote, collective, originary past hangs on a two-fold justification: he asserts that "as forests were once everywhere in the geographical sense, so too they were everywhere in the fossil record of cultural memory" (x) and that forests have "the psychological effect of evoking memories of the past; indeed, that they become figures for memory itself. They are enveloped [...] in the

---

8 Similar tree imagery pervades Tolkien's letters. After C.S. Lewis's death, Tolkien wrote: "I have felt [...] like an old tree that is losing all its leaves one by one: this feels like an axe-blow near the roots" (*L* 341).

aura of lost origins." Between forests and origins exists a form of correspondence "through the medium of recollection, [...] the former provide a sort of correlate, or primal scene, for poetic memory itself" (156, 164).

Although Harrison does not comment on Tolkien's representations of trees and forests, his study nevertheless provides analytical tools helpful in understanding the power and duality of the forest trope in Tolkien's works. For our discussion, three points are particularly important: first, Tolkien's representations of trees and forests display the characteristic features of modernity's nostalgic, mystifying gaze, for which forests are framed by "a halo of loss [...]" (156). Writing at a time when forests had long been receding into vanishing horizons, Tolkien reveals himself as a late heir to the Romantic imagination. Second, Tolkien's forests function as memory metaphors on both the thematic and the structural/narrative levels, namely in the way Tolkien employs processes resembling metaphoric modes and traditions. Harrison's observation about forests as primal prefiguration of the operations of poetic memory is useful in laying the foundations of this argument. Third, since Western civilization cleared its space – as Harrison points out: literally – in the midst of forests, its religious, juridical, civic, and domestic institutions established themselves in dialogue with and opposition to the surrounding sylvan fringe. As a result, the role forests have played in the cultural imagination of the West is a highly elusive, ambiguous, and paradoxical one (ix, x). In the religious, mythological, folkloric, and literary narratives of the West, forests appear simultaneously as places of lawlessness *and* justice, danger *and* enchantment, entrapment *and* freedom. Forests are places where perceptions are confounded and logical distinctions no longer apply: in forests the inanimate may suddenly become animate and the ordinary may be supplanted by the fabulous (x). Within the conflicting tensions of this precise representational tradition we can locate Tolkien's forest. While all woods in Middle-earth display some of the characteristics mentioned above, certain clusters of motifs have been scattered across different parts and different elements of the narrative(s): motifs traditionally associated with the dangers of the forest, Tolkien has attributed to the Old Forest and Mirkwood, while motifs accentuating fantastic enchantment are more closely connected with Lothlórien. Fangorn seems to comprise the contradictory clusters to the greatest extent.

Schama's work, like Harrison's, shows an interest in the mystification of forests, but focuses on the discrepancy between imaginary construct and historical reality. Schama's art-historical perspective is relevant because of Tolkien's own artistic endeavours, but also because the artistic tradition Schama traces has tremendous impact on the collective visual imagination that informs Tolkien's visual and literary depictions of trees. Although Tolkien's status as a visual artist is precarious and his drawings and paintings remained for the most part a private hobby, some of his work was published as illustrations of his fiction and in calendars. Trees dominated Tolkien's artistic imagination for decades,[9] in particular the mythical *Tree of Amalion*, of which existed already several coloured pencil versions when Tolkien agreed to produce another one that would serve as the cover design of *Tree and Leaf*. Discussing the plans for this design with Rayer Unwin, Tolkien wrote:

> I have among my 'papers' more than one version of a mythical 'tree,' which crops up regularly at those times when I feel driven to pattern-designing. They are elaborated and coloured [...] and the tree bears besides various shapes of leaves many flowers small and large signifying poems and major legends. (*L* 342)

The love of detail and intricacy that characterizes the various manifestations of *The Tree of Amalion* illustrates Tolkien's professional interest in medieval manuscripts, but, even more so, his artistic favouring of the free imagination over any mimetic principles governing landscape art. Decorative rather than realistic, his trees are stylized emblems of arboreal abundance. The variety of leaves and flowers on their curling branches evokes not just different individual trees, but different species.[10] This suggests that the aesthetic principles that inform their composition are rooted in the fantasy realm of *Faërie* rather than in the empirical world, rendering their formulaic visualization veritable analogues to the literary metaphors Tolkien employs.

Schama's interest in forests and the collective visual imagination led him to examine three aspects that are pertinent with respect to Tolkien: first, the imaginary construction of the European forest as authentic native homeland, quasi-extension of the fabled primeval Hercynian forest; second, in the tradition of pagan mythol-

---

9   Cf. Hammond & Scull, especially 64f. (fig. 62) and 67 (fn. 73-77).
10 Cf. John R. Holmes, "Art and Illustrations by Tolkien," *J.R.R. Tolkien Encyclopedia*, ed. Michael D.C. Drout (New York, Routledge 2007), 27-32, here 32.

ogy, the concept of the forest as living natural sanctuaries; third, developments in landscape painting that depict the forest not merely as a location within a larger narrative, but as a protagonist in its own right: "The story [...] *is* the forest. This [...] wood is not 'the setting'; it is the history itself" (100).

Schama's reflection on narratological focus lends itself well to a comparison with Tolkien's representational techniques, as does Schama's analysis of the amalgamation of Christian and pagan traditions that inform Western landscape painting. Similar to landscape paintings evoking mythological dwelling places of the divine whilst at the same time transcribing representational conventions of Christian churches to create pictorial echoes of consecrated spaces, so the boughs and branches of Tolkien's Lothlórien, bursting with foliage, create a canopied tabernacle and sanctuary of Elvendom. Charged with memory of a threatened or bygone time,[11] trees in Tolkien's work serve as reflections and reminders of an honoured past (or, as is the case with the White Tree of Gondor, a glorious future). Writing like the historian of Benjaminian coinage about what is endangered or lost and casting it as an object of longing, Tolkien's sylvan landscapes emanate an aura of memory and loss. The world he portrays as the Third Age is a world in which only remnants of the old forests remain. This indicates "a loss of wholeness that, Tolkien claims, once existed" (Saguaro & Thacker 142).

Reminiscent of Romantic sensibilities Tolkien designs a triadic model that posits an original wholeness, followed by loss, leading up to the hope of eventual restoration. In this ultimately Neoplatonic figure of thought – famously cited in Milton's 17th century epic poems – memory is what ties the different phases together. Drawing on multiple cultural, mythological, literary, and artistic traditions, Tolkien's rendition posits forests as a central thematic element (forests preserve memory, acting as its emblems and guardians), chooses the poetic form considered its most apt equivalent (relying on the intrinsic power of the poetic

---

11 This holds true on the fictional level, but also on the level of reality: it does not require the comparative glance into contemporary forestry history to understand that the mystic authority of Tolkien's sylvan landscapes – foils for romantic longing and a myth of lost origin – contrast starkly with the economic realities of private forest ownership and timber profiteering during the twentieth century.

word and its innate connection with memory), and also echoes the topic on a structural level (by employing a triadic composition).[12]

Sylvan Spaces, Societies, and Characters

Many trees that the reader encounters in *The Hobbit* and *The Lord of the Rings* are familiar – as is the case with the other flora of Middle-earth. They bring to the literary landscape "connotations of special properties and lore" and rouse cultural memory (Hazell 68). But Tolkien's invented trees also have an inherent history, innate personality, and metaphoric potential. Conforming with Helms' fourth internal law, they have objective (fictional) reality and physical energy, and are shaped by and respond to formative events and influences. Tolkien's famous letter to the *Telegraph* attributes the hostility of the Old Forest to the injuries it sustained, Fangorn's suspicion to the destructive frenzy of Saruman and his Orcs, Mirkwood's darkness to the evil effect of Sauron's presence, and Lothlórien's beauty to the Elves' love of trees.

It has been observed that all of Middle-earth seems to be alive, appears as a protagonist in its own right, and that anthropomorphized nature has its own agency, experiences, and narrative(s), evoking an overall sense of ancient, mythical time (Curry, "Defending Middle-earth" 282).[13] But Tolkien attributes consciousness to nonhuman entities to various degrees, and although not all trees of Middle-earth appear animated (some form inconspicuous elements of greater landscape-tableaux or serve mere functional purposes as landmarks, hiding places, or sleeping quarters in the manner of Brisbois' Passive Ambient nature), trees and forests do stand out in the way many have independent life (Brisbois' Active, Essential, Independent, and Wrathful Nature). The consciousness trees exhibit "mimics human awareness" (McMahon & Csaki 181) and is paired with great potential for action and change, constructive as well as destructive.

---

12 Zipes comments on this structure when he lists Tolkien along with C.S. Lewis under the heading "romantic anticapitalist writers of fairy tales [...], who look back conservatively to the past for salvation" (185).
13 In describing nature as alive, dynamic, and (self-)transformative, Tolkien shows himself once more under the influence of Romanticism's reconceptualization of nature, which rejected the Baconian "mortification" of nature and dissecting scientific gaze, and instead bestowed onto nature a new sense of agency.

The following sections examine the Old Forest, together with Mirkwood, as examples of sylvan spaces that harbour memory (of injuries or, as in the case of Mirkwood, of a time of blessing); Lothlórien as a paradigmatic memory-scape resonating with the old Nordic belief in forests as sanctuaries of the divine (echoed in the powerful Elvish enchantment that resides in these woodlands); and Fangorn, the wood that is home to the most impressive of Tolkien's tree-like creatures, the Ents.

Mirkwood and the Old Forest

The dwarves' and Bilbo's entry into Mirkwood and, seventy-seven years later,[14] Frodo and company entering the Old Forest are described in similar terms. Far from being welcoming, both forests' gloominess is oppressive and disquieting: "There was no movement of air down under the forest-roof, and it was everlastingly still and dark and stuffy" (*H* 124) and "after a while the air began to get hot and stuffy. The trees grew close again on either side, and they could no longer see far ahead" (*LotR* 112).

The journey from light into darkness, characteristic of any entry into a forest environment, in Tolkien's descriptions transcends realistic representation and gains a metaphoric, even epistemological, dimension: entering the forest is tantamount to moving from the time of the 'here and now' into a realm of mysterious timelessness, standstill, and memory. Perceptions become less clear and the cognitive functions of the everyday are suspended. As Hazell reminds us, the name "Mirkwood" is a reference to the *Elder Edda*, where Mirkwood is a mysterious realm that separates the warring Niflungs and Huns (68). As such it appears as a space of transition, specifically, on the way into hostile territory. But the name is indicative also of the above-mentioned loss of clarity and definition. The uncertainty and cognitive ambiguity of these realms becomes manifest in formulations with unmistakable metaphoric overtones. So we learn that the hobbits upon entering the Old Forest "could see only tree-trunks of innumerable sizes and shapes: straight or bent, twisted, leaning, squat or slender, smooth or gnarled and branched; and all the stems were green or

---

14 *The Lord of the Rings*, Appendix B, 1089 and 1091.

grey with moss and slimy, shaggy growths" (*LotR* 111). When the protagonists enter the forests, the cognitive destabilization is almost immediately followed by their companies getting lost.

Both forests embody memory and imaginative power in a particular fashion: Mirkwood, once "Greenwood the Great," still retains the memory of the Elves that resided there in the past. Even though the evil effect of Sauron's presence is making itself felt, the forest is still indebted to the days of the Elves. In a characteristic triadic structure the forest is described as a once blessed realm. At the end of the Watchful Peace (according to Appendix B in the year 2460 of the Third Age, *LotR* 1087) Sauron returns to Dol Guldur and Thranduil's people are forced into hiding in a northern enclave of the forest. Only then does the forest become "Mirkwood." But after Sauron's defeat, the realm of the Wood-elves is re-established and flourishes again. Greenwood/Mirkwood is renamed once more and becomes Eryn Lasgalen (Wood of Greenleaves). Wholeness, loss, and renewal mark the three phases, and the memory of the past ties together a deprived present with a redeemed/fulfilled future.

However, memory plays yet another important role in the depiction of Mirkwood because Tolkien's description is also indebted to representational conventions characteristic of the fairy-tale forest. Zipes observes in his analysis of the forests of the Brothers Grimm that fairy-tale forests are rarely themselves enchanted but are *sites* where enchantment takes place. Saguaro and Thacker (142) point out that Zipes' description also applies to Tolkien's depiction of Mirkwood, where the memory of the Wood-elves and the presence of Sauron contribute most of the enchantment and danger rather than the forest itself.[15] The forest appears marked by an inherent continuity that preserves and transmits, even in times of growing disharmony, the memory (of beauty, harmony, benevolence, etc.) of the past.

Zipes recognizes another feature of the fairy-tale forest that also comes into play in Tolkien's work: because forests retain the cultural memory of having once been a communal possession, they level social distinctions and are

---

15 In this context it is to be understood that the beech and oak trees of Mirkwood, favoured by the Wood-elves, are mostly benign, and the dangers Beorn warns Thorin's company against, are rather connected with the presence of evil creatures, loss of orientation, lack of food etc. (Hazell 70).

privileged sites for changes of destiny (Zipes 70). In Tolkien's texts, facets of these characteristics become manifest. When the protagonists enter the sylvan realms, their hidden attributes are more clearly revealed (to themselves and others), the dynamics of the companies change, and the ability of little folk to do great deeds emerges (Hazell 70). As spaces of initiation and transition, Tolkien's forests, just as the fairy-tale forests, have (trans-)formative power and touch on questions of selfhood and identity. We should take note that Tolkien's forests are thus charged with memory in an at least threefold sense: within the subcreation of the secondary world (the memory of a time of harmony associated with the Elves); in relation to the historical reality of the Primary World (activating the cultural memory of forests as collective possession); and in the consciousness Tolkien's woods display of the fairy-tale traditions of oral literature. This last form of (fairy-tale) memory is also activated in the ways in which knowledge about forests is preserved, namely in half-forgotten stories, children's tales, and ancient names the origins of which are lost in time. Tom Bombadil reminds the hobbits that the Old Forest was named thus for a reason, "for it was indeed ancient, a survivor of vast forgotten woods [...]" (*LotR* 130). Merry, when asked whether the "stories about it" were true, refers to the memory of children's tales, "old bogey-stories [...] nurses used to tell" (*LotR* 110), and to hearsay.[16] These passages allude to a leitmotif of Tolkien's, namely that popular, folkloric knowledge – often conveyed in metaphorical speech – is valuable and preserves a broader, more authentic form of knowledge than the mere logical and conceptual.

Flieger (264) considers the Old Forest "Tolkien's version of the standard fairy tale dark wood on the order of those in 'Snow White' and 'Hansel and Gretel'." But the forest's hostility to "two-legged creatures" – although explained in the text (*LotR* 130) and the quoted letter through the memory of many injuries as an aftermath of ancient ill-intention and "the secondary response of an endangered environment" (Dickerson & Evans 141) – appears to heighten any threat, dangers, or evil fairy-tale forests might harbour. "Strangled" and "blackened" is not just its appearance but its malicious heart. Ambient, Essential, Independent,

---

16 "At night things can be most alarming, or so I am told;" "They do say the trees do actually move [...];" and "or at least I have heard so" (*LotR* 110). Similarly, Elrond remarks "of the Old Forest many tales have been told" (*LotR* 265).

Wrathful, (still) Passive, (but soon) Active – with its intelligence, mobility, and malice, the Old Forest seems to embody all of Brisbois' categories at once. Most clearly this is articulated in Old Man Willow, the first aggressive foe the hobbits encounter, and a tree villain like no other in Tolkien's work. Traditionally, the willow tree (because of the acrid taste of its bark) was associated with the bitterness of grief (Hazell 75). Chance (*Tolkien's Art* 155) interprets Old Man Willow as an underworld figure, as "Tree of Death," activating the biblical memory of the Tree of Knowledge of Good and Evil in Eden. Eco-conscious analyses interpret Old Man Willow, based on the environmental destruction he has witnessed, as an "element of the environmental concern expressed in the novel" (Brisbois 212). One may certainly diagnose a kind of cause-and-effect relationship between environmental damage and Wrathful nature, seeing Old Man Willow as a cautionary metaphor. However, his depiction is countered by the appearance of Tom Bombadil, who represents a complementary principle and positive counterpart, associated with growth, revivification, and concord with/in nature (Chance, *Tolkien's Art* 156 and Hazell 30). Together with Goldberry, Tom Bombadil stands for harmony, balance, and cyclical renewal. Although he is "master" of the forest, he does not seek dominance or complete control, but only intervenes to restore balance (Hazell 30). Prime example of Brisbois' Independent but Essential nature, this forest character is uninvolved in the power-struggles of Middle-earth, and accordingly the Ring of Power has no effect on him (*LotR* 133). An antithesis to both Sauron and Saruman, Tom Bombadil embodies the wholly sympathetic *Waldmann*, a man of the woods (Schama 100), with echoes also of the Green Man of folklore, a pagan representation of nature itself (Dickerson & Evans 209).

Lothlórien

Lothlórien is the fairest forest realm in Tolkien's legendarium and a privileged site of memory. Echoing classical, Norse, and Christian traditions, the "living land" (*LotR* 356) of Lothlórien represents a sylvan sanctuary, in which the harmony, beauty, and love of a blessed past remain alive. The special relationship of the Elves, who dwell in Lothlórien, to trees is expressed in their name "Galadhrim" (tree people), based on the Sindarin *galadh* (tree).

Once called "Laurelindórinan" (Land of the Valley of the Singing Gold), the land later became simply Lórien (Land of Gold) or Lothlórien (Dreamflower, *LotR* 467) – and a dreamlike-quality certainly appertains to the realm. The travellers first see the elven realm, allegorically heightened, "as if it glowed still in memory of the sun that had gone" (*LotR* 353). In accordance with established representational conventions pertaining to dwelling places of the divine, the heart of Elvendom is described in topographical superlatives, amidst "mallorn-trees taller than any they had yet seen," "ever climbing up like a green cloud," with widespread branches reaching a "height that could not be guessed" (*LotR* 353). In a characteristic fusion of the practical and the spiritual, trees are honoured here as dwelling places of the Elves and sites of sacred (quasi-religious) veneration.[17] Canopied by living boughs (*LotR* 354), the chamber of Celeborn and Galadriel in Carad Galadhon (City of Trees) appears like a tabernacle, invoking the ancient Germanic etymological linkage of foliage and holy sanctuary.[18] A natural memory chapel and prime site of the sublime is also the old spiritual centre of Cerin Amroth, surrounded by a "circle of white trees," reminiscent of "Spring-time in the Elder Days," and "the heart of the ancient realm as it was long ago" (*LotR* 350).[19] A third site of particular spiritual significance (besides the walled city and the hill of Cerin Amroth) and presented as a shrine within a sanctuary is the "enclosed garden" (*LotR* 361) that houses Galadriel's well. Placed amid a sacred grove and surrounded by yet another "high green hedge" (*ibid.*), it is depicted in the medieval *hortus conclusus* tradition (Hazell 35f.).

Like Rivendell nestled in nature (and hidden by it), the sylvan arcadia of Lothlórien is a protected realm that can be entered only with the permission of its inhabitants. The most striking feature besides its beauty is the peculiar experience of time, timelessness, and memory it conveys: Celeborn and Galadriel themselves display no sign of age, "unless it were in the depths of their eyes; for these were [...] the wells of deep memory" (*LotR* 354). "Frodo felt that he was

---

17 Tolkien quotes the Norse belief that forests housed the gods, and – in the depiction of Galadriel – classical and Christian imagery connected with the Aphrodite/Venus and Mary cults.
18 Caras Galadhon first appears as a green hill encircled by a great green wall. When seen from afar, one cannot decide whether it is "a hill of many mighty trees, or a city of green towers" (*LotR* 351).
19 "Malinornelion" translates into "gold beech tree" (Fonstad 184), calling up the image of natural cathedrals/sanctuaries. Interestingly, the mallorns, though undeniably alive, seem to have no distinct personality. Planted by Galadriel, they typify Ambient/Passive nature.

in a timeless land that did not fade or change or fall into forgetfulness" (*LotR* 351). And Sam notes that "[n]othing seems to be going on, and nobody seems to want it to" (*LotR* 361). In Lothlórien, time stands still, and there is no evil and no sickness. Frodo's first impression of the realm articulates this aura of a prelapsarian world (Brisbois 207):

> It seemed to him that he had stepped through a high window that looked on a vanished world. A light was upon it for which his language had no name. All that he saw was shapely, but the shapes seemed at once clear cut, as if they had been first conceived and drawn at the uncovering of his eyes, and ancient as if they had endured for ever. He saw no colour but those he knew, gold and white and blue and green, but they were fresh and poignant, as if he had at that moment first perceived them and made names for them new and wonderful. In winter here no heart could mourn for summer or for spring. No blemish or sickness or deformity could be seen in anything that grew upon the earth. On the land of Lórien there was no stain. (*LotR* 350f.)

Although there are seasons that to some extent correspond with the seasons in the rest of Middle-earth, they seem more clement and – like the entire sylvan realm – remote from the meticulously constructed sense of history that characterizes the rest of Middle-earth. "In Rivendell there was memory of ancient things; in Lórien the ancient things still lived on in the waking world" (*LotR* 349). Those who enter lose their sense of time ("some days so far as they could remember;" "they could not count the days and nights that they had passed there" *LotR* 358, 481f.).

Not only does the perception of time change in this realm of permanent '*praeteritus stans*,' but also the perception of shapes and colours and, indeed, perceptual experience in general: the olfactory (the visitors note the "fragrant grass," *LotR* 350), the auditory ("the South Wind [...] sighed among the branches. Frodo stood still, hearing far off great seas upon beaches that had long ago been washed away" *LotR* 351), and even the tactile experience is heightened and more immediate ("never before had [Frodo] been so suddenly and so keenly aware of the feel and texture of a tree's skin and of the life within. He felt a delight in wood and the touch of it, neither as forester nor as carpenter; it was the delight of the living tree itself" *LotR* 351). Reminiscent of Nietzsche's plea, in "On Truth and Lie in an Extra-Moral Sense," for the revival of dead metaphors, every aspect of

Lothlórien seems endowed with new life and greater immediacy.[20] The effect on the visitors is profound and results in their healing (in body and soul), an activation of memory, and a greater knowledge of the self. Aragorn, "standing still and silent as a tree," but with a light in his eyes, "was wrapped in some fair memory; and as Frodo looked at him he knew that he beheld things as they once had been in this same place" (*LotR* 352). The trees' (physical) power of renewal translates into power to (bodily and spiritually) rejuvenate. As he contemplates the past, Aragorn's physique changes and time is reversed: "the grim years were removed from the face of Aragorn, and he seemed clothed in white, a young lord tall and fair" (*ibid.*). As a space of healing Lóthlórien is perceived also by the other travellers. In the first stage of their recovery, they forget the sorrows of the outside world (*LotR* 355). Later, when strengthened, they come to terms with the loss of Gandalf by collectively and individually remembering him in conversation and song. Walking among the ancient mallorns provides the sustenance necessary on this path of recovery – nourishment of the soul, as important as sleep and food ("they did little but eat and drink and rest, and walk among the trees; and it was enough" *LotR* 358).

Songs are characteristic of Lóthlorien's specific mélange of beauty, memory, loss, and recovery on many different levels. As part of their healing process, the travellers cast their memories of Gandalf into "song or rhyme" (*LotR* 359). They thus mimic the principle way in which memory and ancient knowledge are preserved in this realm: "up on the hill they could hear the sound of singing falling from on high like soft rain upon the leaves" (*LotR* 354). Sam sums up the experience of Lóthlorien in the following metaphor: "I feel as if I was *inside* a song, if you take my meaning" (*LotR* 351). The insights and forms of knowledge gained in Lóthlorien, based on the perceptible rather than the intelligible, are intuitive and "pre-critical" in the Blumenbergian sense ("He knew somehow [...]" *LotR* 360). And while poetry and song are their most apt expression, the content of that knowledge can be troubling, as it not only touches on the experience of loss, but also on novel (and possibly disquieting) forms of acquaintance with the self. In non-rational ways, Lóthlorien makes known to its visitors their innermost desires, granting them glimpses at their

---

20 Tolkien articulates his avowal of uniqueness/individuality through the use of arboreal metaphors most clearly in *TL* 51.

strengths, but also their greatest weaknesses. This becomes apparent in the "trials" all travellers experience, and which Boromir is unwilling to talk about (*LotR* 358). When Frodo and Sam look into the mirror of Galadriel, they get a privileged insight into the complex connections of past, present, and future, and the aspects of potentiality that connect them.

Lothlórien's unique linkage to time and timelessness becomes apparent one last time at the departure of Frodo's company. Galadriel's lament expresses her knowledge of the future fate of her wood. The Fourth Age will bring the passing of the Elves and holds no future for this realm (*LotR* 373). Her parting words to Sam, whose passion as "gardener and lover of trees" endears him to the Lady of the Wood, iterate: "For our spring and our summer are gone by, and they will never be seen on earth again save in memory" (*LotR* 375). Galadriel's parting gift to Sam will prove invaluable as it ensures in the last chapter the ecological well-being of the Shire and beyond. The last glance of Galadriel shows her as her entire realm has been depicted all along: "present and yet remote, a living vision of that which has already been left far behind by the flowing streams of Time" (*LotR* 373). This description is echoed one final time when, with inverted perception, the travellers' departure appears to them as Lothlórien's receding in time: "For so it seemed to them: Lórien was slipping backwards, like a bright ship masted with enchanted trees, sailing on to forgotten shores, while they sat helpless on the margin of the grey and leafless world" (*LotR* 377).

Fangorn

The primeval antiquity of Fangorn forest stands out even by comparison with other forests of Middle-earth. "It is old, very old [...] and full of memory," Legolas observes upon first entering Fangorn (*LotR* 491). More than any other forest of Tolkien's subcreation, Fangorn conforms with Harrison's statement that "[t]he forests were *first*" (1). Although by the end of the Third Age much of it was fast disappearing under the axe, Fangorn is the most impressive image of the original grandeur of the ancient forests. Its cavernous woodland interiors seem inspired by Roman descriptions of the primeval *Urwald* of the Hercynian forest that extended to the ends of the known world – in Pliny's words "unimaginably ancient, literally prehistoric [...] coeval with the world, which surpasses all marvels by its almost immortal destiny" (quoted in Schama 83). With the walking and talking Ents and the avenging Huorns, Fangorn is one of Tolkien's most powerful memory metaphors.

Perceived as dim, stuffy, and "frightfully tree-ish" (*LotR* 462), the forest is "not evil," but full of "watchfulness, and anger" (*LotR* 491). Treebeard and the Ents – shepherds, tree-herders, and sentient caretakers of the forest – personify the organically living wood: "*The* Ent, I am [...] *Fangorn* is my name according to some, *Treebeard* others make it" (*LotR* 464) and "Treebeard is Fangorn" (*LotR* 499). But the Ents also personify the wood's deep memory.[21] Pippin's description of Treebeard echoes the description of Celeborn's and Galadriel's eyes as "wells of deep memory." However, it also evokes the world tree Yggdrasil, pillar of the world, with its far extending roots and its branches holding up the heavens:

> One felt as if there was an enormous well behind them, filled up with ages of memory and long slow, steady thinking; but their surface was sparkling with the present; like sun shimmering on the outer leaves of a vast tree, or on the ripples of a very deep lake. I don't know, but it felt as if something that grew in the ground – asleep, you might say, or just feeling itself as something between root-tip and leaf-tip, between deep earth and sky had suddenly waked up, and was considering you with the same slow care that it had given its own inside affairs for endless years. (*LotR* 463)[22]

Although it is stated elsewhere that Tom Bombadil is "eldest," Treebeard could also lay claim to that appellation, for Gandalf describes him as "the oldest living thing that still walks beneath the Sun upon the Middle-earth" (*LotR* 499).[23] Since Treebeard's memory reaches back to the earliest of times, he assumes the role of a guardian of memory with some authority. When first encountering hobbits, he is suspicious of the newcomers and double-checks the "old list," made "a long, long time ago" (*LotR* 464), of the free-peoples of Middle-earth. Upon their parting as friends, he informs them that he "has put their names into the Long List. Ents will remember it" (*LotR* 586). According to Aleida Assmann's conceptual distinction between storage memory (*Speichergedächtnis*)

---

21 Cf. *L* 190: "Treebeard [...] has a great memory" (*L* 190).
22 Cf. Dickerson & Evans 127. The analogy with Yggdrasil and the Norns (representing past, present, and future) at its roots could be read as a reference to Treebeard's power to change destinies.
23 See also Gandalf's "riddle" concerning the Ents (*LotR* 544). Treebeard himself grants that honour to the Elves (*LotR* 464), which he credits with teaching the trees to speak and names them before Ents in the Old Lists.

and functional memory (*Funktionsgedächtnis*), the Ents primarily represent storage memory (130-42). But they also epitomize the act of remembering (functional memory), marked by their decision at the Entmoot, when – based on their memory of the trees' maltreatment – they change from merely aware but Passive or Independent nature to Active/Essential nature. This turning point, after what long appeared as helplessness to combat adverse forces, marks the "Rise of the Ents" and the beginning of their (and the Huorns') active involvement as agents of change in Middle-earth. Accordingly, memory in Fangorn is not passive and retrograde (as memory appeared in Lothlórien), but the basis of future-oriented action.

Beyond the level of secondary creation, Fangorn as memory metaphor relates to the primary world in three principle ways. In a letter to W.H. Auden, Tolkien spelled these out: "I did not consciously invent [the Ents] at all. The chapter called 'Treebeard' […] was written off more or less as it stands. […] But looking back analytically I should say that Ents are composed of philology, literature, and life" (*L* 212). The Ents' indebtedness to philology can be explained by Tolkien's scholarly interest in linguistic memory and development. The etymology of the name "Ents" combines Old Norse and Old English elements and suggests an association of trees and giants. But also Treebeard's acute awareness of the connection between names, history, and stories is important in this context. Tolkien characterized Old Entish as a language that preserves in particular ways the connection of name, narrative, and memory: "Real names tell you the story of the things they belong to in my language […]. It is a lovely language, but it takes a very long time to say anything in it" (*LotR* 465). Tolkien commented on the Ents as linguists and on the historical and linguistic awareness embedded in their language in Appendix F, where he makes particular mention of their "desire for speech," their "skill […] in tongues," and the fact that Entish was never represented in writing (*LotR* 1130f.). Too complex for others to learn, their speech remained secret and, like any other, once committed to the Ents' memory was never forgotten.

The Ents' indebtedness to literary memory hangs, according to Tolkien, on one attractive and one repulsive force. The letter to Auden details that the Ents owe their name to the "eald enta geweorc" ("the ancient work of giants," Tolkien, *Beowulf* 306) of the 10th-century Anglo-Saxon poem "The Wanderer" (*L* 212,

445), a lament of the fleeting days of glory, whose Latin-inspired *"ubi sunt"* (Where are?) formula also served as linguistic inspiration for the lament of the Rohirrim (*LotR* 508). Tolkien mentions in the same letter his "bitter disappointment and disgust [...] with the shabby use made in Shakespeare of the coming of 'Great Birnam wood to high Dunsinane hill,'" (*Macbeth* 4.1.92-94) and adds: "I longed to devise a setting in which the trees might really march to war" (*L* 212). Thus the idea of the Huorns' march to Helm's Deep and the Ents' attack on Isengard was born.

Besides these concrete influences and stimulations,[24] Tolkien's narrative (re)presentation bears witness that Fangorn, much like the other forests of Middle-earth, is indebted to oral literature. The memory of the Ents (also called Onodrim) is preserved in folkloric form: songs, legends, rhymes, and children's tales. While Aragon thought Ents "were only a memory of the ancient days, if indeed they were ever more than a legend," Legolas objects: "every Elf in Wilderland has sung songs of the old Onodrim" (*LotR* 499). Gandalf quotes a "riddle" concerning the Ents (*LotR* 544) and explains to Théoden their coming "out of the shadow of legend" with a reference to children's stories: "There are children in your land who, out of the twisted threads of story, could pick the answer to your question. [...] You have seen Ents, O King. Ents out of Fangorn Forest, which in your tongue you call the Entwood [...]: to them you are but the passing tale" (*LotR* 549f.) Because Ents represent memory – which is metaphorically related to story-telling and trees/forests – the king himself, by comparison, appears just as a short-lived tale. This inversion indicates how Tolkien relativizes human history within the larger memory of natural history, and it supplies one of the most poignant articulations of his ecological stance for which the Ents are frequently cited as the most potent representations and advocates (Dickerson & Evans 119, 127-29).

As guardians of memory associated with storytelling, the Ents of Fangorn occupy a unique position between past, present, and future. As for Tolkien's assertion that Ents are also composed of "life" and "experience" (*L* 212), while his immediate explanation hints at a gendered approach to wilderness vs. cul-

---

24 Among them the Finnish folk epic *Kalevala* (especially Runo I, 51-59). For more literary resonances see Jones 58-68.

tivated landscape/gardening (Entwives), one may also identify resonances of his preservationist engagement on behalf of trees as informative of his imaginary construction. The representation of the Rowan Quickbeam (Bregalad) especially points in this direction. Quickbeam, who appears as Treebeard's younger (more "hasty") counterpart, is described as a singing and soft-spoken Ent who, despite his deceptively light-hearted manner, conveys a harrowing tale of environmental destruction (*LotR* 483). Hazell explains that rowans are prized for their protective powers against evil forces and points out the resemblance of Quickbeam's home to the setting of Boromir's attack on Frodo (81) – an instructive parallelism that illustrates the textual memory associated with trees as well as Tolkien's sincerity about preservationist issues.

The Party-Tree and the White Tree of Gondor

From the Party-tree standing "proudly" inside the main pavilion in the opening chapter (*LotR* 26) to the White Tree of Gondor dominating the last book, Tolkien's text abounds with mythological, religious, historical, and linguistic references. Depicting the dependability of trees, Tolkien is keenly aware that the words for "tree" and "trust" are etymologically linked (Hazell 81). In the Bible, the tree is a persistent image, particularly of beginnings and endings, significant people and highly historical events (Kilby 62f.) In *The Lord of the Rings*, the flowering of the White Tree is a reassurance of the ultimate victory over evil and intimately connected with time, memory, and renewal. As Gondor's heraldic symbol, the White Tree crowned by seven stars is reminiscent of the symbolism in the Book of Revelation, and the finding of the sapling (affirming the legitimacy of the king) is narratively framed by multiple allusions to the Apocalypse (*LotR* 970-72; Rev. 21:10-11, 23; Kilby 62f.). The barren mountainside location, where the sapling springs up, is analogous to Isaiah's prophecy of the coming of Christ as "a tender plant [...] a root out of a dry ground" (Isaiah 53:2). This seems affirmed by Gandalf's comment that life within the tree may – like a memory – "lie sleeping through many long years" (*LotR* 972). While holding present the memory of the past (through its precursors in Tolkien's legendarium it is a memorial of the Eldar, connected with light and knowledge), the shooting tree also points to the future of the Fourth Age.

Likewise striking is the structural correspondence between the Bible's opening imagery of a garden containing the tree of life and the closing imagery of the same tree in the heavenly New Jerusalem – a juxtaposition that loosely corresponds with the narrative framing in *The Lord of the Rings* of the Party-tree and its renewal through the mallorn Sam plants in the concluding chapter to replace the felled party-tree (*LotR* 1023). The old tree, housed in the party-tent, anticipated Galadriel's flet, built around the central trunk of a great tree. It also resembles the tree Barnstock, around which Völsung's hall is built. Through the allusions to Barnstock (*The Saga of the Volsungs*, ch. 2 and 3) and Donar's Oak, it is tied to Norse mythology. By way of typological correspondence, it is connected to biblical (New Testament) hope and renewal, tying together ages, realms, mythologies, and literatures.

Conclusion

Trees and forests are central to Tolkien's tale and its metaphoric and metaphysical structure. Tolkien conceives of forests and trees in terms of memory and originary plenitude. Drawing on multiple sources and inspirations (mythological, religious, literary, linguistic, and historical), his arboreal creations convey the fullness of meaning the Old English "*treow*" holds: tree, truth, fidelity, trust, pledge, agreement, favour, and kindness (Hazell 81).

Woodland realms appear as memoryscapes on many different levels: as Active, Passive, Essential, Ambient, Independent, and Wrathful nature. But they also echo the depth of cultural memory, classical, Norse, and Christian – often cast in experiences of loss and longing (of or for an imagined unity, harmony, or time of plenty, constructed within the narrative reality or transcending it). Many individual trees carry lore and metaphorical, mythological, or religious significance, like the Party-tree or the White Tree of Gondor. Forests like the Old Forest and Mirkwood metaphorically represent woodlands' powerful memory of environmental injustice, on the one hand, and devoted stewardship on the other. Lothlórien represents positive retrograde memory and its nourishing powers. Fangorn/Treebeard represent deep memory (storage memory and functional) that leads to action and the creation of a future that resembles the best of the past. Nearly all forests illustrate nature's power and the protective/palliative properties of plant life. This holds true also for sylvan spaces this essay did not discuss: the trees of the Woody End offer a hiding place when the Black Riders first arrive. The Chetwood provides shelter when Aragorn and the hobbits need to avoid pursuit after leaving Bree. In Hollin, the ancient Elven-home Eregion, giant holly trees (famed for their palliative powers) survived and offer refuge, showing that an Elvish atmosphere still lingers. Under the ash-trees and oaks of Ithilien, Frodo and Sam find one last "comfortable refuge" (*LotR* 697) before entering the Black Land. After leaving Ithilien, staves "made of the fair tree *lebethron*" and endowed with a "virtue [...] of finding and returning," support them during their darkest hours (*LotR* 694). Drúadan Forest, home of the Wild Men, shelters the Rohirrim as they approach Minas Tirith by the forgotten road. In Firien Wood, Éomer renews his oath to King Elessar. And as the story is drawing to a close and is itself about to become a memory ("they rode gently down into the beginning of the trees as afternoon was wearing away," *LotR* 1027), the last plants named on the journey to the Grey Havens are oak and hazel, known for their protective and magical powers. The effect they have on the company is exemplified by Sam, who in the following sentence is described as being "deep in his memories" (*LotR* 1028).

As memory metaphors, trees and forests influence spatial and temporal representations. Nature supplies an ideal model of cyclical time, a rhythm of renewal and rebirth, which Tolkien fuses with (fictional) historical time and religious time, pairing aspects of pagan mythology with a Christian teleology of redemption. In a triadic figure of thought, trees serve in a deprived present as emblems of a great past and glorious future (Gondor's White Tree crowned by stars). But they also serve as metaphorical formulation of a Time of the Now *and* of the Past, a space of stand-still and reflection, simultaneously detached from and imbued with (hi)story. As spaces of initiation and transition, tree-realms resonate with epistemological overtones and are cast as sites of heightened identity perception. But they also draw on established fairy-tale conventions, which they cite in conjunction with other folkloric traditions as well as literary and linguistic sources. Tolkien draws on Germanic and fairy-tale traditions when he uses the idealized forest realm for a performative critique of power. The power-defying rise of the Ents demonstrates this most impressively. Memory is inscribed into the names (and languages) of trees, woodlands, and sylvan societies. The written memory of runes, the characters used in *The Lord of the Rings*, is associated with tree-branches – and, within Tolkien's subcreation – with the forest folk of the Elves (Appendix F, *LotR* 1128).

One could say that Tolkien's trees and forests resemble runes in the way they possess dual properties, one immediate/practical (on the level of the narrative) and the other representational/metaphorical (on the level of extra-textual references activating the readers' collective and individual memory). On many levels, the analysis of Tolkien's arboreal and sylvan imagery brings to light the fascinating juncture of converging storylines, showing how Tolkien's conservative project – reclaiming cultural, literary, and linguistic memory – converges with his conservationist one – his agenda of ecological and environmental justice. Through the power of the poetic word, the woodland wilderness not only is vindicated but cast as the privileged site of collective memory.

About the Author

Doris McGonagill received her Ph.D. from Harvard University's Department of Germanic Languages and Literatures in 2006 and is currently holding a position as Professor at Utah State University. Publications include her recent monograph *Crisis and Collection: German Visual Memory Archives of the Twentieth Century* (Königshausen & Neumann 2015), "A New Science of Beauty", an entry on Albrecht Dürer in *A New History of German Literature*, as well as articles on German authors Else Lasker-Schüler and W. G. Sebald, Austrian novelist Christoph Ransmayr, and German artist Gerhard Richter. An essay on the representation of urban environments as memory sites in the work of W. G. Sebald appeared in the *Jahrbuch für Internationale Germanistik* in 2014. Most recently, her interest in the intersection of visual and literary culture led her into the realm of fairy tale and folklore with an article titled "Romantic Imagination and Cultural Construction: The Topography of the Grimms' Fairy Tale Forests," accepted for publication in the collection *New Approaches to Teaching Folk and Fairy Tales* (eds. Christa Jones and Claudia Schwabe, University Press of Colorado).

Bibliography

Assmann, Aleida. *Erinnerungsräume: Formen und Wandlungen des kulturellen Gedächtnisses*. Munich: C.H. Beck, 2006.

Blumenberg, Hans. *Paradigms for a Metaphorology*. Translated by Robert Savage. Ithaca NY: Cornell University Press and Cornell University Library, 2010.

Brisbois, Michael J. "Tolkien's Imaginary Nature: An Analysis of the Structure of Middle-earth." *Tolkien Studies* 2 (2005): 197-216.

Burns, Marjorie. *Perilous Realms: Celtic and Norse in Tolkien's Middle-earth*. Toronto: University of Toronto Press, 2005.

Carroll, Jane Suzanne. "A Topoanalytical Reading of Landscapes in *The Lord of the Rings* and *The Hobbit*." *J.R.R. Tolkien: The Hobbit and the Lord of the Rings*. Ed. Peter Hunt. London and New York: Palgrave Macmillan, 2013. 121-138.

Chance, Jane. *Tolkien's Art: A Mythology for England*. Revised edition. Lexington KY: University Press of Kentucky, 2001.

(ed.). *Tolkien the Medievalist*. London and New York: Routledge, 2003.

Curry, Patrick. *Defending Middle-earth. Tolkien, Myth and Modernity*. 2nd edition. 1st edition 1997. Boston MA: Houghton Mifflin, 2004.

"Defending Middle-earth: Tolkien, Myth and Modernity." *The Green Studies Reader: From Romanticism to Ecocriticsm*. Ed. Laurence Coupe. London and New York: Routledge, 2000. 282-287.

Deep Roots in a Time of Frost. Essays on Tolkien. Cormarë Series 33. Zurich and Jena: Walking Tree Publishers, 2014.

Dickerson, Matthew T. and Jonathan Evans. *Ents, Elves, and Eriador: The Environmental Vision of J.R.R. Tolkien*. Lexington KY: University Press of Kentucky, 2006.

Dubs, Kathleen and Janka Kaščáková (eds.). *Middle-earth and Beyond: Essays on the World of J.R.R. Tolkien*. Newcastle upon Tyne: Cambridge Scholars Publishing, 2010.

Flieger, Verlyn. *Green Suns and Faërie: Essays on Tolkien*. Kent OH: Kent State University Press, 2012.

Fonstad, Karen Wynn. *The Atlas of Middle-earth*. Rev. ed. Boston MA: Houghton Mifflin, 1991.

Gray, William. *Fantasy, Myth and the Measure of Truth: Tales of Pullman, Lewis, Tolkien, MacDonald and Hoffmann*. New York: Palgrave Macmillan, 2009.

HAMMOND, Wayne G. and Christina Scull (eds.). *J.R.R. Tolkien: Artist and Illustrator*. Boston MA: Houghton Mifflin, 1995.

HARRISON, Robert Pogue. *Forests: The Shadow of Civilization*. Chicago IL: University of Chicago Press, 1992.

HAZELL, Dinah. *The Plants of Middle-earth: Botany and Sub-Creation*. Kent OH: Kent State University Press, 2006.

HELMS, Randel. *Tolkien's World*. Boston MA: Houghton Mifflin, 1974.

HOLMES, John R. "Art and Illustrations by Tolkien." *J.R.R. Tolkien Encyclopedia*. Ed. Michael D.C. Drout. New York: Routledge, 2007. 27-32.

HUNT, Peter (ed.). *J.R.R. Tolkien: The Hobbit and the Lord of the Rings*. London: Palgrave Macmillan, 2013.

JONES, Leslie Ellen. *Myth & Middle-earth*. Cold Spring Harbor: Cold Spring Press, 2002.

KILBY, Clyde S. *Tolkien and The Silmarillion*. Wheaton IL: Harold Shaw Publishers, 1976.

KOCHER, Paul H. *Master of Middle-earth: The Fiction of J.R.R. Tolkien*. Boston MA: Houghton Mifflin, 1972.

LIGHT, Andrew. "Tolkien's Green Time: Environmental Themes in *The Lord of the Rings*." *The Lord of the Rings and Philosophy*. Eds. Gregory Bassham and Eric Bronson. Chicago IL: Open Court, 2003. 150-163.

MCMAHON, Jennifer and B. Steve Csaki. "Talking Trees and Walking Mountains: Buddhist and Taoist Themes in *The Lord of the Rings*." *The Lord of the Rings and Philosophy*. Eds. Gregory Bassham and Eric Bronson. Chicago IL: Open Court, 2003. 179-191.

NIETZSCHE, Friedrich. "On Truth and Lying in an Extra-Moral Sense." *Friedrich Nietzsche on Rhetoric and Language*. Eds. and trans. Sander L. Gilman, Carol Blair, and David J. Parent. New York and Oxford: Oxford University Press, 1989. 246-257.

SAGUARO, Shelley and Deborah Cogan Thacker. "Tolkien and Trees." *J.R.R. Tolkien: The Hobbit and The Lord of the Rings*. Ed. Peter Hunt. London and New York: Palgrave Macmillan, 2013. 139-155.

SCHAMA, Simon. *Landscape and Memory*. London: Vintage, 1996.

SIEWERS, Alfred K. "Tolkien's Cosmic-Christian Ecology: The Medieval Underpinnings." *Tolkiens Modern Middle Ages*. Eds. Jane Chance and Alfred K. Siewers. New York: Palgrave McMillan, 2005. 139-156.

TOLKIEN, J.R.R. *Beowulf. A Translation and Commentary, with Sellic Spell*. Ed. Christopher Tolkien. London: HarperCollins, 2014.

The Lord of the Rings. New York: Houghton Mifflin Company, 1994.

The Letters of J.R.R. Tolkien. Ed. Humphrey Carpenter, with the assistance of Christopher Tolkien. New York: Houghton Mifflin Company, 2000.

The Silmarillion. 1977. New York: Houghton Mifflin Company, 2001.

ZIPES, Jack. "The Enchanted Forest of the Brothers Grimm: New Modes of Approaching the Grimms' Fairy Tales." *Germanic Review* 62.2 (1987): 66-74.

Peter Hodder

A New Zealand Perspective on the Tectonics of Middle-earth

Abstract

Tolkien modelled his Middle-earth on lands of which he had knowledge: England and selected parts of continental Europe. However, on occasion he describes volcanic eruptions and his landscapes carry the imprint of successive episodes of mountain-building and submergence beneath the sea. These events have been interpreted previously as the result of Middle-earth being tectonically active by applying aspects of the theory of plate tectonics – a theory that post-dates Tolkien's writing. This paper provides evidence that the tectonic history of Tolkien's Middle-earth resembles that of New Zealand: each land's geography resulting from changes between episodes of extensional and compressional tectonic regimes, and between times of vigour (typified by raising mountains and volcanism) and quiescence. Of course the details vary, but there is sufficient similarity to provide a justification for requiring Middle-earth to be recognised as tectonically active and for selecting New Zealand as a locale for the filming of *The Lord of the Rings* and *The Hobbit*.

Imagining Landscapes

Rather similar to the hoary question of the priority of chicken or egg, we might ask whether the story or the map of the landscape on which the story takes place comes first. All readers of *The Hobbit* or *The Lord of the Rings* have noticed the maps on the end-papers of his books. Grotta (89) asserted: "Tolkien once advised that in an adventure story it is essential for the author to draw a map first; otherwise he is likely to encounter 'great discrepancy'." Of the maps relevant to *The Silmarillion*, Christopher Tolkien wrote (*SME* 219): "Though it [the map] was not drawn initially in a way that would suggest that my father intended it to endure, it was the working map for several years, and it was much handled and much altered." Thus, the map is a precursor to the author constructing a "secondary world in which your mind can enter" (*OFS* 36), in which the author "wishes in some measure to be a real maker or hopes that he is drawing on reality: hopes that the peculiar quality of this secondary world (if not all the details) are derived from Reality or are flowing into it" (*OFS* 61).

This is not so different from Brotton's (14-15) representations of presumed reality by map-makers:

> A metaphor, like a map, involves carrying something across from one place to another. Maps are always images of elsewhere, imaginatively transplanting their viewers to faraway, unknown places, recreating distance in the palm of your hand. Consulting a map ensures that faraway is always close at hand.

In short, "[m]ap-makers do not just reproduce the world, they construct it" (Wood 66).

Analogies have long been proposed between the landscapes in J.R.R. Tolkien's Middle-earth that were the settings of *The Hobbit* and *The Lord of The Rings* and the landscapes of Europe and especially England (Campbell 405-408). Tolkien himself notes in one of his letters:

> Middle-earth is not an imaginary world. [...] The theatre of my tale is this earth, the one in which we now live, but the historical period is imaginary. The essentials of that imaginary place are all here (at any rate for inhabitants of N.W. Europe), so naturally it feels familiar, even if a little glorified by the enchantment of distance in time. (*L* 239)

In a contemporaneous letter, he makes it clear that he draws on his own experiences of England (*L* 235):

> There is no special reference to England in the 'Shire' – except of course that as an Englishman brought up in an 'almost' rural village of Warwickshire on the edge of the prosperous bourgeoisie of Birmingham (about the time of the Diamond Jubilee [of Queen Victoria]) I take my models like anyone else – from such 'life' as I know.

However, experiences in the Swiss Alps (*L* 391) are also considered by Pike (439) to have influenced Tolkien's geography. Even so, Tolkien notes:

> And though I have not attempted to relate the shape of the mountains and land masses to what geologists say or surmise about the nearer past, imaginatively this 'history' is supposed to take place in a period of the actual Old World of this planet. (*L* 220)

Two words in this quotation require specific comment, *viz.*, 'period' and 'Old World'.

With reference to the use of the term 'Old World', Tolkien could reasonably be expected to draw on knowledge of landscapes with which he was familiar, as Middle-earth cartographer Karen Fonstad posited (Fonstad xi). Thus, it would be tempting for some inferences about the geology of Middle-earth to be similarly Eurocentric, as has been shown previously (Sarjeant 334). From this it is a short step to inferring the likely climate of Middle-earth (Radagast/Lunt 1-8), which somewhat unsurprisingly given initial assumptions in the model used, turns out to be similar to that of Western Europe, although there are similarities with other parts of the world, including "north of Dunedin in the South Island of New Zealand [which] might be considered the ideal location to film a motion picture based in the Shire" (Radagast/Lunt 6).

Tolkien's use of the words 'a period' could be taken to suggest that he considered his landscape to be unchanging. If so, old time-worn landscapes might be prime candidates for analogies with Middle-earth. One such is Spring Pound, north of Alice Springs in Australia, which a party of several geologists mapping the area in the 1970s likened to Mordor, on the basis of its dark coloured rocks and its overall appearance, following aerial photographic surveys in 1969 ("Second Annual Report for EL2510"). Indeed, the name of this particular 'pound' – an ancient geomorphic feature in Australia in which hard rocks now surround a near circular area of readily eroded soft rocks – was changed from Spring Pound to Mordor Pound. No reference to the origin of the name is made in a scientific publication on the pound's geology (Langworthy and Black 51), one of the authors of which, Alan Langworthy, is generally credited with making the analogy between the pound and Tolkien's Mordor. Indeed, it has been more recently suggested that the Australian "Mordor is an extraordinary area that the geology fraternity has kept quiet about for 30 years" (Breen 14). This may be because the complex contains kimberlites, rocks which may be diamond-bearing, and has been prospected by Conzinc Riotinto of Australia, probably for uranium ("Second Annual Report for EL2510"). It may be no coincidence that greater recent publicity for the Australian Mordor ("Mordor Pound: The Geology of Lord Sauron's 'Australian Home'") coincided with the use of elements of the New Zealand landscape as sets for Peter Jackson's film trilogy. However, drawing an Australian analogy to one Tolkien locality pales by comparison with the landscape and landform analogies found in New Zealand.

At least three 'ages' of Middle-earth can be inferred from *The Silmarillion*: the three sections ("Ainulindalë", "Valaquenta", and "Quenta Silmarillion") that comprise most of this work are set in the 'First Age', "Akallabêth" is set in a subsequent 'Second Age', and predates the last section "Of the Rings of Power and the Third Age", which closes this 'prequel' to *The Hobbit*. Thus, it can be inferred that Tolkien accepted the concept that the geology of Middle-earth changed over time, and this may be reflected in the fact that his first map "was much handled and much altered" (*SME* 219). An ideal real-world candidate for Middle-earth would be an area whose geological history was in some measure comparable to the ages described in *The Silmarillion*: as argued later in this article, New Zealand appears such a candidate.

From Geological Myth-making to Plate Tectonics

A geology of Middle-earth that changes over time appears to have its origins in Tolkien's obsession with Atlantis (Grotta 166), of which the most obvious manifestation is the foundering of the island of Númenor, as punishment for the inhabitants' quest for immortality. There have been many attempts to locate a real Atlantis island, which by 1969 had been emphatically assigned to Santorini (Galanopaulas and Bacon 125), confirmed thirty years later by Friedrich (97-159) in the context of wider considerations of archaeology and culture. Sprague de Camp (10-16) continued a long-standing preference of Atlantis being thought of as an idea in Plato's mind. This stance is consistent with Gillis's concept of Atlantis never being discovered because it was an island 'on the move', ever at the margins of the explored world (Gillis 21). It was effectively a creation of the mind. In a similar way, Lemuria can be considered an idea in scientist Sclater's mind (213) to explain the differences in distribution of lemurs between Madagascar, Africa and India. His idea spawned suggestions from other scientists for the location of Lemuria to explain this and other biogeographic distributions, none of which has been found to exist (Ramaswamy 51). In the same way that the exploration of the oceans continually displaced Atlantis, increasing understanding of the Earth's geological processes and their effect on flora and fauna have required the continual displacement of Lemuria, and its relegation – like Atlantis – to an idea in the mind.

An alternative to explaining the distribution of plants and animals by their using continents and land-bridges (that ended up being creations of the mind) is to envisage the continents themselves on the move, an idea propounded independently by the Norwegian meteorologist Alfred Wegener (1) and the American geologist F.B. Taylor (179) in the early twentieth century. While these ideas had some success in accounting for paleontological distributions, because there was no obvious means of propelling the continents across the face of the Earth, such notions were readily dismissed as fantasy – or modern-day myths – by the scientists of the day (Takeuchi *et al.* 91). Within Britain's academe, Arthur Holmes of the University of Edinburgh later suggested a more dynamic Earth with its crustal movements driven by convection currents. In 1944 he published this idea not in a scientific paper, but in a textbook. Holmes attempted to realise his imagined mechanism with a mechanical model using rotating cylinders to move viscous liquids that in turn dragged overlying strata into valleys, observing (412): "Actual currents in the substratum must of course be far more complicated than those of the ideal cycle which alone has been considered here – but so are the orogenic features [principally mountains] we seek to understand."

It seems unlikely that Tolkien would have been aware of the development of such ideas. Against this background, Tolkien's portrayal in text of a dynamic geology for his Middle-earth seems both unusual and prescient.

The idea of a dynamic Earth with tectonic plates split at the mid-ocean ridges, colliding to raise mountains (like the Rockies and Himalayas currently and the Appalachians and the European Alps rather longer ago), and subducting to cause volcanoes and earthquakes (e.g., the Pacific rim), although a develop-

Figure 1. The floors of the oceans were envisaged to be in motion from their origin at mid-ocean ridges (right) to when they were forced under the edge of another plate (left). At this collision zone mountains were pushed upwards. [Cartoon believed to be drawn by John Holden]

ment of the continental drift ideas of Taylor and Wegener in the early 20th century, is a comparatively recent concept, dating from the 1960s. One of the idea's first proponents, Harry Hammond Hess, chose to present his ideas as 'geopoetry' (599), perhaps as a defence against possible ridicule by scientific colleagues of the day. This suggests that the early ideas of plate tectonics still had a myth-like quality about them. Hess thought that the mechanism that might 'drive' the plates could be a variant of Holmes' proposed convection currents in the Earth's mantle. This speculation of the mechanism of plate tectonics and its effects were the subject of a number of now largely forgotten cartoons first published in 1977 by Holden and Vogt (573).

While one cartoon included a god raising mountains while a subterranean devil simply watched on (**Figure 1**), in another the devils have work to do. **Figure 2** shows devils attending to leaky plumbing which feeds molten rock

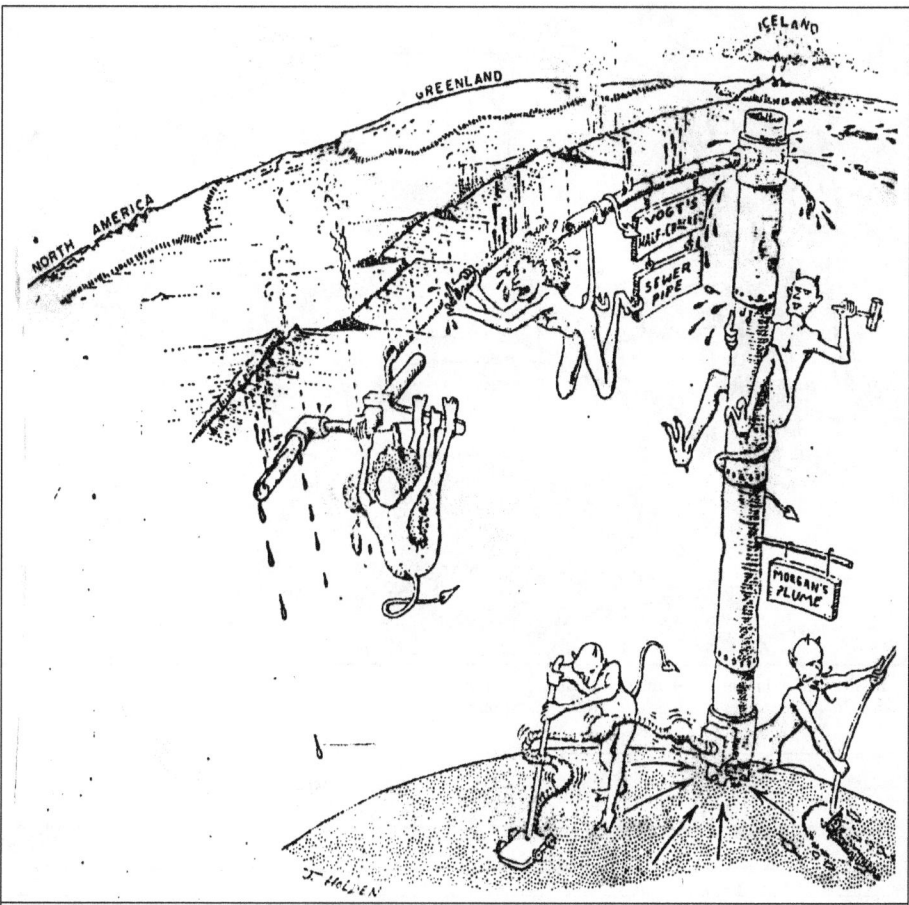

Figure 2. Volcanism from a 'plume' rising from the Earth's mantle at the mid-ocean ridge. The devils were said to be not to scale.
[Source: Holden & Vogt 576, fig. 6]

from the lower regions of the mantle to a mid-oceanic spreading centre. Rather more benign in appearance than the orcs of Moria or Mordor (Russell 140), the devils were said to concoct "strange chemistry of ocean island tholeiites, hawaiites, balonites, and similar hot spot generated rocks, attributed to the culinary habits of X Vulcan *et al.* (regurgitated material, in preparation)".

One cartoon showed a mantle-dwelling fish – *Asthenicethes aseismotathes* – which, as it swam around the Earth, exhaled blobs of magma which rose to the surface to form chains of volcanoes – the intra-plate volcanoes of which

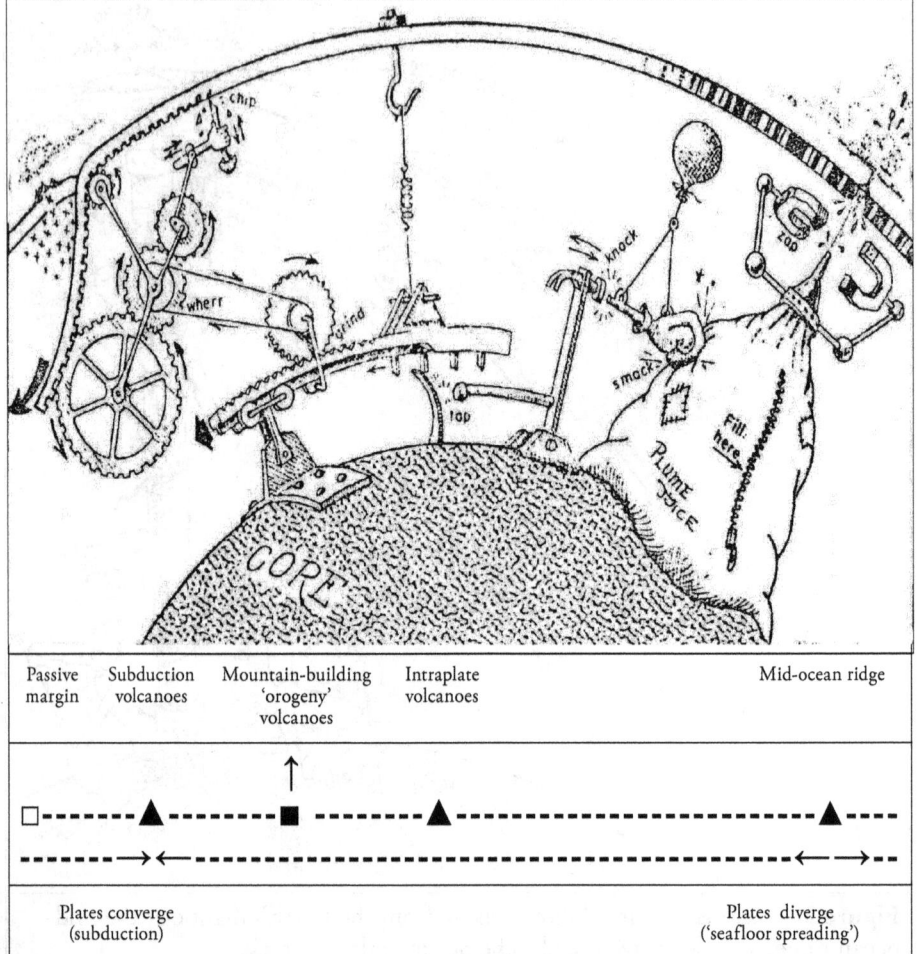

Figure 3. *Upper*: The rate of new plate formation (at right) was required to be the same as the rate of subduction (at left). Volcanoes at the extreme left of the picture are formed by the eruption of rocks made molten by their being subducted. [Source: Holden & Vogt 576, fig. 9]
Lower: Sketch showing the essential features of tectonic environments.

the Hawaiian Islands are the classic example. Still another cartoon portrayed a gravitational anchor theory explaining the origin of Hawaii, for which the caption (Holden and Vogt 574) noted: "According to this hypothesis even the motion of California can be explained although the motions of Californians remain as mysterious as ever."

Figure 3 shows new rock being magnetised and incorporated into the crust at 'spreading centres' – at the right of the sketch, the crust being pulled back into the inside of the earth as if it were an escalator or a conveyor belt at the left. The rate at which new crust is formed at spreading centres needs to be the same as that at which it returns to the mantle if the Earth is to remain the same size. (Incidentally the magnetic 'stripes' that match up on either side of the spreading centres were probably the most important evidence for sea-floor spreading because the alternating magnetic polarity of the stripes matched a magnetic timescale determined independently.)

Thus, a generation of young geophysicists in the late 1960s could be considered to be 'sub-creators' of an almost mythical Earth 'driven' by an internal engine whose operation was essentially unknown and whose history could be but dimly inferred. At the time it was proposed the theory of plate tectonics explained much about the oceans, but it still required much imagination in its application to the rest of the Earth. The past forty years have seen much of the initial imagination and speculation replaced by evidence and data. To scientists plate tectonics is now a credible explanation of how the planet works and is a cornerstone to the current understanding of its geological history. However, there is much that still remains imperfectly understood: theorising and myth-making continue.

The Tectonics of Tolkien's World

In 1974 Robert Reynolds, a student at Swansea University, compiled a map of Middle-earth showing four intersecting tectonic plates (67), as shown in **Figure 4**.

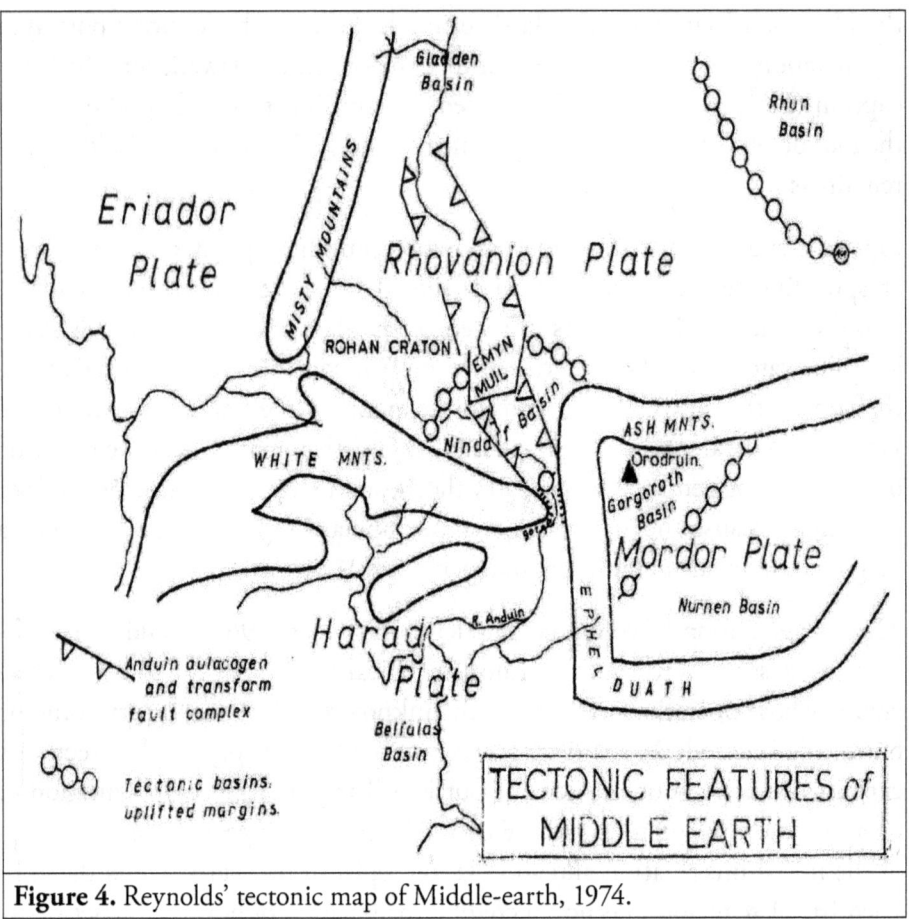

Figure 4. Reynolds' tectonic map of Middle-earth, 1974.

This is a remarkable application of a scientific theory in its infancy to a fictional landscape, albeit one that drew heavily on what was known of the plate tectonics of Europe and Africa. He wrote (67):

> Within the context of the plate tectonic model of lithospheric evolution the portion of Middle-Earth under review resembles southern Europe with areas of high relief joining and dividing, enclosing basins and troughs. My Eriador and Harad continental plates (see map [Figure 4]) correspond to Europe and Africa and have collided squashing between them several microplates. Translation and rotation of other crustal blocks due to dextral movement of the southern continental plate has occurred deflecting mountain chains and creating compressional basins. Just as in Europe evidence for violent orogenic activity [most noticeably earthquakes and volcanoes, e.g., in Greece and

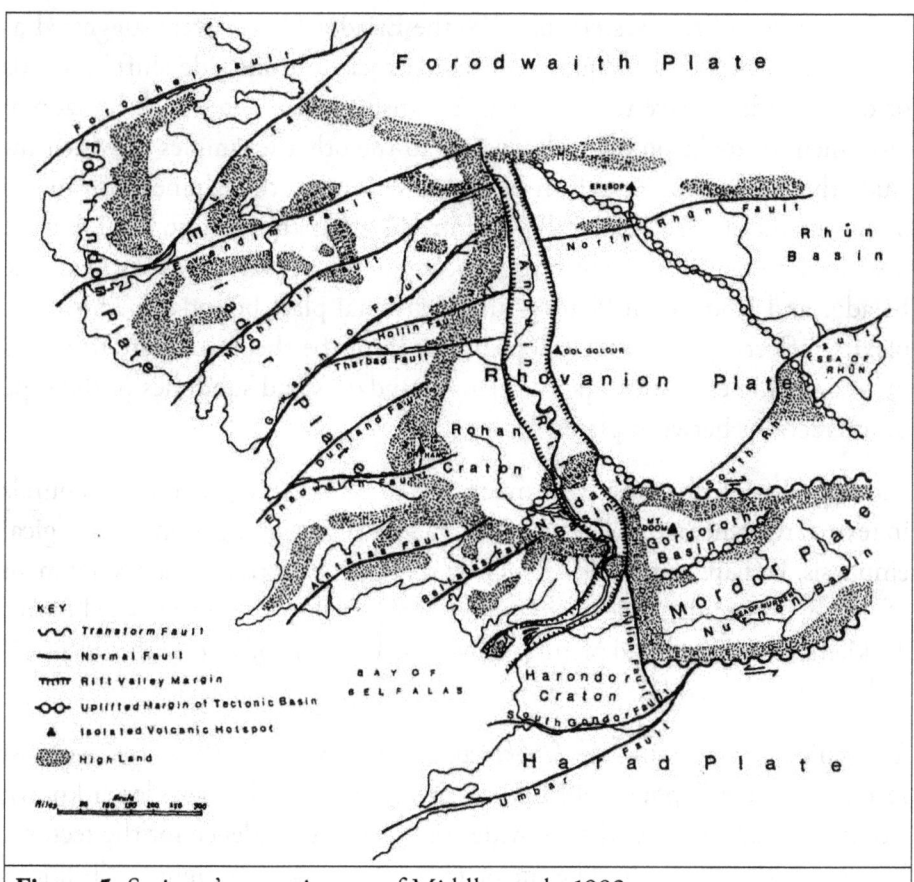

Figure 5. Sarjeant's tectonic map of Middle-earth, 1992.

Italy] decreases northward from Mediterranean to cool temperate latitudes, although ancient worn down orogens are in evidence in the northwest.

While Reynolds conceded that "age correlations are impossible, hence difficulties arise in dating the phases of plate collision" (67), he later recognised (69) a series of orogenic phases that contribute to the form of his map. Had *The Silmarillion* been available to Reynolds at that time, his chronology of tectonic events would probably have been more detailed.

By 1992, by which time there was a greater understanding by geologists of plate tectonics, the tectonic map of Middle-earth, as drawn by Sarjeant (337), had become more complex **(Figure 5)**.

Rivers on one of the western plates – the Eriador Plate – were suggested as the location of "normal faults", in which rocks on one side shift upwards or downwards relative to the other. A transform fault, in which horizontal movement of rocks on one side relative to the other (examples of which include the San Andreas Fault in North America and the Alpine Fault in the South Island of New Zealand) was introduced as the western boundary of the Mordor Plate. The Anduin River occupies the rift valley pulling apart the Eriador and Rhovanian Plates – an extensional plate boundary. This complexity reflects the increasing sophistication of the theory of plate tectonics in recognizing different types of plate boundaries and subtleties of the type of interactions between plates.

Although Sarjeant's map is very much a tectonic one, the paper itself abounds in textual references to Tolkien's landscapes and has a strong geomorphological emphasis. Perhaps unsurprisingly, given that Sarjeant's paper is a development of that by Reynolds, Sarjeant concludes (339): "All in all, in geological terms, Tolkien's descriptions and pictures of Middle-earth are of a world that, geologically at least, is very like our own."

Tolkien's landscapes in *The Hobbit* and *The Lord of the Rings* are the most recent in the development of Middle-earth. It is one of Tolkien's lesser known works, *The Silmarillion*, that provides the strongest evidence for the tectonic history of Middle-earth. The major tectonic changes wrought on Tolkien's world deduced from each chapter of *The Silmarillion* are given in **Table 1** in the form of a stratigraphic sequence – the oldest at the bottom, the youngest at the top: the way a geologist sees the world. The sequence of chapters shows not only a sequence of significant tectonic events, but also that these episodes occur at both 'regional' and 'global' scales, and are interspersed with periods of relative tectonic quiescence, just as occurred on the 'real' Earth, and, as shall be shown later, in New Zealand in particular.

Three 'ages' are identified in *The Silmarillion* and the paleogeography of the world deduced subsequently by cartographer Karen Fonstad at these times forms the basis of a similar variation of tectonism with time, shown in **Table 2**.

Table 1. Major tectonic events inferred in *The Silmarillion*

Time as chapter in *The Silmarillion*	Regions				
	Western lands (Aman)	Belegaer (Sundering Seas)	Middle-earth		
			North	West (Beleriand)	East
Rings of Power …					■ Volcanism in Mordor
Akallabêth	■ Aman and Eressëa (Valinor) 'taken away'	■ Númenor develops and then founders			
XXIV			■ Thangorodrim 'ruined'; mines of Morgoth unroofed	■ Beleriand founders	■ Volcanism in Mordor (inferred by Fonstad 1991)
XXIII					
XXII					
XXI				*Climatic deterioration*	
XX			■ Eruptions of Thangorodrim		
XIX				■ Beleriand 'ruined', since near to volcanoes	
XVIII			■ Iron Mountains erupt		
XVII				□	
XVI			□	□	
XV			□	□	
XIV					
XIII			■ Siege of Angband; Iron Mountains erupt		
XII	□				
XI	■ Pelóri further elevated				
X				□	
IX			■ Volcanism at Angband		
VIII	■ Foundering of part of Valinor				
VII				□	
VI					
V	■ Gap made in Pelóri	■ 'Island ferry' (see text)			
IV				□	□
III			■ volcanism; siege of Utumno		□
II					
I	■ Pelóri Mounts elevated		■ Melkor 'builds' Utmno fortress		

Legend for ages	
Third	
Second	
First	

Inferred extent of orogeny / tectonism	
'Local'	■
'Regional'	■
'Global'	■
Tectonic quiescence	□

Table 2. Analogues for tectonism inferred from Fonstad's chronology

	Middle-earth event *	Geological inference	Regime†
THIRD AGE	Mordor active	Volcanism active at Mordor	■◄
	New lands to the west	Sea-floor spreading active in Belegaer	◄►
SECOND AGE	Valinor 'taken away'		
	Last of Beleriand is submerged		
	Númenor 'falls'		
	The raising from the depths of the sea of Númenor	Intraplate volcanism; or incipient initiation of a plate boundary	◄►
	Further raising of the Pelóri; further darkening of the Shadowy Seas		■
	'Convulsion' of lands to NW, i.e., most of Beleriand; breaching of Blue Mts to form Gulf of Lune; formation of Tower Hills and west-east ridge of Ered Luin	Rise in sea-level and or collapse of ocean floor (rifting?)	◄►
The Great Battle	Destruction of Thangorodrim in the War of Wrath		■
The western Road	Possible destruction of Ered Engrin during War of Wrath	Rapid erosion?	□
... and the return to Endor	Valar raise Pelóri higher	Orogeny	■
	Melkor escapes to Midde Earth; piles the towers of Thangorodrim (the highest peak in Middle-earth) at gates of Angband	Massive volcanism (edifice 5 miles in base diameter and 35,000 feet high)	■
	Valar opens the deep chasm (the Calacirya) to light Eressëa	Tectonic quiescence, with erosion dominant?	□
The Noontide of Valinor ...	Uprooting of the island; the point NE to the Bay of Balar, the greater portion SW to the Bay of Eldamar – Tol Eressëa – the Lonely Isle	Migration and accretion of "exotic terranes"	►◄
The Awakening of the Elves and the Second Great Battle	New rivers, e.g., Sirion	Drainage of 'new' lands derived from rapid erosion of mountains	□
	Echoriath – a two-stage gigantic active volcano	Orogeny, mountain-building and contemporaneous active erosion	■
	Raising of central highlands of Dorthonion and Hithlum; Iron Mountains distorted and broken		
	Eastern end of Great Gulf merges with Sea of Helcar	Sea-floor spreading	◄►
	Belegaer widens and deepens		
	Valar 'break land to the northeast, thence to Utumno'		■
	Elves awake at Cuviénen, "an eastern bay of the Inland sea of Helcar, formed by meltwaters of the pillar of Illium."		□

	Middle-earth event *	Geological inference	Regime†
The Spring of Arda and the settling of Aman	Melkor raises the Hithaeglir - Mountains of Mist (S, p. 34), probably also Ered Nimrais (the White Mountains)	Orogeny	■
	Valar raise the Pelóri mountains as defence	Orogeny in western lands	■
	The Valar settle Aman, west of the Belegaer (the Sundering Seas)		□
	Ossë ferries Valar to the West, perhaps using the 'island ferry' that was later used to carry the Elves	"Exotic terranes" (for explanation, see text)	►◄
	Melkor 'struck the lights of Illuin and Ormal'; Almaren destroyed	Volcanic eruptions, the resulting calderas are the Sea of Helcar and the Sea of Ringol	■
	Either Ered Engrin or the Iron Mountains, raised by Melkor as "a fence to his citadel" of Utumno	Orogeny (Ered Engrin said to be "block-faulted")	■
	Valar set the 'lanterns' – mountains – at Illuin and Ormal	Possible minor volcanism to north and south of the Great Lake	□
FIRST AGE	Valar settle on Isle of Almaren in Great Lake	Almaren may be an island within a volcanic derived lake (akin to Mokoia Island in Lake Rotorua)	□
In the Beginning	Melkor routed to the Outer Darkness (but his influence continues)		
	Arda a scene of conflict between the 'building' by Valar and the 'destroying' by Melkor		■

* Derived from Fonstad.
† Times of inferred tectonic quiescence are shown as □; tectonically vigorous times are shown as: ◄► for extensional regimes; ►◄ for inter-plate collisional regimes; ■◄ for subduction-related tectonism; ■ for orogeny where tectonic regime is unspecified.

Features of Middle-earth Tectonism

The northern realms of Tolkien's world, the stronghold of Melkor, are the most tectonically active. A land of mountain ranges and volcanoes, hosting mines of "divers metals", it seems likely to be subduction-related. The description of the eruptions of Thangorodrim as "great rivers of flame that ran down swifter than Balrogs, and poured over the plain [...] [which] became a burned and desolate waste, full of choking dust, barren and lifeless" (*S* 151) is highly suggestive of pyroclastic flows (e.g., the central North Island of New Zealand). This style of volcanism is characteristic of volcanoes in subduction settings, where one tectonic plate is pushed and/or pulled beneath another. The numerous ranges across the region in a generally east-west orientation suggest repeated orogeny caused by subduction directed to the north or northeast.

In turn, this might suggest that the Belegaer (or Sundering Seas), a prominent feature of the first two ages, might be underlain by a spreading centre. This idea is supported by the re-growth of the Meneltarma – the central peak of the island of Númenor, destroyed at the end of the Second Age, for which an analogy has been drawn with the myth of the destruction of Atlantis (Day 15) – atop the 'Great Rift' (Fonstad 52). Being borne westwards on the plate to the west of this mid-ocean rift seems the likely mechanism of the western lands of Aman and Eressëa being "taken away" at the end of the Second Age. Tolkien's Second Age is inferred to have been one of widespread tectonic activity, following on from the tumultuous events at the end of the First Age, which included Beleriand becoming the 'Lands Under the Waves' (Fonstad 38). Rather than being attributed to sea-level rise (or climate change), the cataclysmic description of the demise of Beleriand suggests its foundering is a consequence of widespread tectonism:

> the northern region of the western world was rent asunder and the sea roared in through many chasms and there was confusion and great noise; and rivers perished or found new paths; and the valleys were upheaved and the hills trod down and [the river] Sirion was no more. (*S* 252)

Much earlier, in the First Age, plate movement associated with the precursor of the Belegaer rift may likewise be an explanation for some of the movements of the 'Island Ferry', an event which Tolkien describes in the following way (*S* 57):

> Ulmo uprooted an island which had long stood alone amid the sea, far from either shore [...] and with the aid of his servants he moved it, as if it were a mighty ship, and anchored it in the Bay of Balar into which Sirion [river] poured its water. Then the Vanyar and the Noldor embarked upon that isle, and were drawn across the sea, and came at last to the long shores beneath the Mountains of Aman [...] But the eastern horn of the island, which was deep-grounded in the shoals off the mouths of Sirion, was broken asunder and remained behind.

The remainder of the island returned across Belegaer, to be "stood alone in the Bay of Edemar; and it was called Tol Eresseä, the Lonely Isle" (*S* 59).

Although the end-positions of the island fragments resemble the consequences of simple spreading from a mid-ocean rift, the re-location of the Noldor (Elves) to Aman from Beleriand requires that the portion of the island fated to be Tol Eresseä journeyed from Balar in the opposite direction to that inferred for initial plate motion in Belegaer and its successor sea. The most probable explanation is a northerly migration of the axis of the west-east orientation of the spreading centre. Where the locations of the plate boundaries are uncertain, geologists have referred to the regions subject to these types of movements as "exotic terranes". Van Andel (163) has pointed out that "the idea of exotic terranes has caught the fancy of many a geologist concerned with the Pacific, and examples have multiplied like rabbits [...]", asserting that "to a surprising degree geologists are romantics." Tol Eresseä could represent such an exotic terrane.

In fact, there is a suggestion that the Island Ferry may have been used previously: to ferry the Valar to Valinor. Thus, two episodes involving exotic terranes may have taken place there. The movement of terranes across the planet borne on the tectonic plates that comprise the Earth's surface, so that rocks of varying ages become adjacent to each other and ultimately joined ("accreted") to each other, has become an accepted explanation

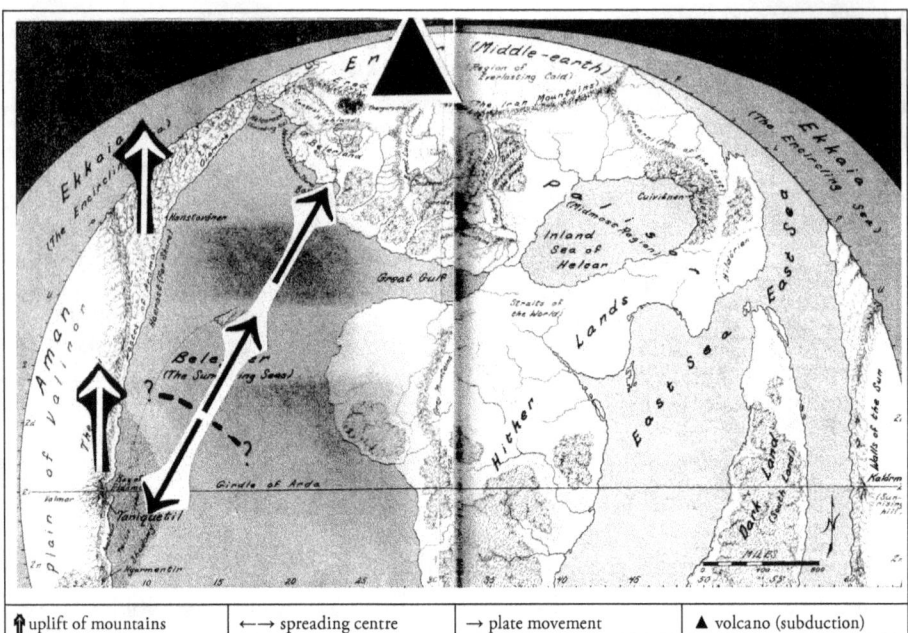

Figure 6. Tectonics of the First Age – I, modified from Fonstad (4). The early movement of the Island Ferry requires a northward spreading of the Belegaer from a rift to the south, in an unspecified location. During this time there is presumably oblique subduction to the West enabling the raising of the ranges of the Pelóri. There is subduction-related volcanism in the North.

among geologists. As is discussed later, there are two episodes of terrane accumulation in New Zealand's geological history which can be seen to parallel the two episodes of terrane migration and accumulation required for Middle-earth.

During the Third Age, at the end of which the events described in *The Hobbit* and *The Lord of the Rings* take place, tectonic activity is confined to Mordor. This volcanic region is considered by Fonstad to be located in the area shown in the First Age as the Inland Sea of Helcar. She asserts its existence in the Second Age, although conceding there is no textual evidence for this. There seems no particular reason to require its initiation as a region of tectonic significance before the end of the Second Age; indeed, it is reasonable to

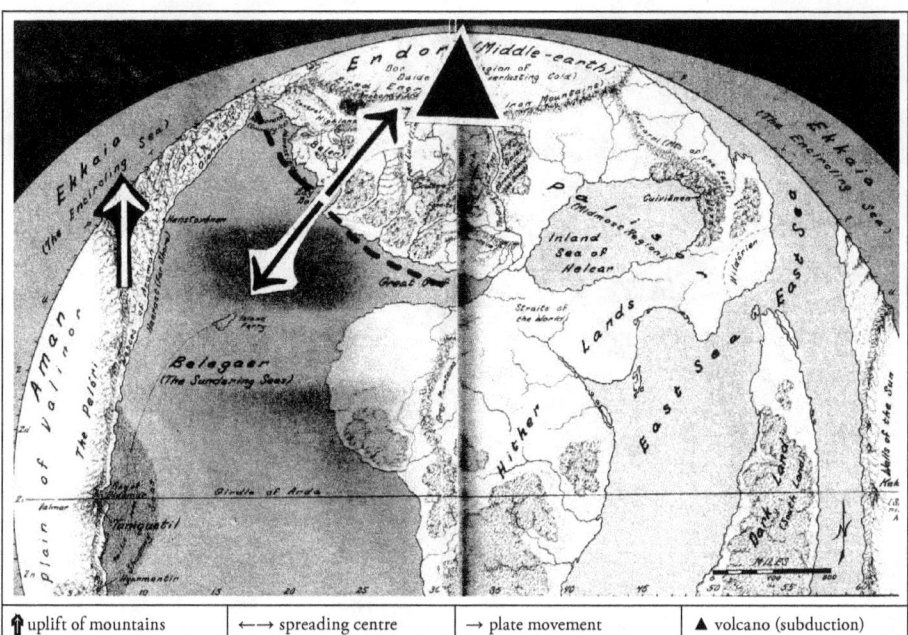

| ⇑ uplift of mountains | ←→ spreading centre | → plate movement | ▲ volcano (subduction) |

Figure 7. Tectonics of the First Age – II, modified from Fonstad (4). The later movement of the Island Ferry requires the rift or spreading centre to have taken up a new position close to the coast of the Great Gulf and the Bay of Balar, in order to return the Island Ferry to become Tol Eresseä. Subduction-related volcanism to the northeast and orogeny (mountain-building) in the west continue.

suggest that its initiation might be a consequence of the "global" tectonism characterising the onset of the Third Age.

Thus, textual analysis of *The Silmarillion* reveals that within each of the three ages the landscape undergoes significant changes. Fonstad's paleogeographic maps of Middle-earth (Fonstad 4), overprinted with inferred tectonic regimes from **Table 1** and **Table 2**, are shown for Tolkien's First Age on **Figure 6** and **Figure 7**.

Fonstad's paleogeographic maps of Middle-earth (Fonstad 38, 62), overprinted with inferred tectonic regimes from **Table 1** and **Table 2**, are shown for Tolkien's Second Age on **Figure 8**, and his Third Age on **Figure 9**, respectively.

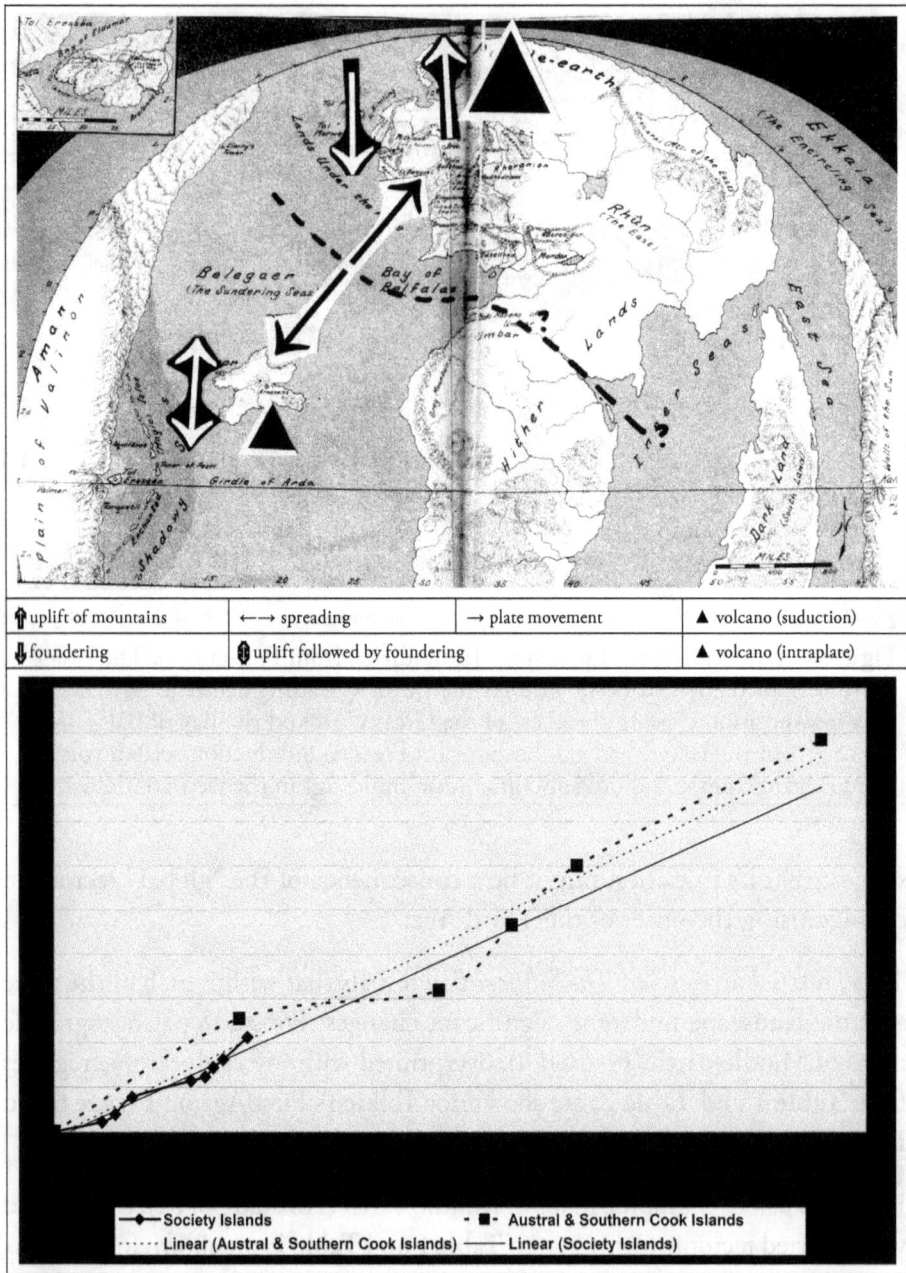

Figure 8. *Above:* Tectonics of the Second Age, modified from Fonstad (38). Here the spreading centre may have migrated south somewhat in order for Beleriand to be able to founder at the end of the age: subsidence is common in

Figure 8. (*continued*) extensional settings. Uplift and subduction-related volcanism continue in the north. Númenor is likely to be a plume-related volcano which, once carried by plate movement away from the upwelling mantle source which "feeds" the volcano, subsides beneath the sea.

Below: To the northeast of New Zealand are the Society Islands whose ages increase with distance away from Mehetia (a historically active volcano), and the Southern Cook Islands which give a less clear relationship of age with distance from the volcanically active Macdonald seamount. These relationships suggest the Pacific plate has been travelling across stationary mantle plume in the mantle – weaknesses in the oceanic crust through which mantle-derived melts are erupted. (Plotted data from McDougall & Duncan 275).

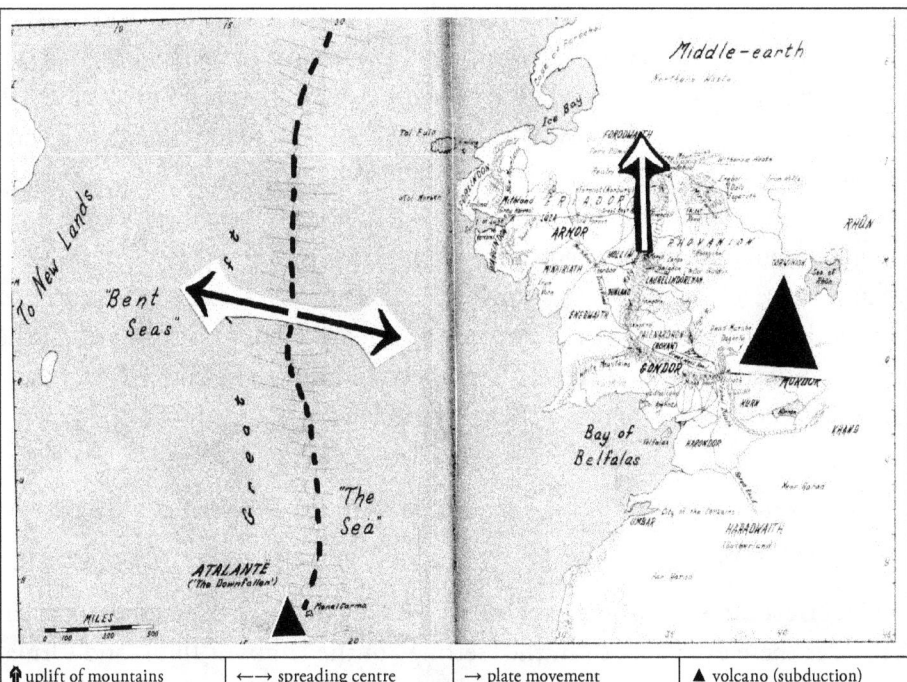

⇑ uplift of mountains | ←→ spreading centre | → plate movement | ▲ volcano (subduction)

Figure 9. Tectonics of the Third Age, modified from Fonstad (62). The spreading centre is now aligned roughly north-south, with subduction occurring beneath the landmasses to west (the "new lands") and east. Uplift of mountains probably continues along the line of the Misty Mountains, with active volcanism in Mordor. In the south, the island of Meneltarma is likely to be a small volcano associated with the mid-oceanic rift ("Great Rift"), a spreading centre.

That these maps are very different implies profound changes to the landscape within and between the "ages". Thus, Middle-earth can be inferred to be tectonically active throughout its geological history. Furthermore, if the imagined landscape were to be realised, an analogy with an actual region of Earth that had been tectonically active might be appropriate. Of course, there are many parts of the planet that would serve this purpose: New Zealand is but one.

Correlation of Tectonism in Middle-earth with New Zealand

New Zealand has been at a plate boundary for most of its existence, initially rifting away from Gondwanaland, and thereafter being subject to a number of tectonic episodes of varying intensity before assuming its present configuration. A correlation between Fonstad's interpretations with significant events in New Zealand's geotectonic history as summarised for the past 500 million years in tabular form (Thornton rear cover) is given in **Table 3**, showing a history of the tectonic plates alternating between being compressed (associated with mountain-building) and extended (sea-floor spreading), interspersed with periods of quiescence (characterized by sedimentation). This correlation is complemented by another interpretation of New Zealand's geotectonic history spanning the last 65 million years in **Table 4** (King 611). In both these correlations, there are several strong 'tie-points', as described below.

Correlation of the "striking" of the lamps of Illuin and Ormal with the Tuhua Orogeny

This correlation is uncertain, but is suggested by the relative quiescence which precedes these events: both in the "setting" of the lamps at Illuin and Ormal in Middle-earth, and in eastern Gondwanaland.

Correlation of first movement of Island Ferry with the Rangitata Orogeny

The earlier movement of the 'Island Ferry' might be correlated with the Permian-Cretaceous accretion of terranes around 140 million years ago. This culminated

Table 3. Correlation of tectonics of Middle-earth and New Zealand for the last 500 million years

MIDDLE-EARTH	
Event	Regime
Volcanism at Mordor	■◄
New lands to west	◄►
Valinor 'taken away'	
Last of Beleriand is submerged	
Númenor 'falls'	
The raising from the depths of the sea of Númenor	◄►
Further raising of the Pelóri	■
'Convulsion' of lands to NW, i.e., most of Beleriand	◄►
Destruction of Thangorodrim	■
Possible destruction of Ered Engrin during War of Wrath	□
Valar raise Pelóri higher	■
Melkor escapes to Midde Earth; makes Thangorodrim	■
Valar opens the deep chasm (the Calacirya) to light Eressëa	□
Uprooting of the island; Tol Eressëa – the Lonely Isle	►◄
New rivers, e.g., Sirion	□
Echoriath – gigantic volcano	■
Raising of central highlands of Dorthonion and Hithlum	
Eastern end of Great Gulf merges with Sea of Helcar	◄►
Belegaer widens and deepens	
Valar break land to the northeast, thence to Utumno	■
Elves awake at Cuviénen	□
Melkor raises the Hithaeglir - Mountains of Mist	■
Valar raise the Pelóri mounts	■
The Valar settle Aman,	□
Ossë ferries Valar to the West	►◄
Melkor 'struck the lights' of Illuin and Ormal'; Almaren destroyed	■
Melkor raises "fence to his citadel" of Utumno	■
Valar set the 'lanterns' of Illuin and Ormal	□
Valar settle Isle of Almaren	□
Melkor routed	
Arda a scene of conflict between 'building' by Valar and 'destroying' by Melkor	■

NEW ZEALAND		
Regime	Age *	Event †
■◄	5 – 0 Ma	Kaimai Tectonic Event
◄►	From 5 Ma	Opening of Le Havre Trough
■◄		Stretching, rotation and uplift
□	11 – 5 Ma	Sedimentation and basin-filling Sedimentation and basin-filling
■◄	10 Ma	Volcanism
►◄ ■◄	19 – 16 Ma	Kiwitahi Tectonic Event
►◄ ■◄	From 23 Ma	Waitemata Tectonc Event
□	65 – 23 Ma	"Going grey" † "Going under" ‡
	65 Ma	Cretaceous/Tertiary boundary
◄►	85 Ma	Tasman Sea rifts
◄►	95 Ma	Fractures, rifts
■◄	142 – 65 Ma	Sedimentation, like Torlesse
■◄	140 Ma	Rangitata Orogeny
►◄	248 – 142 Ma	Collision of *Murihiku* and *Torlesse* terranes
□ ■◄		*Muri-hiku* Rocks / *Torlesse* Rocks
■◄ □	290 – 248 Ma	
■◄	370 – 354 Ma	Tuhua Orogeny
□	417 – 370 Ma	Sedimentation
□	443 – 417 Ma	Sedimentation in east
□	490 – 443 Ma	Shallow sedimentation in east, deeper in west
►◄ □	540 – 490 Ma	Ultramafic and granites in collision zone

* in millions of years
† prolonged sedimentation episode
‡ prolonged submergence under ocean

Table 4. Correlation of tectonics of Middle-earth and New Zealand for the last 65 million years

MIDDLE-EARTH	
Event	Regime
Volcanism at Mordor	■◄
New lands to west	◄►
Valinor 'taken away'	
Last of Beleriand is submerged	
Númenor 'falls'	
The raising from the depths of the sea of Númenor	◄►
Further raising of the Pelóri	■
'Convulsion' of lands to NW, i.e., most of Beleriand	◄►
Destruction of Thangorodrim	■
Possible destruction of Ered Engrin during War of Wrath	□
Valar raise Pelóri higher	■
Melkor escapes to Midde-earth; makes Thangorodrim	■
Valar opens the deep chasm (the Calacirya) to light Eressëa	□
Uprooting of the island; Tol Eressëa – the Lonely Isle	►◄
New rivers, e.g., Sirion	□
Echoriath – gigantic volcano	■
Raising of central highlands of Dorthonion and Hithlum	
Eastern end of Great Gulf merges with Sea of Helcar	◄►
Belegaer widens and deepens	
Valar break land to the northeast, thence to Utumno	■
Elves awake at Cuviénen,	□
Melkor raises the Hithaeglir – Mountains of Mist	■
Geological history continues …	

NEW ZEALAND		
Regime	Age *	Event †
◄► ■◄	0 Ma Present	Extension in N; subduction, & compression
◄► ■	5 Ma Base Pliocene	Extension and subduction volcanism
■◄	10 Ma Late Miocene	Volcanic arc active
◄► ■◄	20 Ma Early Miocene	Norfolk Basin opens
□	25 Ma Late Oligocene	Extension to north; widespread sedimentation
■◄ ►◄ □	40 Ma Middle Eocene	Incipient subduction; Rifting, but also widespread sedimentation
□ ◄►	55 Ma Latest Paleocene	Post-rift passive margin; foundering implies extension
◄►	65 Ma Latest Cretaceous	Separation of NZ from Gondwanaland
Geological history continues …		
* in millions of years		

in episodes of uplift and reduced sedimentation, which is recognized in New Zealand's geological history as the Rangitata Orogeny.

Correlation of the widening of Belegaer with the break-up of Gondwanaland

This major episode in New Zealand's geological history has been described as its becoming "a place of our own" (Thornton 105). The spreading of the sea-floor as New Zealand separated from Australia and Antarctica can be considered analogues of the widening of Belegaer. Under such a tectonic regime the Echoriath is more likely to result from rift-related volcanism than from a subduction-related eruption like that from the Crater Lake in Montana (Fonstad 22).

Correlation of the transition between First and Second Age with the Waitemata Tectonic Event

There was a significant change to the configuration of plate boundaries in New Zealand around 25 million years ago (Kamp 65), which has been recently interpreted as the Waitemata Tectonic Event (Kear 361). Collision between the Pacific and Indo-Australian plates occurred then, but, perhaps more importantly, this is the time of the emplacement of the "allocthons" (rocks moved some distance from their original place of deposition) in Northland and East Cape – the northernmost and easternmost parts of the North Island. In these allocthons, rocks of very different ages ("terranes") are found in unexpected locations: sometimes younger rocks underlie older ones. "Terranes" are described in New Zealand as amalgamating about 120-150 million years ago (Adams *et al.* 235), with accretion starting much earlier (mid Permian), and possibly continuing to the mid-Cretaceous (Howell 487). However, there are also similar younger episodes of lateral movement of continental fragments which seem responsible for the East Coast Allocthon, around 15 million years ago (Bradshaw 375), and the older Northland Allocthon in the Oligocene, about 25 million years ago (Ballance and Spörli 259; Bradshaw 375). This corresponds to diverse and widespread tectonic events in Middle-earth at the end of the First Age, of which Christopher Tolkien (*The Children of Húrin*, dust-jacket) wrote in 2007:

> There are tales of Middle-earth from times long before *The Lord of the Rings*, and the story told in this book [*The Children of Húrin*] is set in the great country beyond the Grey Havens in the West where Treebeard once walked, but which were drowned in the great cataclysm that ended the First Age of the World.

Correlation of end of the Second Age with Kiwitahi Tectonic Event

The construction and destruction of Thangorodrim and the possible destruction of the Ered Engrin are suggestive of a time of high tectonic intensity, and seem consistent with a renewed pulse of New Zealand volcanism around 15 million years ago. This tectonic event may be more widespread than just in New Zealand (Cambray and Cadet 145), suggesting that the raising of the Pelóri may, for example, be a similar type of episode. This transition represents perhaps the most dramatic change to the geology of Middle-earth. The onset of volcanism at the end of the First Age, culminating in the destruction of Thangarodrim, was followed by the "foundering" of Beleriand, which comprised much of the lands to the east of the Belegaer Sea.

Correlation of Third Age with Kaimai Tectonic Event

The volcanism of Mordor, the only evidence of tectonic activity apparent in *The Hobbit* and *The Lord of the Rings*, can be associated with volcanism of the central North Island of New Zealand, specifically Mount Ruapehu. This is the most recent of the three episodes of volcanism within the Kaimai Tectonic Event with an age-range of 5-2.5 million years (Kear 361). This subduction-dominated tectonic regime was preceded by episodes of rifting northwest of New Zealand and stretching, rotation and uplift. This type of environment could lead, on the one hand, to lands being "taken away", i.e. moved, to downwarping and submergence on the other.

The end of the "Third Age" brings us to the present-day, for which the current tectonic setting of New Zealand is shown in **Figure 10**.

Realising an Imagined World

Finding analogies between the real and the imagined is important in the planning stages of a film. The making of *The Lord of the Rings* trilogy provided an opportunity for New Zealand film-maker Peter Jackson to consider New Zealand as Middle-earth. In seeking appropriate landscapes Jackson is recorded (Brodie 13) as saying:

> The way the location process works is that generally a location scout goes out in advance and canvasses the whole country for potential places. We made up a list of what we needed, which obviously came from the book because Tolkien describes the locations very vividly in *The Lord of the Rings*. You can just imagine them in your mind's eye so it was pretty mandatory for the location scouts to read the book. [...] So while there were a whole lot of

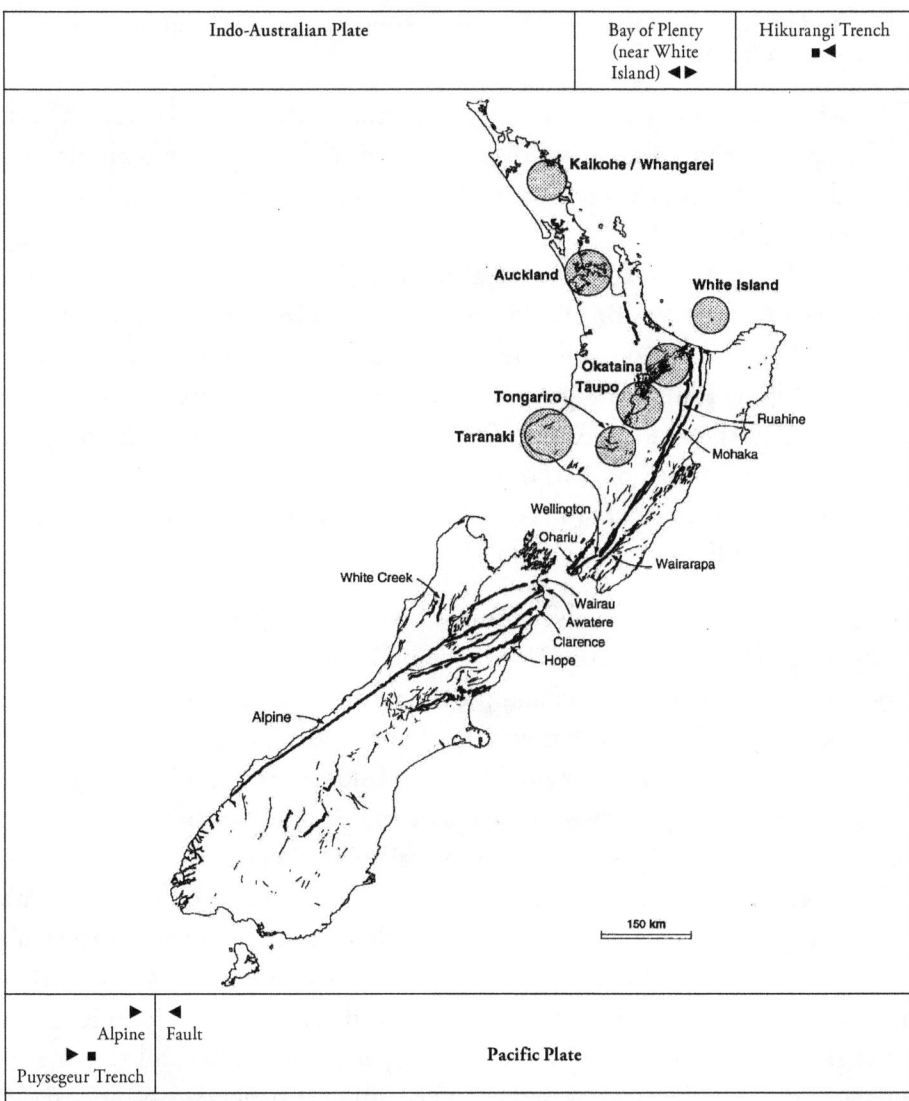

Figure 10. New Zealand at the boundary between the Pacfic and Indo-Australian Plate. Volcanic centres are shown as circles. Those in the centre of the North Island are fed from magma formed by the melting of the Pacific plate being subducted to the west at the Hikurangi Trench. Volcanoes at Auckland and Kaikohe/Whangarei are not subduction-related, but are "hotspots" – small versions of the Hawaiian Islands. The major fault lines passing through both North and South Islands are related to the transpressional boundary between the Indo-Australian and Pacific Plates. An extensional regime is developing "behind" the subduction zone in the Bay of Plenty to the north. Note the opposing, i.e. easterly, direction of subduction of the Indo-Australian plate beneath the Pacific Plate to the south.

considerations, first and foremost the question was always 'is this like it was described in the book?'

The active volcano of Ruapehu in the central North Island – even though not erupting at the time of filming *The Lord of the Rings* – was an obvious candidate to be cast as Mount Doom, with the surrounding volcanic landscape as Mordor (Brodie 31). The eroding pastoral landscapes of soft geologically young volcanic rocks near the rural township of Matamata were deemed evocative of the Shire (Brodie 15), while the rushing streams in the South Island's glacially carved landscape – a consequence of rapid uplift associated with the Alpine Fault (see **Figure 10**) – seemed highly appropriate for "facing the Nazgul at the Ford of Bruinen" (Brodie 87). These landscapes and their geology – the heritage of eons of tectonic activity – are but a few examples that serve to justify Tourism New Zealand's billboard: "Two years to film the trilogy; millions of years to build the set" (Thompson 314).

A masterstroke in portraying New Zealand as Middle-earth could be considered to be the promotional map – "New Zealand home of Middle-earth" – developed by Film New Zealand (Thompson plate 11), and likely modelled on one of Tolkien's Middle-earth that was developed and sold by Weta Workshops ("Lord of the Rings Parchment Map of Middle-earth"). The typography used, the sailing ships shown to the north and west of North Island, and the icons that represent filmed locations are all reminiscent of medieval maps, while the compass rose is probably as close a replica of that used in Tolkien's map as copyright permits (**Figure 11**). McNaughton (xii) describes the map as showing the "film locations and production activity medievalised so that the whole project was given a pre-industrial, if not exactly Neolithic, aura, with the workers identified as tanners, coopers, and the like, all floating in nomadic space." Of course, as Barker and Mathijs (110) reiterate, New Zealand was never like this, even if Europe in the Middle Ages was.

On an early version of the "New Zealand Home of Middle-earth" website, for example, producer Barry Osborne described actors and staff as "being engulfed in this landscape and in this wonderful happy village of Hobbiton [which] for all intents and purposes was very real and really existed", while Ian McKellen who acted the role of Gandalf said on the same website, "Middle-

Figure 11. Poster: New Zealand Home of Middle-earth

earth is a real place and it's New Zealand." In a later commentary, Porter (69) expressed similar sentiments:

> The country's geographic diversity accords with the vision of a legion of readers who love Tolkien's book (although complaints that New Zealand has appropriated an essentially English story continue to divide groups of book and film aficionados). To those with no prior experience of Tolkien's masterwork, New Zealand's rich landscape creates a memorable sensory experience. The lushness of the area close to Matamata replicates the near-idyllic Shire of Frodo's young hobbithood. The breathtaking glory of the Southern Alps

presents a formidable winter challenge, not only for Hobbits but drivers, hikers and skiers. The lonely silence complementing the view of plains and mountains from Mount Sunday echoes Éowyn's inner fears and longings. So many individual places within the country resemble Tolkien's description that audiences who fell in love with Middle-earth shown on screen decided they wanted to visit the country where filming occurred.

Thum (231) claims that Peter Jackson and his film production team have successfully made a sub-creation of Tolkien's work; certainly Carl (151) considers tourism interests appear to think so. The actors' identification with New Zealand as Middle-earth was seen by Wiggins (107) as giving them a part in that creation, an implicit longing inferred as present in all human beings. Tolkien would likely be horrified: on the one hand believing that fantasy should be left for the imagination and the written word, with no place in the animated visual arts such as in cinema or theatre (Birzer 38); and on the other asserting that God was the author of the history of Middle-earth (Birzer 25). By implication, Middle-earth is more than a mere reality: it is a God-created world, through the invention of which Tolkien, as its sub-creator, is "worshipping God more effectively than the mere realist" (Shippey 34).

However, the sub-created world becomes imperfect: natural assets are wasted, opportunities are foregone, and advantages are lost. This makes Jackson's sub-creation of New Zealand as a setting for *The Lord of the Rings* even more pertinent. Once heralded as "God's own country" (Bracken 5), New Zealand could be considered to have "fallen". For example, there has been environmental degradation since European settlement introduced farming practices that turned native forests on the North Island's young volcanic landscape around the Waikato town of Matamata into rolling downlands reminiscent of England, and, thereby, Tolkien's Shire. New Zealanders have destroyed habitats for unique flora and fauna, dammed rivers for irrigation and electricity generation, and extracted coal and gold to feed a resource-hungry nation and world. However, there may yet be a way of forestalling the "fall" for New Zealand as Middle-earth — through the "eucatasprophe" proposed by Tolkien himself (OFS 60). This could take the form of adopting a philosophy of sustainability (*Creating our Future: Sustainable Development of New Zealand*), but would need political will ("Environment Commissioner Welcomes National Reporting Plans"). Thus, while the sub-created Middle-earth may be more than real, regrettably, New Zealand is merely real.

Conclusion

An analysis of Tolkien's *The Silmarillion*, the precursor in time to *The Hobbit* and *The Lord of the Rings* identifies episodes of volcanism, submergence of landscapes, the raising of mountains and the movement of islands, which is highly suggestive of Middle-earth being a region that geologists would describe as "tectonically active". This enables correlations with significant tectonic episodes in New Zealand's geological history, thereby strengthening the identification of Middle-earth landscapes with those in New Zealand that were highlighted in Peter Jackson's film trilogy *The Lord of the Rings*.

Correlations between the tectonic regimes of Middle-earth and New Zealand could not be expected to be perfect. However, there is an alternation and variation in the inferred style and intensity of tectonics of Middle-earth that is certainly more in keeping with the dynamic geological history of New Zealand than it is with many other landscapes that have been proposed as analogues to Middle-earth. If nothing else it provides a geological justification – if it was needed – for the choice of New Zealand as the landscape settings for *The Lord of the Rings* film trilogy and for the succeeding films of *The Hobbit*.

About the author

Peter Hodder's research interests in the geochemistry and tectonics of volcanic landscapes developed while he was at the University of Waikato (Hamilton, New Zealand). They are here joined with elements of his more recent research in the history and sociology of science, including the different ways in which those versed in arts and science perceive the world about them. He is currently based at Victoria University of Wellington – at the centre of Middle-earth.

Bibliography

ADAMS, Chris. J., Hamish J. Campbell, Ian J. Graham and Nick Mortimer. "Torlesse, Waipapa and Caples Exotic Terranes of New Zealand: Integrated Studies of Their Geological History in Relation to Neighbouring Terranes." *Episodes* 21 (1998): 235-240.

BALLANCE, John D. and Bernard Spörli. "Northland Allocthon." *Journal of the Royal Society of New Zealand* 9 (1979): 259-275.

BARKER, Martin and Ernest Mathijs. "Seeing the Promised Land from Afar: The Perception of New Zealand by Overseas *The Lord of the Rings* Audiences." *How We Became Middle-earth: A Collection of Essays on The Lord of the Rings.* Eds. Adam Lam and Nataliya Oryshchuk. Zurich and Berne: Walking Tree Publishers, 2007. 107-128.

BIRZER, Brad. *J.R.R. Tolkien's Sanctifying Myth: Understanding Middle-earth.* Wilmington DL: ISI Books, 2003.

BRACKEN, Thomas. "God's Own Country." In *Lays and Lyrics: God's Own Country and Other Poems.* Wellington: Brown, Thomson and Co., 1893. 5-9.

BRADSHAW, John D. "Northland Allocthon: An alternative hypothesis of origin." *New Zealand Journal of Geology and Geophysics* 47 (2004): 375-382.

BREEN, Rosalie. "In the Land of Mordor Where the Shadows Lie." *AUSGEO News* 66 (2002): 14-15.

BRODIE, Ian. *The Lord of the Rings Location Guidebook.* 2nd edition. Auckland: HarperCollins, 2002.

BROTTON, Jerry. *A History of the World in Twelve Maps.* London: Penguin, 2013.

CAMBRAY, Herve and Jean-Paul Cadet. "Testing Global Synchronism in Peri-Pacific Volcanism." *Journal of Volcanology and Geothermal Research* 63 (1994): 145-164.

CAMPBELL, Alice M. "Maps." *J.R.R. Tolkien Encyclopedia. Scholarship and Critical Assessment.* Ed. Michael D.C. Drout. New York: Routledge, 2007. 405-408.

CARL, Daniela S. *Cultural Representation of New Zealand's Landscapes in the Films of The Lord of the Rings and its Implications for Tourism.* MSc Thesis. Victoria University of Wellington, 2004.

Creating our Future: Sustainable Development for New Zealand. Wellington, Parliamentary Commissioner for the Environment, 2002.

DAY, David. *Tolkien's Ring.* London: HarperCollins, 1994.

EKMAN, Stefan. *Here Be Dragons. Exploring Fantasy Maps and Settings.* Middletown CT: Wesleyan University, 2013.

"Environment Commissioner Welcomes National Reporting Plans" 20 February 2014. 2 April 2014. < http://www.pce.parliament.nz/media/media-releases/environment-commissioner-welcomes-national-reporting-plans/>

FONSTAD, Karen. *The Atlas of Middle-earth.* Revised edition. London: Grafton, 1991.

FRIEDRICH, Walter L. *Fire in the Sea: the Santorini Volcano: Natural History and the Legend of Atlantis.* Cambridge: Cambridge University Press, 2000.

GALANOPAULAS, Angelos G. and Edward Bacon. *Atlantis: The Truth Behind the Legend.* London: Nelson, 1969.

GILLIS, John R. *Islands of the Mind: How the Human Imagination Created the Atlantic World.* London: PalgraveMacmillan, 2004.

GROTTA, Daniel. *J.R.R. Tolkien Architect of Middle Earth.* Philadelphia: Running Press, 1992.

HESS, Harry Hammond. "History of Ocean Basins." *A Volume to Honour A.F. Buddington.* Eds. A.E.J. Engel, Harold L. James and B.F. Leonard. Boulder: Geological Society of America, 1962. 599-620.

HOLDEN, John C. and Peter R. Vogt. "Graphic Solutions to the Problem of Plumacy." *EOS: Transactions of the American Geophysical Union* 58 (1977): 573-580.

HOLMES, Arthur. *Principles of Physical Geology.* London: Nelson, 1944.

HOWELL, David G. "Mesozoic Accretion of Exotic Terranes Along the New Zealand Segment of Gondwanaland." *Geology* 8 (1980): 487-491.

KAMP, Peter J.J. "Late Oligocene Pacific-wide Tectonic Event." *Terra Nova* 3 (1991): 65-69.

KEAR, David. "Reassessment of Neogene Tectonism and Volcanism in North Island, New Zealand." *New Zealand Journal of Geology and Geophysics* 47 (2004): 361-374.

KING, Peter R. "Tectonic Reconstruction of New Zealand: 40 ma to Present." *New Zealand Journal of Geology and Geophysics* 43 (2000): 611-635. [These descriptions with accompanying maps are also available at <http://www.gns.cri.nz/what/earthhist/nz_origins/paleo/index.html>]

LAM, Adam and Nataliya Oryshchuk (eds.). *How We Became Middle-earth: A Collection of Essays on The Lord of the Rings.* Zurich and Berne: Walking Tree Publishers, 2007.

Langworthy, Alan P. and Lance P. Black. "The Mordor Complex: a Highly Differentiated Potassic Intrusion with Kimberlitic Affinities in Central Australia." *Contributions to Mineralogy and Petrology* 67 (1978): 1-62.

"*Lord of the Rings* Parchment Map of Middle-earth." 6 February 2014. <http://www.mightyape.com.au/product/Lord-of-the-Rings-Parchment-Map-of-Middle-Earth-by-Weta/20679357>

McDougall, Ian and R.A. Duncan. "Linear Volcanic Chains – Recording Plate Motions?" *Tectonophysics* 63 (1980): 275-295.

McNaughton, Howard. "Foreword: Straddling the Date Line in *The Lord of the Rings*." *How We Became Middle-earth: A Collection of Essays on The Lord of the Rings*. Ed. Adam Lam and Nataliya Oryshchuk. Zurich and Berne: Walking Tree Publishers, 2007. vii-xx.

"Mordor Pound: the Geology of Lord Sauron's 'Australian Home'." 2002. 8 February 2014 <http://www.ga.gov.au/about-us/news-media/news-2002/mordor-pound-the-geology-of-lord-saurons-australian-home.html>

"New Zealand Home of Middle-earth." 13 April 2009. <http://www.nzhomeofmiddleearth.com/>

Pike, W.S. "An Appreciation of the Weather in *The Lord of the Rings*." *Weather* 57 (2002): 439-446.

Porter, Lynnette R. "Postcards from the Shire: Global Impressions of New Zealand After *The Lord of the Rings*." *How We Became Middle-earth: A Collection of Essays on The Lord of the Rings*. Ed. Adam Lam and Nataliya Oryshchuk. Zurich and Berne: Walking Tree Publishers, 2007. 67-86.

Radagast the Brown [aka Dan Lunt]. "The Climate of Middle Earth." 4 February 2014. <http://www.bristol.ac.uk/university/media/press/10013-english.pdf>

Ramaswamy, S. *The Lost Land of Lemuria: Fabulous Geographies, Catastrophic Histories*. Berkley, CA: University of California Press, 2004.

Reynolds, Robert C. "The Geomorphology of Middle-earth." *The Swansea Geographer* 11 (1974): 67-71.

Russell, Gary. *The Lord of the Rings: The Art of the Fellowship of the Ring*. London: HarperCollins, 2002.

Sarjeant, William A.S. "The Geology of Middle-earth." *Proceedings of the J.R.R. Tolkien Centenary Conference 1992*. Ed. Patricia Reynolds and Glen H. GoodKnight. *Mythlore* 80 (Milton Keynes) & *Mallorn* 33 (Altadena), 1995. 334-339.

Sclater, Phillip L. 1864. "The Mammals of Madagascar." *Quarterly Journal of Science* 1 (1864): 213-219.

"Second Annual Report for EL25101 Mordor West Period Ending 20/11/2008." Rum Jungle Uranium Ltd. 11 February 2014. <http://www.geoscience.nt.gov.au/ntgsjsput/bitstream/1/74834/1/EL25101_2008_A.pdf>

SHIPPEY, Thomas A. *The Road to Middle-Earth*. London: Grafton, 1992.

SPRAGUE DE CAMP, Lyon. *Lost Continents: The Atlantis Theme in History, Science and Literature*. New York: Dover. 1970.

TAKEUCHI, Hotochi, Seiya Uyeda and Hiroo Kanamori. *Debate About the Earth*. Revised edition. San Francisco: Freeman Cooper, 1970.

TAYLOR, Frank. B. "Bearing of the Tertiary Mountain Belt on the Origins of the Earth's Plan." *Geological Society of America Bulletin* 21 (1910): 179-226.

THOMPSON, Kristin. *The Frodo Franchise. How The Lord of the Rings Became a Hollywood Blockbuster and Put New Zealand on the Map*. Auckland: Penguin, 2007.

THORNTON, Jocelyn. *The Reed Field Guide to New Zealand Geology*. 2nd edition. Auckland: Reed, 2003.

THUM, Maureen. "The Sub-Creation of Galadriel, Arwen and Éowyn: Women of Power in Tolkien's and Jackson's *Lord of the Rings*." *Tolkien on Film: Essays on Peter Jackson's Lord of the Rings*. Ed. Janet Brennan Croft. Altadena CA: Mythopoeic Press, 2004. 231-258.

TOLKIEN, John Ronald Reuel. *The Letters of J.R.R. Tolkien*. Ed. Humphrey Carpenter, with the assistance of Christopher Tolkien. London: George Allen & Unwin, 1981.

"On Fairy-stories." *Tree and Leaf*. London: Unwin Books, 1964. 11-70.

The Children of Húrin. Ed. Christopher Tolkien. London: HarperCollins, 2007.

The Silmarillion. Ed. Christopher Tolkien. Boston MA: Houghton Mifflin, 1977.

The Shaping of Middle-earth. (*The History of Middle-earth* volume 4). Ed. Christopher Tolkien. First published 1986. London: HarperCollins, 1993.

VAN ANDEL, Tjeerd H. *New Views on an Old Planet: A History of Global Change*. 2nd edition. Cambridge: Cambridge University Press, 1994.

WEGENER, Alfred. *The Origin of Continents and Oceans (Die Entstehung der Kontinente und Ozeane)*. Braunschweig: Friedr. Vieweg & Sohn, 1915.

WIGGINS, Kayla McKinney. "The Art of the Story-teller and the Person of the Hero." *Tolkien on Film: Essays on Peter Jackson's The Lord of the Rings*. Ed. Janet Brennan Croft. Altadena CA: Mythopoeic Press, 2004. 103-122.

WOOD, Denis. "How Maps Work." *Cartographica* 29 (1992): 66-74.

Gabriel Ertsgaard

"Leaves of Gold There Grew":
Lothlórien, Postcolonialism, and Ecology

Abstract

Lothlórien is an ecological utopia whose harmonious enchantments contrast with the destructive magical technologies of Sauron and Saruman. Yet the Elves have their own imperialist history, and due to the power of the One Ring, the Elves' sustainable civilization is inextricably entangled with Sauron's eco-catastrophic magic. They must let their civilization fail to save Middle-earth. The fall of Mordor and Lothlórien, though, cannot guarantee Middle-earth a socially or ecologically harmonious future, but simply creates space for new generations to determine their own destinies. We cannot directly map the power dynamics of our world onto Middle-earth, but there are enough intriguing parallels for some profitable borrowing. Our first world consumer civilization, for all of its positive aspects, is entangled with socially and ecologically harmful global structures, and even the conservation movement has historical links to colonialism. Unlike the Elves, though, we cannot retreat from this world, so we must seek a solution within it.

Introduction

Lothlórien, where the golden mallorn trees grow, is an ecological utopia, cultivated and perfected by Lady Galadriel's loving enchantments. Yet when we first discover this seemingly timeless realm in Tolkien's *The Lord of the Rings*, a shadow of loss already hovers over it. The Elves know that to defeat Sauron, Frodo must destroy the One Ring. Although they will do everything in their power to help the Ring-bearer, his success comes for them at a great cost: the enchantments girding and protecting Lothlórien will be undone. Thus, in order to save Middle-earth from Sauron's destructive magic, they must sacrifice their own sustainable civilization. The Elves, though good, admirable, and even heroic, also have a history of imperialist ambition. This contributes to much of the strife in *The Silmarillion*. Unlike Sauron and Saruman, though, these ambitions do not cause the Elves to lose reverence for the natural world. This allows them to make their difficult choice and ultimately leave Middle-earth.

Tolkien denied that his work was allegorical, but invited readers to find "applicability" in it (*FR* xi). Those of us who enjoy the benefits of a first world lifestyle, may find that applicable resonances hit uncomfortably close to home. We also have a civilization worth preserving, but even before addressing global inequalities, our rate of consumption exceeds what the planet can support. We must find our way toward a "choice of the Elves", but we have no other realm to depart for. Tolkien's narrative does not provide a solution to our dilemma, but perhaps it can help us organize our imaginations to better serve our sustainability efforts. Postcolonial ecocriticism, by illuminating how themes of power and nature intersect, can help us clarify useful resonances between Middle-earth and our world. Therefore, this essay will first sketch an approach to postcolonial Tolkien ecocriticism, next examine the stewardship ethic alongside the Elves' imperial history, and then consider both the aesthetics and the fall of Lothlórien. Finally, with Tolkien's vision to guide us, we will look again at our own world.

Applicability and Postcolonial Ecocriticism

Tolkien's concept of applicability in literature and his expressed environmental sensibilities provide a foundation for Tolkien ecocriticism. Regarding the former, he writes: "I think that many confuse 'applicability' with 'allegory'; but one resides in the freedom of the reader, and the other in the purposed domination of the author" (FR xi). Liam Campbell, exercising that "freedom of the reader," argues in *The Ecological Augury in the Works of JRR Tolkien*:

> When we read of the crisis facing, not only the peoples, but also the natural world of Middle-earth, when we encounter imagined trees, grasslands and flowing waters which are 'threatened by a machine-loving enemy' bereft of an environmental conscience [...] it is no great leap of faith, using 'applicability' as our watchword, to see the environmental crisis facing our own reality reflected. (Campbell 37)

Campbell quotes the phrase "machine-loving enemy" from a letter by Tolkien to the *Daily Telegraph*. In the letter, which was prompted by the newspaper's prior reference to "a kind of Tolkien gloom, where no bird sings," Tolkien clarifies,

> In all my works I take the part of the trees as against all their enemies. Lothlórien is beautiful because the trees were loved; elsewhere forests are represented as awakening to consciousness of themselves. The Old Forest was hostile to two-legged creatures because of the memory of many injuries. Fangorn Forest was old and beautiful, but at the time of the story tense with hostility because it was threatened by a machine-loving enemy. (*L* 419-20)

Tolkien also criticizes "the torture and murder of trees" and "the savage sound of the electric saw" in this letter (*L* 420). Between Tolkien's invitation to discover applicability in his works and his overt expressions of environmental concern, Tolkien ecocriticism has a strong foundation.

Postcolonial ecocriticism, though, is more complex, so we should clarify the relationship between postcolonial and ecological concerns. In the introduction to *Postcolonial Ecologies: Literatures of the Environment*, Elizabeth DeLoughrey and George Handley suggest four intersections between postcolonial and ecological theories (24-25). We can orient ourselves by applying each intersection to Tolkien's work. Illustrative examples must suffice, for a comprehensive study of Tolkien and postcolonial ecology is beyond the scope of this essay. Even so, this section will prepare us for a careful look at Tolkien's Elves and Lothlórien.

"First, an ecological frame is vital to understanding how geography has been and still is radically altered by colonialism, including resource use, stewardship, and sovereignty" (DeLoughrey and Handley 24). This intersection is a valuable lens for the diverse geography of Tolkien's Middle-earth, which includes a range of interactions between sentient beings and the environment. Tom Bombadil in the Old Forest and the Ents in Fangorn Forest are the purest manifestations of the preservationist ideal, whereas Sauron and Saruman devastate landscapes. Others fall in between these two extremes. Elves adapt nature to their needs, creating harmonious forest-gardens. Hobbits are pastoralists, but sometimes battle the Old Forest. Human societies show a wide range of responses to nature.

As for geography being "radically altered by colonialism," let us particularly consider Saruman. Campbell observes that Saruman "craves power and seeks to gain mastery over others" (96). This proves ecologically destructive because "as Saruman gathers his forces and his strengths about him, it is predominantly at the expense of the land itself" (Campbell 99). Saruman's occupation of the Shire echoes both colonialism and globalization. Matthew Dickerson and Jonathan Evans point out in *Ents, Elves, and Eriador* that Saruman introduces "food production solely for export," with harmful social and ecological consequences (207). John Elder (xi), in his foreword to Dickerson and Evans, writes of Saruman: "Not only does he raze the forests, poison the waters, and denude the soil surrounding his Isengard stronghold [...] but he also brings the destructive impulse of Mordor back to the Shire itself [...] Saruman's projects resonate with many destructive outcomes of political and commercial globalization today."

However, there are complications with a postcolonial reading of this episode. Daniel Smith-Rowsey (134) acknowledges that "the portrayal of Hobbits as bucolic and multi-faceted is [...] a positive articulation of subaltern consciousness," but he also notes that "they are still Caucasian, English-speaking, male-normative, and marked as European in hundreds of ways." Smith-Rowsey specifically analyzes Peter Jackson's *The Lord of the Rings* films, but his critique equally fits Tolkien's novels. Thus, we should keep in mind Tolkien's distinction between allegory and applicability. Because of the Hobbits' English coding, Saruman's occupation of the Shire would be an imperfect allegory for post-Columbian colonialism, but it still has applicable resonances. Although the dynamics of Middle-earth are not identical to those of our world, Tolkien's work has rich resources for imagining how colonialism might harm and reshape geography. Smith-Rowsey's question regarding the Hobbits' subaltern status, however, segues into DeLoughrey and Handley's next intersection.

"Enlightenment dualisms of culture/nature, white/black, and male/female were constituted through the colonial process" (DeLoughrey and Handley 24). These same Enlightenment dualisms have a complicated place in Tolkien's work. Brian McFadden (164) notes: "While Tolkien abhorred racism and the denial of dignity to different races, he still had the tendency to create oppositions (dark and light, good and evil, beauty and ugliness, Elf and human, and so on) that might be interpreted as racism by readers trained to read against the text." McFadden (166) adds: "Tolkien was a human being and would have admitted himself to be fallible; his society, also, had not yet become as self-aware or as self-critical with respect to colonialism and racism as it is today." Tolkien, then, while consciously opposing racism and, as Jane Chance (173) notes, both literal and metaphorical apartheid, relied on the same binary hermeneutic so often deployed as a tool of oppression. As DeLoughrey and Handley argue (25): "The 'cultivation' that presumably constituted the post-Enlightenment European male subject was increasingly distanced from women, the poor, and peoples of color. Likewise, these naturalized others were likened to a construction of nature that was increasingly seen to require masculine European management."

However, Tolkien's work destabilizes this "masculine European management" by depicting not only diverse societies, but also diverse social and ecological arrangements. As Patrick Curry notes in *Defending Middle-earth* (67): "The alliance against Mordor is only just cobbled together (thanks mainly to Gandalf) among people with drastically different cultures, languages, habits, and agenda." Nor is it hard to make the leap from Tolkien's ecologically motivated dissatisfaction with modernity to his willingness to respect and depict alternative modes of life. Perhaps the best critical approach, as modeled by McFadden, Chance, and Smith-Rowsey, is to acknowledge both the problematic binaries in Tolkien's work and the elements that can destabilize them. Indeed, such an approach may help us analyze the Elves' surrender of power, which is arguably the breakdown of a hegemonic system. The Elves, however, occupy an ambivalent space, for they simultaneously reflect both humans and the non-human other. This points towards DeLoughrey and Handley's third intersection.

"The ecocritical interrogation of anthropocentrism offers the persistent reminder that human political and social inequities cannot be successfully and sustainably resolved without some engagement with the more-than-human world and deep time. [Both] the more-than-human world and deep time" (DeLoughrey and Handley 25) are important factors in Tolkien's books. As Campbell (153) notes: "Tolkien's works are alive with beings and races that are by definition non-human. Humanity (when understood as the race of men) in Tolkien's cosmology is but one component in the sphere of creation, and is forced to take its place alongside (as opposed to being considered superior to) the non-human." Middle-earth is filled with diverse beings and terrains, and these received Tolkien's careful attention. If "ecocritical postcolonialism attempts to imagine something beyond the confines of our human story, an imagination that is essential to modes of sustainability," as DeLoughrey and

Handley (25) assert, then Tolkien's "engagement with the more-than-human world" certainly deserves respectful consideration.

As for deep time, few authors have incorporated this theme as integrally as Tolkien. Andrew Light's excellent essay "Tolkien's Green Time" from *The Lord of the Rings and Philosophy* explores this in detail, so a few comments here will suffice. Although Tolkien's eon-spanning *The Silmarillion* was only published posthumously, it echoes through his other work. As Tolkien writes of *The Lord of the Rings*, "This tale grew in the telling, until it became a history of the Great War of the Ring and included many glimpses of the yet more ancient history that preceded it" (*FR* viii). *The Silmarillion* traces that history back to the world's creation. According to Dickerson and Evans (30), this has ecological implications, for "Tolkien's Middle-earth [...] has an inherent purpose; it is the deliberate creation of Ilúvatar, and no decision of Elf, Dwarf, Man, or Hobbit can diminish its inherent goodness or change the purpose for which it was made: to cause its inhabitants to rejoice in its glory both by participation and by attribution and to make Ilúvatar glad." This engagement with deep time, then, leads to a stewardship ethic that ascribes innate value to the more-than-human world. The Elves' sacrifice of power (and therefore Lothlórien) in order to preserve the rest of Middle-earth flows out of this deep, ancient stewardship ethic. We will explore the Elves' sacrifice further on, though, so let us now turn to DeLoughrey and Handley's last intersection.

"Finally, the field of postcolonial studies has long been engaged with questions of agency and representation of the nonspeaking or subaltern subject [...] the question of who can 'speak for nature'" (DeLoughrey and Handley 25). Significantly, Tolkien distributed the authority to "speak for nature" across diverse races and creatures. Gandalf is an embodied angel, Tom Bombadil can be seen as an incarnation of nature, and the Ents are an ancient race physically resembling the trees they tend. The Elves have the most developed environmental aesthetic of all the "children of Ilúvatar," but Hobbits and wild men have their own attentive ways of relating to the natural world. Even the Dwarves voice their particular love for stone and mountain in Tolkien's works. The Orcs, though, express no appreciation for nature, and the dark-skinned Swertings are silent. This brings to mind Chinua Achebe's (174) famous complaint about *Heart of Darkness*: "It is clearly not part of Conrad's purpose to confer language on the 'rudimentary souls' of Africa. In place of speech they made 'a violent babble of uncouth sounds.' They 'exchanged short grunting phrases' even among themselves. But most of the time they were too busy with their frenzy."

Still, Sam Gamgee's empathetic curiosity regarding a dead Swerting warrior's motives, home, and family in *The Two Towers* (341) differs substantially from Marlow ontologizing his own ignorance of African languages in *Heart of Darkness*. McFadden (159) writes of Tolkien's dead Swerting scene: "The ultimate barrier to communication is death [...]. However, Tolkien allows death to be a site of humanization." This does not render the Swertings' silence and the Orcs' malevolence entirely unproblematic. McFadden (166) notes: "Despite acknowledging the evils of racism and recognizing the equality of races, Tolkien may have inherited some of the implicit biases of his time." Through that wide range of voices "speaking for nature," however, Tolkien provides a substantial amount of material that deserves our constructive engagement. Although this brief survey of Tolkien and postcolonial ecology has not touched on all relevant points of contact, it clarifies a framework for exploring such resonances. This should provide an adequate foundation for our more focused look at the High Elves and Lothlórien, so now let us turn to that task.

The High Elves' Burden

Dickerson and Evans (42) convincingly argue that Tolkien's environmental ethic was rooted in a religious concept of stewardship "which sees humans in the roles of both lord and servant, as gardeners and managers, with the rest of nature having intrinsic value." According to Patrick Dobel in a 1977 essay for *The Christian Century*, such an ethic is implicit in the Christian worldview, for "the stewardship imperative assumes that the moral and ecological constraints are respected, and it adds the obligation to distribute the benefits justly. [...] Mistreating his charges, gorging himself on the resources in excess consumption, and not caring for resources will all cause the steward to be 'cut off'" (Dobel 32). Dickerson and Evans (39) identify Denethor of Gondor as one such bad steward, "who seldom even uses the word steward to describe himself, preferring the title *Lord*. Denethor does not hesitate to use exploitative methods to achieve his goals."

They also saw positive stewardship as deeply connected to the Elves' intrinsic purpose, for "the elves seem to be called to this [positive] model of stewardship. When Ulmo argues against summoning the elves to Valinor, he speaks of 'using their gifts of skill to order all the lands and heal their hurts.' This implies [...] the imposition of some structure that might not otherwise exist" (Dickerson and Evans 42). In *The Silmarillion*, Tolkien calls the Elves who both heed the summons and reach Valinor "Calaquendi," or Elves of the light (53). In *The Hobbit*, he refers to them as "High Elves" (151). Valinor, where the Elves enjoy the light of the sacred trees Telperion and Laurelin in the company of the angelic Valar, echoes the Garden of Eden.

However, the stewardship ethic intersects with postcolonial concerns in ways that a strict focus on Christian theology might miss. We can see this by briefly considering the people of Númenor, whose Half-elf first king chooses a mortal, human life, and a remnant of whom founded Gondor. In *The Silmarillion*, Tolkien describes the interactions between the powerful Númenóreans and the humans of Middle-earth: "And coming among them the Númenóreans taught them many things. Corn and wine they brought, and they instructed Men in the sowing of seed and stone, and in the ordering of their life, such as it might be in the lands of swift death and little bliss" (*S* 263). If stewardship includes an "obligation to distribute the benefits justly," then the Númenóreans were good stewards of not only the land, but also of their fellow humans.

But protection and benefit can prove masks of imperialism, as with Kipling's famous poem, "The White Man's Burden." Tolkien was well aware of the degenerate course of colonialism, and did not let the fantasy of Kipling's "White Man's burden" with its "savage wars of peace" rest comfortably. Later in his tale, the Númenóreans "desired now wealth and dominion in Middle-earth [...] Great harbours and strong towers they made [...] but they appeared now rather as lords and masters and gatherers of tribute than as helpers and teachers" (*S* 266-67). Finally, after being corrupted by Sauron and sacrificing the White Tree, "they came no longer as bringers of gifts, nor even as rulers, but as fierce men of war. And they hunted the men of Middle-earth and took their goods and enslaved them, and many they slew cruelly upon their altars" (*S* 274).

The Númenóreans, dissatisfied with their mortal status, both oppress their fellow humans and ecologically devastate their island. The final destruction of the island by Ilúvatar completes a process begun by the imperialist Númenóreans. As Dickerson and Evans note (61-62): "It is a fall that stems from a loss of respect for Númenor, the island realm granted them by the Valar, and it results in the gross mistreatment of not only that land but also other areas of Middle-earth colonized by Men." Denethor in his failure as a steward recapitulates the sad trajectory of his ancestors. In contrast, Gandalf declares to Denethor,

> The rule of no realm is mine, neither of Gondor nor any other, great or small. But all worthy things that are in peril as the world now stands, those are in my care. And for my part, I shall not wholly fail of my task, though Gondor should perish, if anything passes through this night that can still grow fair or bear fruit and flower again in days to come. For I am also a steward. Did you not know? (*RK* 33-34)

As Dickerson and Evans (38) point out: "Gandalf makes no connection between stewardship and rule." By severing this connection, Tolkien undermines the philosophical foundation not only of imperialism, but of any exploitation, human or ecological, justified through dominion rights.

On the stewardship spectrum, the Elves fall between Gandalf and the Númenóreans. Although the Elves' reverence for nature never lapses, they do get caught up in feuds, power struggles, and political wars that have global consequences. The sad history surrounding the Silmarils illustrates this. The great elf king Fëanor captures the light of the two sacred trees in these jewels, the same trees that in their dying give birth to the moon and sun. Animated by such a light, "were they indeed living things, they rejoiced in light and received it and gave it back in hues more marvelous than before" (*S* 67). However, Fëanor's possessiveness of these jewels proves corrosive both to himself and to his civilization. Tolkien suggests that the desire for power was innate to Fëanor's personality, writing of him and his wife: "Nerdanel was also firm of will, but more patient than Fëanor, desiring to understand minds rather than to master them, and at first she restrained him when the fire of his heart grew too hot; but his later deeds grieved her, and they became estranged" (*S* 64).

The desire for the Silmarils and the desire for power are entangled. The Dark Lord, Morgoth, "lusting ever for the Silmarils," corrupts the Elves with tales "of the mighty realms that they could have ruled at their own will, in power and freedom in the East," and stirs up chauvinism by suggesting that humans will possess those realms that could belong to Elves (*S* 68). Similarly, Fëanor "seldom remembered now that the light within them [the Silmarils] was not his own" and "began openly to speak words of rebellion against the Valar" (*S* 69). Although these events are earlier than the fall of Numenor, they follow a similar pattern of corruption, and ultimately lead to the High Elves' exodus from Valinor.

The final sequence of events triggering that exodus begins with a crime against nature. Morgoth and the spider-shaped demon Ungoliant attack and destroy the two trees of light. Yavanna, the trees' creator, declares: "The Light of the Trees has passed away, and lives now only in the Silmarils of Fëanor. [...] Yet had I but a little of that light I could recall to life the Trees, ere their roots decay; and then our hurts should be healed" (*S* 78). But Fëanor replies: "I can unlock my jewels, but never again can I make their like; and if I must break them, I shall break my heart, and I shall be slain [...]. This thing I will not do of free will" (*S* 78-79). For the trees, this refusal is moot. Following the attack on the trees, Morgoth raids Fëanor's stronghold in the latter's absence, killing his father Finwë and stealing the Silmarils. Yet in his refusal, Fëanor clearly falls short of the Elves' highest purpose "to order all the lands and heal their hurts." Tolkien notes: "The Silmarils had passed away, and all one it may seem whether Fëanor had said yea or nay to Yavanna; yet had he said yea at first [...] it may be that his after deeds were other than they were" (*S* 79). But as it is, Fëanor rouses the Elves to war and conquest: "After Morgoth to the ends of the Earth! War shall he have and hatred undying. But when we have conquered and have regained the Silmarils, then we and we alone shall be lords of the unsullied Light, and masters of the bliss and beauty of Arda. No other race shall oust us!" (*S* 83).

Galadriel is among those swayed by this speech. Tolkien writes: "No oaths she swore, but the words of Fëanor concerning Middle-earth had kindled in her heart, for she yearned to see the wide unguarded lands and to rule there a realm at her own will" (*S* 84). When the ship-building Teleri Elves refuse Fëanor the use of their ships, he attacks them and steals their ships, killing many Teleri in the process (*S* 87). Later Fëanor abandons the Elves led by his half-brother Fingolfin, burning the ships rather than sending them back for the others. Tolkien writes of this: "Led by Fingolfin and his sons, and by Finrod and Galadriel, they dared to pass into the bitterest North; and finding no other way they endured at last the terror of Helcaraxe and the cruel hills of ice [...] and it was with a lessened host that Fingolfin set foot at last upon the Outer Lands" (90). In Middle-earth the Elves would wage war on the dark lords Morgoth and Sauron, but also on Dwarves, Men, and each other.

Let us contrast this imperial impulse with the call to stewardship that represents the Elves' true purpose. Here, Tolkien's distinction between magic and enchantment is helpful. In *On Fairy-Stories* Tolkien calls enchantment an "Elvish craft" and clarifies:

> Enchantment produces a Secondary World into which both designer and spectator can enter, to the satisfaction of their senses while they are inside; but in its purity it is artistic in desire and purpose. Magic produces, or pretends to produce, an alteration in the Primary World. It does not matter by whom it is said to be practised, fay or mortal [...] it is not an art but a technique; its desire is power in this world, domination of things and wills. (*OFS* 70-71)

Influenced by this distinction, Patrick Curry (63) argues that our ecological crisis is driven by "the domination of financial and technological magic over enchantment." He concedes that "science as a human activity has perfectly honorable antecedents, and is not intrinsically or necessarily perverted by power-as-domination," but warns "the ideology which is sometimes called scientism [...] has become almost inseparable from both power and profit, and sometimes an object of worship in its own right" (Curry 63-64). Similarly, Campbell (193) argues: "unlike the enslaving and 'bulldozing' technologically-themed magic used by Sauron and others, the enchantments created by the Elves within their lands are used to hold off the evil and environmental devastation which afflicts other landscapes in Middle-earth." At their best, the Elves are good stewards. They care for and protect the life of those lands in which they dwell. Nor do they ever pursue magical technologies without concern for the natural world. Yet they can still be tempted by the imperial fantasies that trigger in other beings ecologically-destructive pursuits of domination.

However, the line between magic and enchantment is not always clear. The boundary blurs between science as a quest to understand nature and science as the nursemaid of technology. (Nor are technology and aesthetics mutually exclusive, as many who have examined a Tesla electric car would concede.) Nerdanel who only wishes "to understand minds" is the wife of Fëanor who would "master them." Some episodes particularly strain Tolkien's schema. One of Fëanor's great failings is his refusal to turn his aesthetic objects into a technology, even to save the trees that gave them light. But this refusal is rooted in a desire for domination encouraged by the Dark Lord, Morgoth. Tolkien clearly saw a link between this desire for domination and the use of science to create nature-dominating technologies. The Elves' enchantments, therefore, always risk entanglement with darker magics, just as disinterested science risks entanglement with destructive forms of technology. Tolkien's response to the atomic bomb reflected this: "The utter folly of these lunatic physicists to consent to do such work for war-purposes: calmly plotting the destruction of the world!" (*L* 116). In *The Lord of the Rings* this entanglement manifests in the connection between the Elves' rings and Sauron's One Ring. Referring to the rings, Campbell (193) writes: "The Elves use a magic of sorts then in order to protect, heal and restore the land or the Earth." However, this entanglement also proves the undoing of enchanted realms like Lothlórien.

Lothlórien Fades

Dickerson and Evans identified the three races' primary relationships with nature as follows: agriculture for the Hobbits, horticulture for the Elves, and feraculture for the Ents (xxi, 31-32). We can think of these as roughly paralleling the sustainable farming of Wendell Berry, the landscape architecture of Frederick Law Olmsted, and the wilderness preservation efforts of John Muir. Significantly, Tolkien made room for all three in his Middle-earth. He seems to have anticipated, at least artistically, William Cronon's (90) petition from "The Trouble with Wilderness": "If wildness can stop being (just) out there and start being (also) in here, if it can start being as humane as it is natural, then perhaps we can get on with the unending task of struggling to live rightly in the world – not just in the garden, not just in the wilderness, but in the home that encompasses them both." As Lothlórien reveals, Tolkien's Elves are particularly adept at making gardens of (not just from) the wilderness.

Tolkien writes of Frodo's first morning in the Lothlórien woods: "As the light grew it filtered through the yellow leaves of the mallorn [...]. Pale-blue sky peeped among the moving branches. [...] Frodo saw all the valley of Silverlode lying like a sea of fallow gold tossing gently in the breeze" (*FR* 448). "Sea of fallow gold" has an enchanted ring, but nothing in the description ensures that the forest is cultivated. Perhaps the enchantment resides in Frodo's vision. When the travelers reach the heart of Lothlórien, though, the landscape has obvious garden qualities:

> To the left stood a great mound, covered with a sward of grass as green as Spring-time in the elder days. Upon it, as a double crown, grew two circles of trees: the outer had bark of snowy white, and were leafless but beautiful in their shapely nakedness; the inner were mallorn-trees of great height, still arrayed in pale gold. High amid the branches of a towering tree that stood at the centre of all there gleamed a white flet. At the feet of the trees, and all about the green hillsides, the grass was studded with small golden flowers shaped like stars. (*FR* 454)

Lothlórien, then, is the quintessential example of "the Elves' preoccupation [...] with the cultivation, refinement, and preservation of the aesthetic qualities of the created world" (Dickerson and Evans 109). The Elves' stewardship is so thorough that "no blemish or sickness or deformity could be seen in anything that grew upon the earth. On the land of Lórien there was no stain" (*FR* 454-55). According to Michael Brisbois (207), this "is a glimpse of the holy, as expressed through the natural perfection of Lórien." Sam Gamgee's impression, "whether they've made the land or the land's made them, it's hard to say," suggests a reciprocal dependence (*FR* 455). Not only are "immortal realms interlaced with the everyday world of physical experience and natural topography," as Alfred Siewers (143) notes, but they are interlaced with the sentient beings who inhabit them. As Brisbois (197-98) observes: "The subtle magic that infuses the Elves is intertwined with the land they live in, suggesting they do not make clear distinctions between culture and nature." Jean-Christophe Dufau (108) makes an even stronger claim: "They can be said to inhabit their trees as a soul does its body – intimately and powerfully."

Over Lothlórien, however, lies the spectre of the One Ring. In *The Silmarillion* Sauron, feigning friendship, teaches the Elves to make Rings of power, "but Sauron secretly made the One Ring to rule all the others" (*S* 287). The Elves perceive Sauron's evil intentions as soon as he dons this Ring (*S* 288). During the war with Sauron, they hide their three most powerful rings,

> yet after the fall of Sauron their power was at work and where they abode there mirth also dwelt and all things were unstained by the griefs of time. [...] the Ring of Sapphire was with Elrond, in the fair valley of Rivendell [...] whereas the Ring of Adamant was in the Land of Lórien where dwelt the Lady Galadriel. [...] Thus it was that in two domains the bliss and beauty of the Elves still remained undiminished [...]. (*S* 298)

Dickerson and Evans (109) describe Rivendell and Lothlórien as "two remaining realms of a much greater Elvish presence in Middle-earth [...] surviving outposts where a remnant dwell before their total and final withdrawal." However, these last vestiges of the Elves' earlier imperial greatness are entangled with Sauron's Ring. In *The Fellowship of the Ring*, speaking of the three rings of the Elves, Elrond insists: "those who made them did not desire strength or domination or hoarded wealth, but understanding, making, and healing, to preserve all things unstained" (*FR* 352). Nevertheless, he fears that "when the One has gone, the Three will fail, and many fair things will fade and be forgotten" (*FR* 352).

Galadriel shares Elrond's fear, saying to Frodo: "Do you not see wherefore your coming is to us as the footsteps of Doom? For if you fail, then we are laid bare to the enemy. Yet if you succeed, then our power is diminished, and Lothlórien will fade, and the tides of Time will sweep it away. We must depart into the West, or dwindle to a rustic folk of dell and cave, slowly to forget and be forgotten" (*FR* 472). Galadriel clarifies the deep attachment the Elves have for their enchanted realm, saying, "the love of the Elves for their land and their works is deeper than the deeps of the Sea, and their regret is undying and cannot ever be wholly assuaged" (*FR* 473). Although the inevitable fading of Lothlórien is both a personal and ecological tragedy for Galadriel, the consequences of a victory for Sauron would be far worse for both her people and her land. The Elves must conspire to destroy the One Ring, dooming their green utopias, to hold back Sauron's tide of complete ecological destruction. Therefore, she tells Frodo: "For the fate of Lothlórien you are not answerable, but only for the doing of your own task. Yet I could wish, were it of any avail, that the One Ring had never been wrought, or had remained forever lost" (*FR* 473).

Galadriel and Elrond's fears are justified. Tolkien describes the final fate of Lothlórien in an appendix to *The Return of the King*. Following Aragorn's death,

> Arwen [...] went out from the city of Minas Tirith and passed away to the land of Lórien, and dwelt there alone under the fading trees until winter came. Galadriel had passed away and Celeborn also was gone, and the land was silent.
>
> There at last when the mallorn-leaves were falling, but spring had not yet come, she laid herself to rest upon Cerin Amroth; and there is her green grave, until the world is changed, and all the days of her life are utterly forgotten by men that come after, and elanor and niphredil bloom no more east of the Sea. (*RK* 428)

The leaves of a mallorn, Legolas explains in *The Fellowship of the Ring*, persist until spring when new buds blossom, but when Arwen passes they have already started to fade (*RK* 434). As Patrice Hannon (36) observes, this elegiac quality pervades *The Lord of the Rings*, "a story of loss and longing, punctuated by moments of humor and terror and heroic action but on the whole a lament for a world [...] that has passed even as we seem to catch a last glimpse of it flickering and fading." For Hannon (37), even "the many quick-moving scenes of flight and pursuit and battle [...] are secondary to the sense the book conveys of things slipping into – or already become part of – the irrecoverable past."

Elves mirror the reader's experience of passing and loss, such as when Haldir mourns beneath golden mallorn trees, "Alas for Lothlórien that I love! It would be a poor life in a land where no mallorn grew. But if there are mallorn-trees beyond the Great Sea, none have reported it" (*FR* 452). His world still exists, but he knows it must fail. Dickerson and Evans (114) insist that

> the sense of failure that accompanies the Elves' passing should not be attributed to flaws inherent in their environmental aesthetic. [...] their failure resides in the effort to resist all change, stemming from their prideful, selfish desire to have things as they once were. Yet their efforts to preserve the beauty of nature keep the memory of Valinor alive not only for themselves but for all races.

The Elves, however, do not at all times "desire to have things as they once were," for they leave Valinor with ambitious visions of carving new empires, and Galadriel herself "yearned to see the wide unguarded lands and to rule there a realm at her own will" (*S* 84). Over millennia they help defeat Morgoth only to see Sauron rise, and help defeat Sauron only to see him return. As Tolkien puts it: "They were valiant, but the history of those that returned to Middle-earth in exile was grievous" (*RK* 519). It is only after this long, exhausting tenure that they seek "at best a truce, in which they may pass to the Sea unhindered and leave Middle-earth forever" (*FR* 452). So the sun finally sets on the Elves' beautiful but troubled empire, their tenure as stewards ends, and to protect the natural world one final time, they surrender the power to protect it in the future.

Before this last surrender, however, a critical episode occurs – one that prefigures Frodo's struggle and temporary failure on the lip of Mount Doom. Frodo, overwhelmed by the task before him, tells Galadriel: "You are wise and fearless and fair, Lady Galadriel [...]. I will give you the One Ring, if you ask for it. It is too great a matter for me" (*FR* 473). Even this late in her time on Middle-earth, the offer of dominant power tempts Galadriel. She responds:

> And now at last it comes. You will give me the Ring freely! And in the place of a Dark Lord you will set up a Queen. And I shall be not dark, but beautiful and terrible as the Morning and Night! Fair as the Sea and the Sun and the Snow upon the Mountain! Dreadful as the Storm and the Lightning! Stronger than the foundations of the earth. All shall love me and despair! (*FR* 473)

Galadriel appears physically transformed by her imperialistic reverie: "She stood before Frodo seeming now tall beyond measurement, and beautiful beyond enduring, terrible and worshipful" (*FR* 473). Infused with the One Ring's power, she would dominate and absorb into her very being the natural world's sublimity – the qualities of morning, night, sea, sun, snow, mountain, storm, and lightning.

But Galadriel is now far wiser than when she left Valinor. She has seen the lust for absolute power gnaw and corrupt lords even more powerful than herself, so she draws back from the precipice "and lo! she was shrunken: a slender elf-woman, clad in simple white, whose gentle voice was soft and sad" (*FR* 474). Galadriel then offers this final repudiation of imperial ambition: "I pass the test

[…]. I will diminish, and go into the West, and remain Galadriel" (*FR* 474). According to Maureen Thum (239), this suggests a positive attitude toward women by Tolkien, for "unlike Eve, who cannot resist evil, Galadriel is able to withstand a temptation that many strong men […] find irresistible." In resisting, though, she also concedes the decline of her realm. Loren Wilkinson (83) claims that the martial heroics in *The Lord of the Rings* are "a diversion for the real world-changing action of the story, which is not about the exercise of power but the surrender of it." Frodo, as the Ring-bearer, carries the literal weight of this sacrifice, but by tying Frodo's task to the Elves' fate, Tolkien rooted the surrender of power even deeper into the spirit of his tale. Galadriel's song for Lothlórien expresses this beautifully:

> I sang of leaves, of leaves of gold, and leaves of gold there grew:
> Of wind I sang, a wind there came and in the branches blew.
> […]
> O Lórien! The Winter comes, the bare and leafless Day;
> The leaves are falling in the stream, the River flows away. (*FR* 482)

This song of cultivation and loss resonates with another hobbit, Sam Gamgee. As Wilkinson (82) notes, "there are two kinds of story in *The Lord of the Rings*: the hero story, and the gardener story." Galadriel has been in her long life both a heroic warrior and a careful gardener, but her gift to Sam is a gardener's gift. She explains, "In this box there is earth from my orchard, and such blessing as Galadriel has still to bestow upon it" (*FR* 486). With this gift, Sam will "restore the Shire to its garden state" after the ravages of Saruman's colonial regime (Wilkinson 82). Thus Galadriel, who can no longer save her own garden realm, places in Sam's hands the power to save his – no magic weapon but enchanted soil, literally a small portion of her earth.

Conclusion

The entanglement between enchantment and magic, ecology and imperialism, is hardly limited to Tolkien's Middle-earth. Richard Grove claims in *Green Imperialism*:

> The seeds of modern conservationism developed as an integral part of the European encounter with the tropics and with local classifications and interpretations

> of the natural world and its symbolism. [...] the environmental experiences of Europeans and indigenous peoples living at the colonial periphery played a steadily more dominant and dynamic part [...] in the growing awareness of the destructive impact of European economic activity. (Grove 3)

Yet despite the contributions of indigenous knowledge, "forest conservation and associated forced resettlement methods were frequently the cause of fierce oppression of indigenous peoples and became a highly convenient form of social control" (Grove 12). In short, the "enchantment" of conservationism has historically been entangled with the "magic" of colonialism.

In Zimbabwe, formerly Rhodesia, white settlers justified their place and privilege through an aesthetic embrace of landscape similar to that of Tolkien's Elves. As David Hughes (7) puts it in *Whiteness in Zimbabwe*: "This rhetoric of 'Rhodesian pastoral' [...] cast Europeans as uniquely capable of appreciating, enhancing, and glorifying the environment." This paralleled a psychological withdrawal from the black majority surrounding them. In Hughes' (xii) words: "In their own minds, they turned away from native, African people and focused instead on African landscapes. [...] Environmental conservation and white identity have produced and shaped each other." Similarly, Tolkien's Elves retreat into their own enchanted nature realms, like Lothlórien, and largely detach themselves from the other races of Middle-earth.

However, in this era of globalization we have no exact parallel to the Elves' eventual withdrawal from Middle-earth. We must figure out how to ethically proceed in a world that will almost certainly remain entangled. The trickiest task for those of us who live in developed nations is bringing our consumption-driven, unsustainable lifestyle under control. As Keith Thomas (301) argues in *Man and the Natural World*: "a growing number of people had come to find man's ascendancy over nature increasingly abhorrent to their moral and aesthetic sensibilities. This was the human dilemma: how to reconcile the physical requirements of civilization with the new feelings and values that same civilization had generated." In other words, how to reconcile magic with enchantment. Thomas (303), who recognized that we are far from accomplishing this, added: "a mixture of compromise and concealment has so far prevented this conflict from being fully resolved. But the issue cannot be completely evaded and it can be relied upon to recur."

The difficulty with changing our lifestyle is that there is much to value in it. Most poor people in developed nations can take hot showers every morning, whereas wealthy landlords three hundred years ago could not. Music and story pervade our culture, despite their commodification. Tolkien fans, in particular, should be sympathetic to finding beauty in popular culture products that certain aesthetes might denigrate. As for horticulture, national and municipal parks both depend on tax revenue which in turn depends on our "economic engine". (Similarly, as the documentary *Milking the Rhino* notes, ecotourism-based conservation efforts in Africa depend on developed world economies.) We are thus entangled with a Ring of Power, consumerism, and cannot simply retreat to Valinor. Tolkien offers us no absolute solution to this predicament in his work. Instead, Gandalf proposes this tentative project: "It is not our part to master all the tides of the world, but to do what is in us for the succour of those years wherein we are set, uprooting the evil in the fields that we know, so that those who live after may have clean earth to till. What weather they shall have is not ours to rule" (*RK* 190).

Strangely, our carbon emissions will at least influence that future weather. Our physical, natural world will change significantly, as the irreversible decline of Antarctica's Thwaites glacier makes clear (Howard). Earth has transformed before – a geological history echoed in *The Silmarillion's* world-rending upheavals – and these present changes, though substantial, are far from the greatest the Earth has ever seen. However, the scale of our human contribution to these changes is unprecedented. Nor is climate change our only ecological concern, though it does contribute to others. In the face of a sharp, human-driven drop in biodiversity, we may justly echo Elrond's fear that "many fair things will fade and be forgotten" (*FR* 352).

The popular slogan "failure is not an option" is inadequate and subtly imperialistic. It assumes the power to impose one's complete agenda, to dominate all things that might resist. But we have passed certain tipping points, and a complete ecological victory is no longer even physically possible. Yet we should still salvage and save what we can, and we "shall not wholly fail of [our] task […] if anything passes through this night that can still grow fair or bear fruit and flower again in days to come" (*RK* 33). Denethor, the bad steward, prematurely capitulates when his potency, his lordship, proves less than supreme. On the other hand, *The Lord of the Rings* is filled with characters who understand that their own actions are necessary but not sufficient to save Middle-earth. Similarly, we should each pursue some necessary task with integrity, support the work of others, and perhaps even take on multiple tasks, but we cannot accomplish all or control what others do. Yet only through the surrender of power, the surrender of imperial fantasies, can we learn the self-restraint necessary to live sustainably.

This reminder is certainly valuable for environmental humanists. In the four decades since *Western Man and Environmental Ethics* set out "to examine how attitudes toward nature and technology have led to an environmental crisis, and how new attitudes might contribute to the survival and quality of life on earth" (Barbour 1), the environmental humanities have flourished, but we have clearly failed to turn back the tide of ecological destruction. Perhaps our volumes are beacons on the ridge, or seeds seeking fertile soil. We sustain a tradition of thought that a willing generation might use to sustain the Earth. But a great deal lies, and must lie, beyond our control – even for scholar-activists who legitimately fill multiple roles.

By embracing our finitude, we might understand why Tolkien considered death a gift, one that only "became a grief" when humans "grew wilful and proud and would not yield, until life was reft from them" (*S* 265). Our individual tenures as stewards are limited, a few decades at most. Then, despite our successes or failures, the mantle must pass to others. Such finitude confers value upon both life and death, the latter limiting the potential weariness of the former. The Elves lack this gift, but after long ages they too surrender power and pass the world's care to others. Thus the Elves' withdrawal, which we cannot imitate, is already an imitation of us. However, by accepting death and limits, we can create space for more than our single species or particular cultures. Rather let us strive to clear fields, to negotiate truces, to bring some things green and lively through the night, and in all of these to see even our limits as blessings.

About the Author

Gabriel Ertsgaard is a Doctor of Letters candidate, Global Studies concentration, at Drew University. His research focuses on the environmental humanities, especially the intersection of literature, spirituality, and ecology. He previously taught English in South Korea and the Republic of Georgia.

Bibliography

Achebe, Chinua. "An Image of Africa: Racism in Conrad's *Heart of Darkness.*" *Things Fall Apart: A Norton Critical Edition.* Ed. Francis Abiola Irele. New York: W. W. Norton, 2009. 169-181.

Barbour, Ian G. "Introduction." *Western Man and Environmental Ethics: Attitudes toward Nature and Technology.* Ed. Ian G. Barbour. Reading, MA: Addison-Wesley Publishing, 1973.

Brisbois, Michael J. "Tolkien's Imaginary Nature: An Analysis of the Structure of Middle-earth." *Tolkien Studies* 2 (2005): 197-216.

Campbell, Liam. *The Ecological Augury in the Works of JRR Tolkien.* Zurich and Jena: Walking Tree Publishers, 2011.

Chance, Jane. "Tolkien and the Other: Race and Gender in Middle-Earth." *Tolkien's Modern Middle Ages.* Ed. Jane Chance and Alfred Siewers. New York: Palgrave Macmillan, 2009. 171-186.

Cronon, William. "The Trouble with Wilderness; or, Getting Back to the Wrong Nature." *Uncommon Ground.* Ed. William Cronon. New York: W. W. Norton, 1996. 69-90.

Curry, Patrick. *Defending Middle-Earth: Tolkien: Myth and Modernity.* New York: Houghton Mifflin, 2004.

DeLoughrey, Elizabeth and George B. Handley. "Introduction: Towards an Aesthetics of the Earth." *Postcolonial Ecologies: Literatures of the Environment.* Ed. Elizabeth DeLoughrey and George B. Handley. New York: Oxford University Press, 2011. 3-39.

Dickerson, Matthew and Jonathan Evans. *Ents, Elves, and Eriador: The Environmental Vision of J.R.R. Tolkien.* Lexington, KY: University of Press of Kentucky, 2006.

Dobel, Patrick. "The Judeo-Christian Stewardship Attitude to Nature." *Environmental Ethics: Readings in Theory and Application.* 5th edition. Ed. Louis P. Pojman and Paul Pojman. Belmont, CA: Wadsworth, 2008. 28-32.

DUFAU, Jean-Christophe. "Mythic Space in Tolkien's Work (*The Lord of the Rings, The Hobbit* and *The Silmarillion*)." *Reconsidering Tolkien*. Ed. Thomas Honegger. Zurich and Berne: Walking Tree Publishers, 2005. 107-128.

ELDER, John. "Foreword." *Ents, Elves, and Eriador: The Environmental Vision of J.R.R. Tolkien*. Matthew Dickerson and Jonathan Evans. Lexington, KY: University of Press of Kentucky, 2006. ix-xii.

GROVE, Richard H. *Green Imperialism: Colonial Expansion, Tropical Island Edens, and the Origins of Environmentalism*, 1600-1860. New York: Cambridge University Press, 1995.

HANNON, Patrice. "*The Lord of the Rings* as Elegy." *Mythlore* 92 (2004): 36-42.

HOWARD, Brian Clark. "West Antarctica Glaciers Collapsing, Adding to Sea-Level Rise." *National Geographic Daily News*. 12 May 2014. <http://news.nationalgeographic.com/news/2014/05/140512-thwaites-glacier-melting-collapse-west-antarctica-ice-warming/>

HUGHES, David McDermott. *Whiteness in Zimbabwe: Race, Landscape, and the Problem of Belonging*. New York: Palgrave Macmillan, 2010.

KIPLING, Rudyard. "The White Man's Burden." 1899. *The Internet Modern History Sourcebook*. 1997. Fordham University. <http://www.fordham.edu/halsall/mod/kipling.asp>

LIGHT, Andrew. "Tolkien's Green Time: Environmental Themes in *The Lord of the Rings*." *The Lord of the Rings and Philosophy: One Book to Rule Them All*. Ed. Gregory Bassham and Eric Bronson. Chicago, IL: Open Court, 2003. 150-163.

McFADDEN, Brian. "Fear of Difference, Fear of Death: The *Sigelwara*, Tolkien's Swertings, and Racial Difference." *Tolkien's Modern Middle Ages*. Ed. Jane Chance and Alfred Siewers. New York: Palgrave Macmillan, 2009. 155-169.

MILKING THE RHINO. Dir. David E. Simpson. Kartemquin Films, 2009.

SIEWERS, Alfred K. "Tolkien's Cosmic-Christian Ecology: The Medieval Underpinnings." *Tolkien's Modern Middle Ages*. Ed. Jane Chance and Alfred Siewers. New York: Palgrave Macmillan, 2009. 139-153.

SMITH-ROWSEY, Daniel. "Whose Middle-Earth Is It? Reading *The Lord of the Rings* and New Zealand's New Identity from a Globalized, Post-Colonial Perspective." *How We Became Middle-earth: A Collection of Essays on The Lord of the Rings*. Ed. Adam Lam and Nataliya Oryshchuk. Zurich and Berne: Walking Tree Publishers, 2007. 129-145.

THOMAS, Keith. *Man and the Natural World: A History of the Modern Sensibility*. New York: Pantheon Books, 1983.

THUM, Maureen. "The 'Sub-Subcreation' of Galadriel, Arwen, and Éowyn: Women of Power in Tolkien's and Jackson's *The Lord of the Rings.*" *Tolkien on Film: Essays on Peter Jackson's The Lord of the Rings*. Ed. Janet Brennan Croft. Altadena, CA: The Mythopoeic Press, 2004. 231-256.

TOLKIEN, John Ronald Reuel. *The Fellowship of the Ring*. New York: Ballantine Books, 1965.

The Hobbit or There and Back Again. New York: Houghton Mifflin, 1997.

The Letters of J.R.R. Tolkien. Ed. Humphrey Carpenter. London: Unwin Hyman, 1990.

"On Fairy-Stories." *Essays Presented to Charles Williams*. Ed. C. S. Lewis. Grand Rapids, MI: William B. Eerdmans Publishing, 1966. 38-89.

The Return of the King. New York: Ballantine Books, 1965.

The Silmarillion. Ed. Christopher Tolkien. New York: Houghton Mifflin, 2001.

The Two Towers. New York: Ballantine Books, 1965.

WILKINSON, Loren. "Tolkien and the Surrendering of Power." *Tree of Tales: Tolkien, Literature, and Theology*. Ed. Trevor Hart and Ivan Khovacs. Waco, TX: Baylor University Press, 2007. 71-83.

Index

A
Ainur as creators of Arda 79-80
applicability versus allegory 208, 210
Aquinas, Thomas 75
    creation as participation 82-83
    on hope 86
    Thomist perspective on Arda's creation 80
    understanding Tolkien 75

B
Barberis, Danièle: relationship between Dwarves and their mines 32-33
binary hermeneutic and racism in Tolkien's works 210-211

C
Cad Goddeu 21, 128
    and Entish mythology 21
colonialism
    environmental consequences 209-210
    Saruman 209-210
creational hope 85, 87, 90
    as future of Elves 88, 90
    versus despair 86-87
Cronon, William 2

D
deep time and Arda's creation 212
definition of nature 31, 34
deforestation
    of Great Britain 19, 25
    of Middle-earth 10, 17, 25
Dickerson, Matthew and Jonathan Evans: *Ents, Elves and Eriador* 31
diversity in Tolkien's works and ecocritical postcolonialism 211-212
divisiveness in *The Lord of the Rings* 98
Dwarves
    and greed 37, 44
    appreciation for nature 39
    as experienced by other characters 30

characteristics 29-30
contrasts to Hobbits 44-45
craftsmanship 39-40, 45
creation 35
love of stone versus practices of evil 41-42, 45
narrative link shared with Goblins (Orcs) 42-43
negative depictions 30
preservation of beauty 33, 41, 45
relationship to artifacts 43
relationship to mithril and other metals 39-40
relationship to nature, environment 29-30, 35, 38-39, 41
relationship to the other races 34-35, 45-46
relationship to their mines 32-33

E
Eiseley, Loren 2
Elves
    and stewardship responsibilities 214-216, 224, 226
    and their relationship with the environment 108, 110, 114
    and trees 120-121
    ecology as aesthetics 107-109
    stewardship, imperialism and the Silmarils 216-218, 224
emanationism 78, 80-82, 84-85
    and Neoplatonism 78-79, 82
Ents
    and Saruman 8-9
    and the War of the Ring 9-10
    artifacts 6-7
    as English mythological tree-trope 21
    as mediators between other culture and wilderness 2-3, 10, 24
    as memory metaphor 160-163
    as vision of a different way to live in and with nature 3, 8
    enmeshment with nature 112, 114
    Entwives and sustainable forestry 7, 10, 130, 135
    etymology and Entish history 161
    origins and motivations 4, 128-129
    place in object-oriented ontology 112
    qualities 1-2, 5-6, 9-10, 128-130
    reasons for extinction 3, 8
    representative of the ideal? 7-8
    stewardship 2
    Treebeard 5
environment: characteristics in Tolkien's works 97

F

Fangorn
    and Elves 17-18
    as memory metaphor 159, 161
    as realisation of Entish culture 6-7
    invasion 8
Flieger, Verlyn
    image of light in Eru's creation 78-79
    on hope in Tolkien's works 85
forest destruction in Tolkien's works 3-4
forest
    and fairy 12
    as commodity 20, 22
    fear 13, 15
    in contrast to tame, individual trees 14
    Old Man Willow as threat 13
    perception of forests by Elves 17
    perception of forests by Hobbits 13-14
    perception of forests by Men of Middle-earth 15-16
    perception of forests by Orcs 16-17
    perception of forests in Middle-earth 11-16, 18, 22, 24
forestry in Great Britain 19-20

G

geochronology for Middle-earth 187-192
geological change in Middle-earth and Atlantis 172
greed in Middle-earth 37-38
growing things and goodness 32, 34, 36-37

H

Harrison, Robert 1-2, 147-148
horse-phenomenology in Tolkien's works 105-106

I

interobjectivity 102

L

'Lay of Leithian' as ecological commentary 109-110
Lothlórien and Elvish horticulture 218-219
Lothlórien
    and the spectre of the One Ring 220
    as sylvan sanctuary 155-156
    fate and imperialistic reverie 221-223

timelessness and memory metaphors 156-158
love for trees versus longing for the sea 133

M
maps and Tolkien's works 172
McIntosh, Jonathan
    Thomist interpretation of Tolkien 81
melancholy
    and Elves 64
    and sea-longing 61
    definition 50-51
    in *The Lord of the Rings* 51, 64
metaphorical versus allegorical readings 144-145
Metaphorology 144
metaphysics of creation in Tolkien's works 75, 84
Milbank, Alison
    Thomist interpretation of Tolkien 81
Mirkwood
    as memory metaphor 153
    origin in *Elder Edda* and narrative function 152-153
motivations for filming *The Lord of the Rings* in New Zealand 196-200

N
natural world influences on Middle-earth's geography 170, 171
nature
    in Peter Jackson's *Hobbit* 101
    and enmeshment of characters 110, 112-113
    and enmeshment with language 107
    as character in Tolkien's works 73-74
    as creational hope 76
    as creative act 77
    healing function 158
    object-oriented ontological reading 96-97
    passive and active nature in Tolkien's works 146-147
    relationship with the different Races 52
    restoration 76

O
object-oriented ontologies 97-98
    definition of ethics in OOO 98-99
    nature as an object 100-101
    relations to environment 99-100, 104-105
Old Man Willow 154-155

P

parallels between Middle-earth's and New Zealand's tectonism 192-196
perspectival change in Tolkien's works 102-106, 113
plate tectonics
    in Middle-earth 178-181, 186-187
    The Silmarillion as source for plate tectonics in Middle-earth 182-186
    theories of origins 175-179
postcolonial ecocriticism 209, 225
    and globalization 225
primal forests in English cultural history 20-21

R

real world places locations in Middle-earth: Spring Pound in Australia 173-174
relationship between creator and creation 77
relationship between Dwarves and Elves 34
relationship to trees as characterising element 131-133
responsibility for nature in postcolonial studies 212-213

S

Schama, Simon 148-149
sea-longing 61-62
    as home-loning 61-62
    in other bodies of water 63
stewardship 1, 8, 10-11, 23, 32, 212-214
    and imperialism 214-215
    forest stewardship 1, 10
sublime nature in Tolkien's works 24

T

"The Mariner's Wife" 133-135
"The Sea Bell" 68-69
Tolkien, John Ronald Reuel
    as landscape expert 23
    relationship to plants and trees 18-19, 22
    woodsmanship versus forestry 25
Tom Bombadil and nature 63
Tree and Leaf 140
trees
    and forests as memory metaphors 140-143, 147-148, 151, 154, 164-165
    and nature as animate beings 151
    and plants and their importance in Tolkien's works 140
    ambivalent nature 141-142
    and biblical connections 163-164

and Elves 124
and Hobbits 125
and their powers 127
artistic representation 149-150
as linking element 125
as living beings in *The Lord of the Rings* 125-126
in Tolkien's works and their Shakespearean origins 127-128
narrative and plot functions 121, 150
Old Man Willow's malevolence 127
romanticism 150
symbolism 123
symbolism of the White Tree 122-123
Trees of Valinor as source of light 121-122

W

water
    and Dwarves 56
    and Elves 56-60
    and Hobbits 52-53
    and Men 53-55
    and Nenya 60
    and rivers 57-58
    and starlight 57
    controlling water in *The Lord of the Rings* 58
    function in the narrative 66-67
    funerary rites in *The Lord of the Rings* 54-55
    healing functions 65-66, 68, 70
    music of creation 62
    narrative function 111
    relationship with Tom Bombadil 63

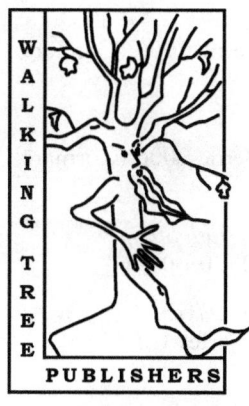

Walking Tree Publishers
Zurich and Jena

Walking Tree Publishers was founded in 1997 as a forum for publication of material (books, videos, CDs, etc.) related to Tolkien and Middle-earth studies.

http://www.walking-tree.org

Cormarë Series

The *Cormarë Series* collects papers and studies dedicated exclusively to the exploration of Tolkien's work. It comprises monographs, thematic collections of essays, conference volumes, and reprints of important yet no longer (easily) accessible papers by leading scholars in the field. Manuscripts and project proposals are evaluated by members of an independent board of advisors who support the series editors in their endeavour to provide the readers with qualitatively superior yet accessible studies on Tolkien and his work.

News from the Shire and Beyond. Studies on Tolkien
Peter Buchs and Thomas Honegger (eds.), Zurich and Berne 2004, Reprint, First edition 1997 (Cormarë Series 1), ISBN 978-3-9521424-5-5

Root and Branch. Approaches Towards Understanding Tolkien
Thomas Honegger (ed.), Zurich and Berne 2005, Reprint, First edition 1999 (Cormarë Series 2), ISBN 978-3-905703-01-6

Richard Sturch, *Four Christian Fantasists. A Study of the Fantastic Writings of George MacDonald, Charles Williams, C.S. Lewis and J.R.R. Tolkien*
Zurich and Berne 2007, Reprint, First edition 2001 (Cormarë Series 3), ISBN 978-3-905703-04-7

Tolkien in Translation
Thomas Honegger (ed.), Zurich and Jena 2011, Reprint, First edition 2003 (Cormarë Series 4), ISBN 978-3-905703-15-3

Mark T. Hooker, *Tolkien Through Russian Eyes*
Zurich and Berne 2003 (Cormarë Series 5), ISBN 978-3-9521424-7-9

Translating Tolkien: Text and Film
Thomas Honegger (ed.), Zurich and Jena 2011, Reprint, First edition 2004 (Cormarë Series 6), ISBN 978-3-905703-16-0

Christopher Garbowski, *Recovery and Transcendence for the Contemporary Mythmaker. The Spiritual Dimension in the Works of J.R.R. Tolkien*
Zurich and Berne 2004, Reprint, First Edition by Marie Curie Sklodowska, University Press, Lublin 2000, (Cormarë Series 7), ISBN 978-3-9521424-8-6

Reconsidering Tolkien
Thomas Honegger (ed.), Zurich and Berne 2005 (Cormarë Series 8), ISBN 978-3-905703-00-9

Tolkien and Modernity 1
Frank Weinreich and Thomas Honegger (eds.), Zurich and Berne 2006 (Cormarë Series 9), ISBN 978-3-905703-02-3

Tolkien and Modernity 2
Thomas Honegger and Frank Weinreich (eds.), Zurich and Berne 2006 (Cormarë Series 10), ISBN 978-3-905703-03-0

Tom Shippey, *Roots and Branches. Selected Papers on Tolkien by Tom Shippey*
Zurich and Berne 2007 (Cormarë Series 11), ISBN 978-3-905703-05-4

Ross Smith, *Inside Language. Linguistic and Aesthetic Theory in Tolkien*
Zurich and Jena 2011, Reprint, First edition 2007 (Cormarë Series 12), ISBN 978-3-905703-20-7

How We Became Middle-earth. A Collection of Essays on The Lord of the Rings
Adam Lam and Nataliya Oryshchuk (eds.), Zurich and Berne 2007 (Cormarë Series 13), ISBN 978-3-905703-07-8

Myth and Magic. Art According to the Inklings
Eduardo Segura and Thomas Honegger (eds.), Zurich and Berne 2007 (Cormarë Series 14), ISBN 978-3-905703-08-5

The Silmarillion - Thirty Years On
Allan Turner (ed.), Zurich and Berne 2007 (Cormarë Series 15), ISBN 978-3-905703-10-8

Martin Simonson, *The Lord of the Rings and the Western Narrative Tradition*
Zurich and Jena 2008 (Cormarë Series 16), ISBN 978-3-905703-09-2

Tolkien's Shorter Works. Proceedings of the 4th Seminar of the Deutsche Tolkien Gesellschaft & Walking Tree Publishers Decennial Conference
Margaret Hiley and Frank Weinreich (eds.), Zurich and Jena 2008 (Cormarë Series 17), ISBN 978-3-905703-11-5

Tolkien's The Lord of the Rings: Sources of Inspiration
Stratford Caldecott and Thomas Honegger (eds.), Zurich and Jena 2008 (Cormarë Series 18), ISBN 978-3-905703-12-2

J.S. Ryan, *Tolkien's View: Windows into his World*
Zurich and Jena 2009 (Cormarë Series 19), ISBN 978-3-905703-13-9

Music in Middle-earth
Heidi Steimel and Friedhelm Schneidewind (eds.), Zurich and Jena 2010 (Cormarë Series 20), ISBN 978-3-905703-14-6

Liam Campbell, *The Ecological Augury in the Works of JRR Tolkien*
Zurich and Jena 2011 (Cormarë Series 21), ISBN 978-3-905703-18-4

Margaret Hiley, *The Loss and the Silence. Aspects of Modernism in the Works of C.S. Lewis, J.R.R. Tolkien and Charles Williams*
Zurich and Jena 2011 (Cormarë Series 22), ISBN 978-3-905703-19-1

Rainer Nagel, *Hobbit Place-names. A Linguistic Excursion through the Shire*
Zurich and Jena 2012 (Cormarë Series 23), ISBN 978-3-905703-22-1

Christopher MacLachlan, *Tolkien and Wagner: The Ring and Der Ring*
Zurich and Jena 2012 (Cormarë Series 24), ISBN 978-3-905703-21-4

Renée Vink, *Wagner and Tolkien: Mythmakers*
Zurich and Jena 2012 (Cormarë Series 25), ISBN 978-3-905703-25-2

The Broken Scythe. Death and Immortality in the Works of J.R.R. Tolkien
Roberto Arduini and Claudio Antonio Testi (eds.), Zurich and Jena 2012
(Cormarë Series 26), ISBN 978-3-905703-26-9

Sub-creating Middle-earth: Constructions of Authorship and the Works of J.R.R. Tolkien
Judith Klinger (ed.), Zurich and Jena 2012 (Cormarë Series 27),
ISBN 978-3-905703-27-6

Tolkien's Poetry
Julian Eilmann and Allan Turner (eds.), Zurich and Jena 2013
(Cormarë Series 28), ISBN 978-3-905703-28-3

O, What a Tangled Web. Tolkien and Medieval Literature. A View from Poland
Barbara Kowalik (ed.), Zurich and Jena 2013 (Cormarë Series 29),
ISBN 978-3-905703-29-0

J.S. Ryan, *In the Nameless Wood*
Zurich and Jena 2013 (Cormarë Series 30), ISBN 978-3-905703-30-6

From Peterborough to Faëry; The Poetics and Mechanics of Secondary Worlds
Thomas Honegger & Dirk Vanderbeke (eds.), Zurich and Jena 2014
(Cormarë Series 31), ISBN 978-3-905703-31-3

Tolkien and Philosophy
Roberto Arduini and Claudio R. Testi (eds.), Zurich and Jena 2014
(Cormarë Series 32), ISBN 978-3-905703-32-0

Patrick Curry, *Deep Roots in a Time of Frost. Essays on Tolkien*
(Cormarë Series 33), ISBN 978-3-905703-33-7

Representations of Nature in Middle-earth
Martin Simonson (ed.), (Cormarë Series 34), ISBN 978-3-905703-34-4

Paul H. Kocher, *The Three Ages of Middle-earth*
Zurich and Jena, forthcoming

Beowulf and the Dragon

The original Old English text of the 'Dragon Episode'
of *Beowulf* is set in an authentic font and bound in
hardback as a high quality art book. Illustrated by
Anke Eissmann and accompanied by John Porter's
translation. Introduction by Tom Shippey. Limited
first edition of 500 copies. 84 pages.

Selected pages can be previewed on:
www.walking-tree.org/beowulf

Zurich and Jena 2009
ISBN 978-3-905703-17-7

Tales of Yore Series

The *Tales of Yore Series* provides a platform for qualitatively superior fiction that will appeal to readers familiar with Tolkien's world:

The Monster Specialist

Sir Severus le Brewse, among the least known of King Arthur's Round Table knights, is preferred by nature, disposition, and training to fight against monsters rather than other knights. After youthful adventures of errantry with dragons, trolls, vampires, and assorted beasts, Severus joins the brilliant sorceress Lilava to face the Chimaera in The Greatest Monster Battle of All Time to free her folk from an age-old curse. But their adventures don't end there; together they meet elves and magicians, friends and foes; they join in the fight to save Camelot and even walk the Grey Paths of the Dead. With a mix of Malory, a touch of Tolkien, and a hint of humor, The Monster Specialist chronicles a tale of courage, tenacity, honor, and love.

The Monster Specialist is illustrated by Anke Eissmann.

Edward S. Louis, *The Monster Specialist*
Zurich and Jena 2014 (Tales of Yore Series No. 3), ISBN 978-3-905703-23-8

Tales of Yore Series (earlier books)

Kay Woollard, *The Terror of Tatty Walk. A Frightener*
CD and Booklet, Zurich and Berne 2000, ISBN 978-3-9521424-2-4

Kay Woollard, *Wilmot's Very Strange Stone or What came of building "snobbits"*
CD and booklet, Zurich and Berne 2001, ISBN 978-3-9521424-4-8

Information for authors

Authors interested in contributing to our publications can learn more about the services we offer by reading the "services for authors" section of our web pages.

http://www.walking-tree.org/authors

Manuscripts and project proposals can be submitted to the board of editors (please include an SAE):

Walking Tree Publishers
CH-3052 Zollikofen
Switzerland

e-mail: info@walking-tree.org

Walking Tree Publishers, Zurich and Jena, 2015

www.ingramcontent.com/pod-product-compliance
Lightning Source LLC
Chambersburg PA
CBHW070731160426
43192CB00009B/1399